New Perspectives on Teaching
and Learning Modern Languages

MODERN LANGUAGES IN PRACTICE

Series Editor
Michael Grenfell, *Centre for Language in Education, University of Southampton*
Editorial Board
Do Coyle, *School of Education, University of Nottingham*
Simon Green, *Trinity & All Saints College, Leeds*
Editorial Consultant
Christopher Brumfit, *Centre for Language in Education, University of Southampton*

The **Modern Languages in Practice Series** provides publications on the theory and practice of modern foreign language teaching. The theoretical and practical discussions in the publications arise from, and are related to, research into the subject. *Practical* is defined as having pedagogic value. *Theoretical* is defined as illuminating and/or generating issues pertinent to the practical. Theory and practice are, however, understood as a continuum. The series includes books at three distinct points along this continuum: (1) Limited discussions of language learning issues. These publications provide an outlet for coverage of actual classroom activities and exercises. (2) Aspects of both theory and practice combined in broadly equal amounts. This is the *core of the series*, and books may appear in the form of collections bringing together writers from different fields. (3) More theoretical books examining key research ideas directly relevant to the teaching of modern languages.

Other Books in the Series
Cric Crac! Teaching and Learning French through Story-telling
    Roy Dunning
Effective Language Learning
    Suzanne Graham
Fluency and its Teaching
    Marie-Noelle Guillot
The Elements of Foreign Language Teaching
    Walter Grauberg
The Good Language Learner
    N. Naiman, M. Fröhlich, H.H. Stern and A. Todesco
Inspiring Innovations in Language Teaching
    Judith Hamilton
Le ou La? The Gender of French Nouns
    Marie Surridge
Motivating Language Learners
    Gary N. Chambers
Switched On? Video Resources in Modern Language Settings
    Steven Fawkes
Target Language, Collaborative Learning and Autonomy
    Ernesto Macaro
Training Teachers in Practice
    Michael Grenfell
Validation in Language Testing
    A. Cumming and R. Berwick (eds)

Please contact us for the latest book information:
Multilingual Matters, Frankfurt Lodge, Clevedon Hall,
Victoria Road, Clevedon, BS21 7HH, England
http://www.multilingual-matters.com

MODERN LANGUAGES IN PRACTICE 13
Series Editor: Michael Grenfell

New Perspectives on Teaching and Learning Modern Languages

Edited by
Simon Green

MULTILINGUAL MATTERS LTD
Clevedon • Buffalo • Toronto • Sydney

Library of Congress Cataloging in Publication Data

New Perspectives on Teaching and Learning Modern Languages
Edited by Simon Green
Modern Languages in Practice: 13
1. Languages, Modern–Study and teaching. I. Series. II. Green, Simon
PB35.N454 2000
418'.007 21–dc21   99-045550

British Library Cataloguing in Publication Data

A CIP catalogue record for this book is available from the British Library.

ISBN 1-85359-472-5 (hbk)
ISBN 1-85359-471-7 (pbk)

Multilingual Matters Ltd

UK: Frankfurt Lodge, Clevedon Hall, Victoria Road, Clevedon BS21 7HH.
USA: UTP, 2250 Military Road, Tonawanda, NY 14150, USA.
Canada: UTP, 5201 Dufferin Street, North York, Ontario M3H 5T8, Canada.
Australia: P.O. Box 586, Artarmon, NSW, Australia.

Typeset by Bookcraft, Stroud.
Printed and bound in Great Britain by Cromwell Press Ltd.

Contents

Notes on the Contributors

Simon Green
Senior Lecturer in Education and German, Faculty of Education, Trinity and All Saints College, Leeds.

Michael Grenfell
Senior Lecturer in Education, Centre for Language in Education, University of Southampton.

David Little
Director of the Centre for Language and Communication Studies and Associate Professor of Applied Linguistics, Trinity College, Dublin.

Gary Chambers
Senior Lecturer in Education (Modern Languages), School of Education, University of Leeds.

Ann Gregory
Senior Lecturer in French and Education, College of Ripon & York St John.

Christopher Brumfit
Director of the Centre for Language in Education and Dean of the Faculty of Educational Studies, University of Southampton.

Anthony Lodge
Professor of French, Department of French, University of St Andrews.

Philip Hood
Lecturer in Education, Centre for Research into Second and Foreign Language Pedagogy, School of Education, University of Nottingham.

John Thorogood
CILT Language Teaching Adviser and Languages National Training Organisation Professional Officer.

Do Coyle
Lecturer in Education, Centre for Research into Second and Foreign Language Pedagogy, School of Education, University of Nottingham.

Kim Brown
Lecturer in Education (Modern Languages), School of Education and Professional Development, University of East Anglia.

Introduction

SIMON GREEN

> New opinions are always suspected, and usually opposed, without any other reason but because they are not already common.
>   John Locke, *An Essay Concerning Human Understanding* (1690)

When is it the right time for us to review the state of modern languages in our education system?

With many others taking stock of their current achievements and future goals as they prepare to cross the threshold to the new millennium, it seems appropriate that we too should pause and ask some pertinent questions about the direction of this major subject. In fact it is important to consider not just its direction, both in the school curriculum and in higher education, but also its very place on the educational agenda.

During the past 15 years the education system has been subjected to unprecedented intervention from central government, through a bewildering series of demands, targets, inspections, assessment tests, guidance, circulars and the like. Each has seemed more urgent than the previous one, and barely has time been taken to draw breath than the next one arrives. There has been little time for judicious evaluation and measured research before the headlong rush to the next panacea.

This book represents an attempt to redress the balance and to concentrate on what Stephen Covey (1989) refers to as 'Quadrant II' activity – that is, to focus more carefully upon what is *important*, as opposed to what is *urgent*. Too often we are forced by circumstance to react to stimuli presented by others – government requirements, inspection demands, assessment criteria, curriculum change – and hence have too little time to spend on what really is crucially important: the very essence of our activity and the core function of the task in hand. The book results from a desire not just to put into context the debates that have raged around the subject itself, but also to answer three deceptively simple questions: where are we now? Where could we be by 2005? And how could we get there?

Our ten authors, considering these three questions and many others, have attempted to find common cause and a possible way ahead. They have each dealt with the questions from the point of view of their own educational background, and have sought to present ways of dealing with particular issues according to their own expertise. The chapters that follow are all written by practitioners in the field who would like to take some time out to reflect on where we are, to challenge easy assumptions and *idées fixes*, to stimulate debate and to suggest new directions. There is a wide range of experience and expertise here, and plenty of informed comment. The chapters are discrete in themselves, but their common threads are, first, a rejection of the status quo, where there is much disquiet and a lack of clear purpose; and second, a celebration of those future possibilities which could bring about so much more, not just for our students but for all who wish for a more effective and purposeful national capability in modern languages.

Over the past 20 years probably no other area of the curriculum has generated so much debate and change as the study of modern languages. In order to accommodate increasing numbers of students, diverse external demands and technological advances, we have in a relatively short space of time lurched from one set of ideas to another on this subject in all sectors of education – primary, secondary, vocational, higher and teacher training. At such a time of rapid change it is not possible to sit back in calm contemplation of all the issues and make reasoned cases for careful progression on all fronts. In England the National Curriculum has once again been reviewed and renewed; we await the impact of the National Literacy Strategy and the National Advisory Centre on Early Language Learning upon later learners of modern languages; all teachers are to be trained in the use of information and communication technology or ICT; the Nuffield Inquiry into modern languages is set to report; the European dimension continues to have a political as well as an educational effect; teacher supply remains critical; and examination entries reflect widening choices. Specialist language colleges are growing in number and influence, more adults are enrolling on language courses, business is certainly taking a belated interest once again, and several cities (for example Sheffield and Leeds) are modelling themselves as multilingual environments. Many students in both further and higher education are at least taking up some language pathway, and student mobility is opening some eyes to possibilities of life and work outside the UK.

Within this vibrant context of uncertainty, challenge, opportunity and ambiguity, this book seeks to address positively and constructively the key issues. It is divided into three parts, with three chapters dedicated to each section. Part I deals with research-based critical analysis, Part II focuses on the current educational context, and Part III is concerned with issues relating to classroom practice, with suggestions for future planning. The

Conclusion draws each of these chapters together and makes some far-reaching proposals for radical change.

In Part I Michael Grenfell examines standard practice in the modern languages classroom from the point of view of pupil attainment, and asks whether a more radical approach to learner independence through strategy training might offer more long-term benefits than would additional language teaching on its own. David Little also pleads for greater learner autonomy, and makes a strong and convincing case for the centrality of languages in any modern curriculum. Gary Chambers focuses on the key issue of motivation amongst teenage learners of modern languages. Basing his contribution on his own research into learners in England and Germany, he identifies the critical phases through which learners pass and suggests ways in which more of them can be encouraged to continue their studies beyond a basic level.

All three contributors to Part I see evidence from their own and others' research that much could be done by both teachers and learners to improve both educational attainment *and* motivation if only there were a coherent approach to methodology and a systematic pattern of provision. This links well with Part II, where the current context of teaching and learning comes under scrutiny and proposals are made about the way forward for all sectors of education. First, Ann Gregory analyses the situation at the primary level, arguing the case for a clear strategy to enhance progress already being made under the National Literacy Strategy and to provide that necessary continuity across the early stages of education. The setting up of the National Advisory Centre for Early Language Learning in late 1999 may go some way towards meeting the challenges raised by Gregory's chapter.

Christopher Brumfit then presents a cogent argument in favour of a national policy for language education in its broadest sense and proposes, as an innovative and essentially liberating approach to language provision, a charter for all language learners. The inclusion of knowledge of languages in a multilingual society is a welcome addition to thinking about citizenship in the curriculum. Finally in this section Anthony Lodge examines recent developments in higher education, including the drive for greater participation by more students in myriad language programmes, and offers a proposal for in-depth study of language over and above cultural and socio-political issues.

How all of these issues are seen in everyday classroom contexts is the subject of Part III. Philip Hood examines the increasingly complex world of ICT and its inevitable impact on both the teaching and learning of modern languages. His answer is to plead, not for more hardware and sophisticated software, but for a more rigorously thought-through methodology that will handle existing provision more effectively and also anticipate and strategically prepare for technological developments. Next, John Thorogood discusses the question of vocational languages and business language training provision. In the final section of Part III, Do Coyle links back to Chambers' first chapter and argues that the key to motivation in the future may well lie in cross-curricular activity that will lend a more relevant focus to language study and emphasise ends over means.

Kim Brown provides an incisive Conclusion, championing the cause of a fresh pedagogy to enliven teachers' practice and giving a cogent and practical demonstration of how that can be achieved within existing constraints.

The purpose of this book is to stimulate debate about what kind of language teaching is appropriate for the new millennium, what skills learners will need to cope with technological as well as linguistic demands and how we can syntheise the two. We are seeking neither a Holy Grail of the One True Method nor a quick and easy answer to complex problems, but rather a convergence of views from practitioners and learners, researchers and trainers, policy-makers and managers so as to make the most effective use of the best that we have got.

More people communicating more effectively in more languages around 2005 would be a good outcome. We hope that this book will help towards making that goal a reality. As les Bleus said in a different context in July 1998: 'La victoire est en nous!'

References

Covey, S. (1989) _The 7 Habits of Highly Effective People_. Simon and Schuster.

Chapter 1
Learning and Teaching Strategies

MICHAEL GRENFELL

The whole impetus behind this book is to reassess the learning and teaching of modern languages as we move into the next century. Such an endeavour involves reviewing issues of policy and practice, in order to develop new ways of thinking about modern languages for the world that is coming into being. Although this initial chapter focuses specifically on learning strategies, these also have implications for the way we teach languages overall. What I have to say will, I hope, make this clear.

The main part of the discussion looks at the way we think about language and how this shapes our assumptions about how to teach it. By introducing aspects of research on second language learning, specifically on learning strategies, I aim to offer pointers to how we might reorient our practice towards a new methodology for the new millennium. My intention is not overly to criticise what passes in the name of communicative language teaching or 'CLT' in modern languages, but to show how we also need to think 'strategically' in the twenty-first century.

First I want to consider today's language practices, together with the assumptions underlying them, in methodological terms.

A Century of Change

There is little doubt that the twentieth century has been marked by an explosion in technology and world communications. As the global economy has developed, so have the means to exchange information, whether in face-to-face contact or through telecommunications. The speed with which communication occurs has increased at a frightening pace, and there is now the need to send out and receive all manner of documents and messages with the briefest of delays. Of course this revolution has radically reshaped our lives, not only in how we view each other and ourselves, but also through the knowledge we now have of the distant corners of our world. Central to this phenomenon is *language*; it is language which lubricates the system, provides the medium for establishing relationships with others, is what we depend on to get our message across as well as the means by which we learn more about what is happening and what is available to us in both our personal and our professional lives.

This focus on language has pervaded our history throughout this century. Systems of world communication began to develop in its early years, at least partly out of military and political expediency. Now as we reach its closing stages it is the media industry that is ubiquitous in its multifarious ways of getting news and entertainment to our doorsteps. Yet the effect of language goes beyond common utilities. Language has also scrutinised, and been scrutinised in, the process of examining who we are as a species and, by implication, our understanding of what we are to become. In this statement I mean to draw attention to the way language has been used this century: to justify both revolution and dictatorship; to establish authority; to express freedom; and to formulate a range of humanist philosophies.

But what has all this got to do with learning and teaching modern languages?

Until comparatively recently, indeed probably until the immediate post-war period, modern languages were seldom learnt as a means to communicate – to transact business, or to interact with others. Learning languages was seen instead as an individual pursuit, a mark of refined culture, the ultimate expression of a disciplined intellect. Mastery was gained through the rigorous application of the mind to learning vocabulary, analysing grammar and, ultimately, gaining access to the world of classical literature. In England as late as the early 1980s competence in foreign language at the age of 16 was judged on the basis of translation tests and written prose which rewarded accuracy and heavily penalised every grammatical transgression. The spoken word was at best a gesture, accorded only a small proportion of marks in final examinations.

This situation has of course changed, and the change was brought about by a twin pincer movement, both top-down and bottom-up. Official reform gave substance to the exigencies of socio-economic development. For modern languages in Europe, the progress of the European Union in forging a 'nation of states' pulled in its wake a whole set of professional requirements for the new European citizen. One of these was the ability to converse with fellow Europeans. The 'threshold level' (Van Ek, 1975) was born, along with numerous language-promoting activities and publications stemming from the Council of Europe, a European institution that brought together some of those most committed to the idea of a multilingual continent. But change also came bottom-up; most noticeably from teachers themselves, who realised that the old-style classical approach to modern languages was neither appropriate nor relevant for the vast majority of the pupil population. Such teachers wanted to reward other 'communicative' features of language besides grammatical accuracy, to stage learning in more manageable amounts, and to develop pupils' linguistic competence in a way that allowed them to 'get by' in another language and culture. Such pressures for change coalesced in curricular reform: first in the English General Certificate of Secondary Education (GCSE), and then in the National Curriculum. Both can be understood as a product of the communicative movement in second language learning.

Communicative language teaching exists in many forms, some of which do not necessarily sit comfortably together. Briefly, however, they all involve some shift in emphasis, away from learning language for its own sake to a focus on the need and ability to understand and to be understood. CLT itself can be understood in terms of both top-down socio-economic and cultural pressures, and bottom-up pedagogic imperatives on the part of those involved in teaching. Its main tenets were formulated within the field of English as a foreign language (EFL), as it was here that the necessity to *use* language, as opposed to simply studying and analysing it, was first expressed in the almost international adoption of English as a near lingua franca. However, the influence of CLT was quickly felt in the world of modern languages, as resonances rang between the two in terms of implications for policy and practice.

Such change, both for modern languages and EFL, should not be understood as simply the result of pedagogic fashion or political trends. Rather, the communicative revolution implicated the very substance of language itself: what we understand it to be and how it operates. Early conceptualisations of language, most noticeably in behaviourist psychology, had presented it as nothing more than a set of skill habits to be acquired through rote learning, but from the 1950s, Chomskyan linguistics began to show its innate, quasi-biological character. The brain can be understood to have a 'language acquisition device' which holds linguistic competence from which individual performance acts are generated.

By the 1970s and 1980s the 'naturalness' of language and the symmetry of process between first and second language learning were being given full-blown expression in the work of the psycholinguist Stephen Krashen, who saw the key to success as residing in a methodological approach which stressed acquisition over learning, the need for comprehensible input, and the redundancy of conscious, explicit knowledge about language. The thrust of this argument can, of course, be seen as directly congruous with CLT and pressures for reform within the world of modern languages. There is the same stress on naturalness, the same emphasis on oral target language, the same doubt cast on grammar knowledge as a route to communicative effectiveness. The study of modern languages has followed in this slipstream ever since. In practice, we find teachers intending to maximise exposure to the target language – particularly, in the early stages, oral language. Published materials are based around 'situational' dialogues which supply the necessary language to act as tourist or host with foreign nationals. Games and pair-work activities form the bedrock of classroom practice, at the expense of an explicit study of grammar. However, the upshot of this type of approach has been disappointing for policy-makers in England. Inspection reports (see OFSTED, 1995) note the lack of truly pupil-initiated language and the way pupils' competence and enthusiasm seem to 'plateau out' within two or three years of starting to learn a language. Why is this so? And why might a 'strategic' approach to learning and teaching better facilitate pupils' progress on both counts?

The 'Communicative' Classroom

Let us imagine a classroom where French is being taught to pupils in the first year or two of secondary school. What goes on?

The teacher enters the class:

Bonjour, les élèves. Asseyez-vous. Sortez vos livres. Mettez les bagages par terre. Ça va?

The teacher then revises a series of numbers which have been previously taught/learnt. Next she moves on to presentation activity.

OK. Regardez les images.

She produces a set of flashcards of items of food and drink; the pupils have met the drinks before, but not the food.

Alors, qu'est-ce que c'est?

She shows a picture of a glass of beer. Other examples follow: wine, coffee, tea, etc. Some pupils put up their hand and answer, others remain uninvolved. The teacher then shows a picture of a cheese sandwich.

C'est un sandwich au fromage. Répétez ...

Pupils repeat in chorus and individually. Once six items have been presented, the teacher moves into a questioning phase.

Alors, c'est un sandwich au fromage, oui ou non?
C'est un sandwich au fromage ou une bière?
Qu'est-ce que c'est?

This latter sequence demonstrates three-stage questioning, as a range of questions is offered by the teacher and answers solicited from the pupils according to the various items demonstrated. This offers increasing opportunities for pupils' independence in answering the questions.

The teacher next uses a range of 'flashcard' games in order to test pupils' memory; for example, removing one card from a sequence and asking the class to spot the missing item, and hiding a card from view and getting the class to guess what it is. All this is great fun and the class show evident enjoyment of the lesson. Now she sets up a role-play:

Alors, nous sommes au café. Je suis la serveuse. Vous entrez.
Bonjour, monsieur, vous désirez?

[*as the customer*] Je voudrais un vin rouge et un sandwich au jambon.

C'est bien, monsieur, voilà. Ça fait trente-cinq francs.

[*as the customer*] Merci, madame, voilà.

Merci, monsieur, au revoir.

[*as the customer*] Au revoir.

She has the class carry out the same type of dialogue with each other according to prompts supplied on cue cards. She then listens as various pairs repeat their dialogue. The lesson concludes with the class copying out the items of vocabulary and writing the model dialogue in their exercise books.

I am not wishing to caricature modern languages lessons. I should also state quite clearly that not only have I conducted very many lessons myself along similar lines, but that I do believe this type of structure has a part to play in any modern languages course. It is not that this form of communicative approach is misguided, rather that it is insufficient on its own. Let us use it, though, as an example, to help us to understand, through exploring the issues underlying current practice in many modern languages lessons, the necessity for adding a personal strategic element to language learning.

In many ways this lesson has all the attributes of a good 'communicative' language-teaching session. It is clearly based around the 'everyday activity' of food and drink. There is the use of an authentic context and the employment of a legitimate conversation to effect the necessary transaction. There is a degree of individual production and a real emphasis on maximising the use of the target language. There is also an element of unpredictability. We can imagine that error tolerance is high in such a classroom. On the face of it, therefore, this is a good strategy for language teaching, and one that might be expected to bear fruit with young learners.

However, on another level we might ask: what is the nature of the linguistic knowledge that is presupposed in such a methodology? Much of the repetition, for example, seems reminiscent of the rote learning characteristic of audio-visual approaches. Is the exposure to the target language supposed to activate an innate 'language acquisition device' in a Krashenite sense? Is a structural sense of dialogue and grammatical utility supposed to be gained through unconscious analysis of syntax and the subsequent generation of new patterns?

And what is going on in this lesson that matters? On the face of it, pupils are successfully conducting a dialogue to order food and drink; except, of course, that this may be a rare experience for these young learners – and they certainly would not expect to be ordering alcoholic beverages. Moreover, it is all 'let's pretend': there is no real café, nor does any food or drink get consumed, nor money exchanged. And the teacher's language is perforce hopping between various levels of classroom discourse: to establish her own relationship with pupils, to deal with classroom management, and to act as the authentic source of French. There are major questions here concerning what is being taught and why. Certainly, memorisation of vocabulary and phrases is at a premium, but what else is there here of value? On many levels the social nature of this interaction is a sham, mimicking the features of communication rather than genuinely communicating. Little wonder, therefore, if the final effect were to produce walking phrase books: individuals equipped with a repertoire of stock phrases but little by way of creating the means for personal expression in the language. We might not be surprised if such an effect were highly demotivating for pupils caught in this way, as so often, on the treadmill of repetition, memorisation and regurgitation.

The main focus for the rest of this chapter is on the argument that raising the prominence of learning-strategy work in modern languages classrooms is one way of alleviating this situation. However, before considering learning strategies *per se*, I want to spend a little more time addressing issues about the nature of linguistic knowledge.

What it is to know a language

What is the nature of linguistic knowledge? We recognise that learning our first language involves a profound process of mental programming, and that this takes place as part and as expression of our developing understanding of the world that surrounds us and of our position in it. We learn language, and in doing so we also learn socio-cultural behaviours and the cognitive skills for living as a fully operational human being. What explicit knowledge we have of language comes later, as an after-the-event awareness of what has already been acquired. It seems that in the natural setting all these aspects progress in an integrated fashion. This is not always the case with learning a second language in a formal situation. Here the various elements are all topsy-turvey, and many features seem to antagonise rather than facilitate the processes of learning.

We know that second language learners already have 'linguistic competence' in another language, but the usefulness of this is questionable. All languages serve a common purpose, of course; the human brain is the same across languages and nationalities; learners certainly try to apply their existing linguistic knowledge to the new language, yet the result often seems to be a hindrance rather than a help. Systematic 'interlanguages' develop, neither one language nor the other, and competencies apparently fossilise or plateau out way before optimal levels are reached.

Learners also already have a formed conceptual view of the world: of self, of objects and of others. They have only a secondary need to translate this world view into another language, including its alien notions, functions, tenses, and ways of expression. And learners already possess a developed personality, which is expressed in and through their first language. Learning a second language takes them back to rudimentary concerns of confidence, assertion and the need for social intercourse.

Any view of modern languages learning and teaching which overplays the similarities between first and second language is therefore overlooking important differences of form and process in the way these languages are acquired and used. We need an understanding of language which places it in its social as well as its psychological context. The problem with many models of learning, for example the Chomskyan notion of universal grammar, is that they have modelled language at an intra-psychological level, with scant regard for its social form and functioning. Yet in many ways communicative language teaching is guilty of doing the opposite: of stressing the social utility of language at the expense of the psychological shifts which have to be made in order to develop linguistic competence. Modern methodologies seem to assume, perhaps mistakenly, that both psychological and socio-cultural theories of learning can be enjoined with little incongruousness, because they can be grouped around the metaphor of communication. The result of this theoretical compromise is sometimes a confusion which gives rise to the type of idealised language learning I have exaggerated above. A strategic approach to learning and teaching offers the possibility of a different tack to pedagogy, and is built more securely on a concept of the nature of language itself.

Strategic and Communicative Action

I wrote above of how, as we have progressed through the twentieth century, the history of language learning and teaching has been intimately bound up with the way language itself has increasingly featured in debate about humankind. Post-modernists have argued that language is relative and transparent: communication is therefore at best approximative. Here is not the place to go into the details of such issues, still less to offer counter-arguments. I should, however, like to draw on the work of the German philosopher Jürgen Habermas (1984; 1987). Habermas does not subscribe to the notion of ultimate linguistic relativity. Rather, he sees in language, its nature and process, a clue to guide modern living. For him, *communicative* action is any action aimed at the effective transmission of knowledge, and at the creation of conditions optimal for this. *Strategic* action, on the other hand, orients actions towards a predetermined, recognisable end or goal. We might see CLT as an example of an attempt to create communicative action through communicative competence; but of course conditions are never optimal, and communication is always being disrupted: by the limited linguistic knowledge (at every level) of those involved, by their social circumstances, and by intervening factors of time and space. How do teachers and learners deal with such conditions?

In the classroom quoted above, problems are kept to a minimum as the teacher controls and guides the discourse towards the intended pedagogic ends. What is learnt is what is transmitted by the teacher to the pupils within these ideal conditions. And because it is knowledge created from these conditions, it is knowledge that only has utility in these conditions. In order to deal with the real world of communication something else is required. In some experiential cases, this 'something else' is simply immediate contact with the foreign culture, when a whole set of knowledges and practices can be brought into operation. However, these are rarely present in modern languages classrooms. Why is this so?

In the Vygotskyan tradition of psycholinguistics, language is the mediator in the world (Vygotsky, 1962; 1978). It is not so much that all thought takes place in language as that the two are very close, and language is the structure around and through which thought is constructed. In the human acquisition of a first language, Vygotsky identified, as did Piaget, a form of language that was not targeted on discourse with others but seemed a kind of 'egocentric' speech; that is, was for no benefit other than that of the speakers themselves. However, unlike Piaget, Vygotsky believed that this form of language, rather than dying away with the mastery of linguistic competence, becomes internalised as 'inner speech', where it acts as a kind of language-based super-ego, constructing and commenting on the world as this presents itself. The thrust of this argument leads to questions about the nature of language, and how thought is generated and processed.

It seems that the human brain is always working to maximise efficiency and speed in dealing with thought and language. There is a time during our first language acquisition when we have to name the world in order to 'know' it. Mistakes are made, as common features are over-generalised: cats are called dogs, and random men in supermarkets 'Daddy'. Eventually, however, language is fine-tuned to conventional sense and meaning. Words and structures learnt in specific contexts are passed into long-term memory, where they are stored to await activation in appropriate situations. Not only do we learn about facts and objects in the world, we learn how to do things: to operate the toilet, to organise a drink, and to write. Much of this learning 'how to do' involves a similar naming of and familiarisation with the objects to be used, but it also involves, as part of the correct procedure for getting things done, sequencing and operationalising them. This series of events might need to be brought to mind in a step-by-step manner, but mostly it is processed as a single unit of action. We do not make coffee every day by naming all the necessary equipment and bringing the recipe to mind – it is all automatised. But we did do this at some stage in the past; it is just that now, in keeping with our principle of maximal efficiency, the brain processes the sequence as an integrated, common event or routine.

What has all this got to do with second language learning and teaching?

The Vygotskyan perspective outlined above forms the basis of modern-day approaches to second language acquisition from a cognitive theoretical model. Cognitive theorists are keen to view all mental processes as various forms of information processing. Facts and objects represent one form of information; how to do things represents another. These two are referred to respectively as *declarative* and *procedural* knowledge. Both are needed to help us navigate our way through the world. Things are constantly learnt and are passed through to long-term memory. We *know*, and we know that we know, but we rarely consider the nature of this knowing. The procedural aspect of life goes on automatically and unattended. However, suddenly there is a problem: the car does not work, or the kettle will not boil. At that point we are catapulted out of routine. The original process is recalled to mind, possibly in sequence, as we check through procedure. We think through the problem in an objective sense, perhaps talking out loud to aid our reasoning. We aim to bring the situation back under control: to that procedural state of equilibrium where all thought processes are working at maximal efficiency, that is, with minimal effort.

In this view of language the world forms part of a dramatic universe which constantly confronts us. Our way of dealing with this confrontation is to establish control over a situation through familiarity with it; to process and proceduralise it as much as possible, leaving the maximum amount of thought available for dealing with the present. Problems are always confronting us, throwing us out of procedure towards greater concentration on current circumstance. Language is the mediator of all this: it lets us communicate with others and with ourselves; it provides the basis for thought; it moves problems to resolution. Language is able to provide us with conceptual schemes for solving problems.

But what about the case of the second language learner? Learning a language is *per se* problematic. It immediately throws us out of procedure into an alien linguistic environment. Here language is no longer the means of solving problems with the world: it is itself the problem. We may have conceptual schemes of the world, but we cannot express them in the second language. We do not have knowledge of the words, or of how to make the structures work for us. Then there is a second order of knowledge in learning another language: as well as knowing how to deal with objects, others and ourselves in life, we must find new language to mediate our actions. A third order of knowledge is the extent to which we are aware of these difficulties and able to design ways of dealing with them.

If we follow through these three orders of knowledge, we can see that our first task is to learn the correct words for the second language world and the linguistic structures to operate them. Our second task is somehow to graft this knowledge on to who we already are and our existing understanding of life. Our third task is to be aware of this procedure and act in ways which maximise its effectiveness.

I referred above to 'communicative' and 'strategic' action, and pointed out that very often modern languages lessons are designed around an ideal notion of communication, or to create the ideal conditions for communication. There is an old adage which asks: 'Are we teaching communication so that language is learnt; or are we teaching language so that communication is learnt?' The ideal *communicative* action I describe suggests that it is the former which most often applies in the modern languages classroom: that communication, if present, is the means and the end to second language learning. Here it is assumed that the three orders of knowledge I have just mentioned are present implicitly in language and can themselves be learned through the process of second language acquisition. However, a consideration of my other action type, the *strategic*, may show us that there are other ways of thinking about modern languages classrooms and teaching than creating ideal communicative conditions. Here communication would no longer be both means and end, but rather the goal towards which strategic action was planned. To this extent there would be a third order of knowledge present in the classroom: that which planned for the processing of the full scope of linguistic information. This knowledge would include vocabulary and grammar, but greater attention would be given to the way such systemic knowledge mapped on to the schematic view of life learners already possessed. Relational concepts, functions and notions, values and organising principles; the socio-cultural aspects of others; the identity of the self, with all its individual differences – all would be essential constituents of this way of dealing with any language problems which presented themselves.

Gaining Control

If learning a first language can be seen as a process of gaining control over self, others and the world of objects, learning a second language might similarly be seen as gaining control over self, others and objects in that second language, except that this second process also involves a transferral of schematic knowledge and the development of systemic knowledge of the new language. Too often in second language learning and teaching the second has been seen as a by-product of the first, or the first as of secondary importance. Sometimes the control I write of has been interpreted simply as command of vocabulary and grammar, but mastery over these aspects of language rarely proves sufficient at any level of practical competence. We have all had the experience of drilling the perfect tense to perfection only to find it non-operationalised in continuous discourse outside of the grammatical exercise. Becoming linguistically competent involves control over the necessary language and structures. However, it also involves control over oneself in operating those words and structures. Moreover it involves control over the social and concrete world as this presents itself, in terms of making sense and meaning and mediating the problems which arise in interacting with it. A strategic view of language learning and teaching offers a different way of conceptualising these problems which will lead to the construction of distinct methodological principles in designing pedagogic activity. 'Strategic' in this sense refers to the way the learner might operate in the world in and through the second language. This is the topic I now wish to address.

Learning Strategies

Research and enquiry about learning strategies arise from a focus on the 'good language learner' (Naiman *et al.*, 1996/1978). The notion is a simple one: what is it that the successful language learner does that the unsuccessful one does not? Furthermore, if we can ascertain what it is, can we then teach it to the less successful?

Why 'strategies'? Early on in the research field it was supposed that successful learners had a set of actions and approaches which they adopted in their language learning, and that these were deliberate and systematic, if not always conscious. The word 'strategy' therefore implies a sense of forethought and pre-planning, if only at an intuitive level. Early researchers (Stern, 1975) arranged for language learners to keep diaries of their work and then analysed these in terms of likely approaches to the tasks of learning. It was possible to demonstrate a whole range of strategies which showed how learners operated on various linguistic levels. Some of these were affective and attitudinal, as successful learners sought out opportunities to engage with the language and those speaking it. Others related to ways of systematising structural knowledge about the language. Mostly, however, all the strategies listed showed how successful learners were active and positive about their language learning, building up a base competence which they developed over a period of time.

Later work focused on the social context of language learning, demonstrating how successful learners readily engaged with others and interacted with their environment. Specifically, it was possible to identify the ways in which successful learners made the most of a little language, called on discourse techniques to control what was being said, and learnt from it (Wong-Fillmore, 1979). On occasion this amounted to pretence, with a learner making as if they understood in an attempt to keep an interaction going from which sense and meaning might eventually be picked up. As successful learners attempted to recreate their world view in the new language the picture that emerged was very much akin to the problem-solving and control of self, others and objects described above. They also attempted to express their existent identities through the new language.

Such social interaction is very much dependent on a context where a high degree of target language is available as the natural medium of discourse. In such situations the conditions for communicative action are indeed ideal. In more formal pedagogic contexts, however, learners often do not have the opportunity to act in this way. Here formal strategies seem to play a more significant role. Such strategies might be closely akin to study skills, or else involve actual grappling with language tasks. The strategies may be deliberate, but not necessarily conscious. O'Malley and Chamot (1990) list a whole set of strategies according to their cognitive and metacognitive character. A *cognitive* strategy is one which involves the learner engaging with the language and trying to make sense of it and in it. Examples might include:

- *Inferencing*   Using available information to guess meanings of new items, predict outcomes, or fill in missing information.
- *Resourcing*   Using target language reference materials such as dictionaries, encyclopedias or textbooks.
- *Deduction*   Applying rules to understand or produce the second language, or making up rules based on language analysis.
- *Repetition*   Imitating a language model, including overt practice and silent rehearsal.

From this brief list it is possible to see how these so-called cognitive strategies can operate on a number of levels involving external sources, mental learning skills and reasoning about sense and meaning in language.

Metacognitive strategies, on the other hand, involve a further step of knowledge: the prefix 'meta' means 'beyond'. Metacognitive strategies are thus those which are beyond cognition. In practice this term is employed to describe all those strategies which involve a degree of planning, self-management and monitoring. Examples could include:

- *Selective attention*   Deciding in advance to attend to specific aspects of input, often by scanning for key words, concepts and/or linguistic markers.
- *Self-monitoring*   Checking one's comprehension during listening or reading, to assess accuracy.
- *Self-evaluation*   Checking the outcomes of one's own language learning against a standard after it has been completed.

In each case, metacognitive strategies involve thinking about a language rather than working in the language itself.

This way of describing strategies implicates my earlier discussion of language learning as information processing, inasmuch as it pertains to strategic action, to language learning as an end, rather than simply a communicative goal. The order of knowledge involved is not so much language for communication's sake as knowledge of how to act on language, and awareness of the outcomes of this acting. It is this second order of knowledge that features in the strategic language-learning context, rather than communicative intent or the language *per se*.

So far this discussion represents strategies in quite an abstract or theoretical way. But there are further, more practical points we can raise about them.

First, it is clear that even within the list of strategies there is a vast range of information involved in operating them. So, for example, consulting a dictionary involves using various other pieces of information on how it is set out and the way rubrics can guide and help in ascertaining the correct meaning. This knowledge is of a different nature from the rules one might apply in order to deduce meaning from language.

Second, therefore, implicit in this distinction is some hierarchy of difficulty: certain strategies are easier to operate than others. Some may also deal with the mechanics of language in a bottom-up way, whilst others operate from a more top-down, holistic level.

It follows, third, that easier strategies might be learned earlier, the difficult ones acquired later. Moreover some strategies might be more useful than others, in so far as they are capable of application in a wider variety of settings.

Fourth, we must recognise the context dependency of strategies inasmuch as they can only ever be applied to particular linguistic situations. Certain language tasks therefore give rise to specific strategies. However, there is also the particular language learner to consider. Listing only the repertoire of possible strategies available to a learner understates the individual variation present in strategy use. In other words, what works for one learner may not work for another. Individual personality, cognitive style and identity will have much bearing on the extent to which any one strategy is employed, or not. Pupils makes choices which form patterns according to their own particular dispositions.

Learning to Learn

The English National Curriculum for modern foreign languages (DfE, 1995) does indeed include references to strategies for learners of modern languages to use in its suggestions concerning 'Language Learning Skills and Knowledge of Language':

Pupils should be taught to:

(a) learn by heart phrases and short extracts, e.g. rhymes, poems, songs, jokes, tongue-twisters;
(b) acquire strategies for committing familiar language to memory;
(c) develop their independence in language learning and use;

(d)   use dictionaries and reference materials;
(e)   use context and other clues to interpret meaning;
(f)   understand and apply patterns, rules, and exceptions in language forms and structures;
(g)   use their knowledge to experiment with language;
(h)   understand and use formal and informal language; and
(i)   develop strategies for dealing with the unpredictable.

Clearly this list relates to my discussion of cognitive and metacognitive strategies. Other language skills are listed in the Curriculum's *Programme of Study Part I*. Pupils should:

- listen attentively, listen for gist and detail;
- follow instructions and directions;
- imitate pronunciation and intonation patterns;
- listen and respond to different type of language; and
- produce a variety of spelling.

It is common in coursebooks for the authors to list these types of skill and to offer language-learning tasks to develop them. Very often, however, they are treated as implicit elements of language learning, tools which may be acquired as a by-product of gaining competence, rather than as the means for doing so. Turning a skill into a strategy requires that it is not only used, but is recognised as a language-learning tool; yet there is little by way of guidance in the National Curriculum on how to unpack the forms of knowledge – social and linguistic, declarative and procedural, cognitive and metacognitive – that might guide teachers in their under-standing of them. There is no sense of the relevance of the hierarchy of difficulty or the order of acquisition in developing such language skills. The National Curriculum covers five years of language learning, and is presumably seen as providing the basis for advanced linguistic skills thereafter in further and higher education. But how are we to operationalise its main tenets in practice? particularly if we take a strate-gic line in helping learners acquire the skills to learn a language, rather than simply teaching the language itself?

   Some research has reported (Grenfell & Harris, 1993; 1994; 1995; 1999) on the possibility of strategy instruction, where learners are indeed taught specific strategies deemed useful to the language-learning process. Just as action research follows a cycle of development involving the identification of problems, the planning and implementation of the modification of prac-tice and the evaluation of outcomes, which together feed into a new cycle of change, so in strategy instruction there is an attempt to create an ongoing programme of change. This programme involves a series of discrete stages:

(1)   preparation/consciousness-raising;
(2)   modelling;
(3)   practice;
(4)   action-planning/goal-setting and monitoring;
(5)   focused practice and fading of reminders; and
(6)   evaluation of strategy acquisition and recommencing the cycle.

In Stage 1, learners reflect on the learning process and the notion of strategy use is introduced.

In Stage 2, certain strategies are presented, explained or demonstrated. These might include any of those already listed. In the early stages, the accent is less on putting specific strategies across to learners than on introducing the idea of thinking about language learning in this way. Strategies might then relate to specific skill areas – listening, speaking, reading, writing – or other ways of thinking about language.

In Stage 3, opportunities are created for the strategies dealt with to be encountered in classroom tasks. The learners therefore get to use them in practice.

In Stage 4, learners further develop their metacognitive awareness in planning to operationalise the strategies and setting themselves goals to do so. Such targets serve to encourage pupils to think about their language learning strategically.

In Stage 5, more practice is provided but learners are encouraged to proceduralise their use so that strategies become a more unconscious, automatic way of doing language.

Finally, in Stage 6, learners are encouraged to reflect on the strategy instruction cycle and to comment on the usefulness of this approach to language. This final stage, just as in action research, also provides a springboard to further work; identifying other strategies which may come to be of use as general awareness of language is developed, together with the means to work with it.

At one level such strategy instruction clearly represents just another aspect of language to teach, and there is some evidence to suggest that teachers, if not learners, might initially feel that strategy work is simply a diversion from the real business of language learning. Moreover this explicit teaching of strategies can overlook individual dispositions in strategy use. Strategies arising out of group discussion can at least offer opportunities for common skills to develop and be focused upon within a class, but some attention will need to be given to those individual learners who simply do not find a particular strategy available or useful to them. Finally, it might be felt that making strategies explicit in this manner will suffer the same fate as any other explicit knowledge taught formally. We know that the presentation, explanation and teaching of grammar does not automatically lead to it being learned. Might the same apply to strategies? Possibly. What is being advocated here, though, is not a return to formal instruction, merely the addition of a strategic view to the already communicative classroom. Another way to approach strategy instruction is to keep the particular mechanism or strategy much more implicit in the early stages. In this case tasks are created which require such or such strategies and these are used in classes. Here it is for the teacher to decide what to teach and when. Only when learners are using the strategies effectively does the teacher invite reflection on what is occurring in the activity; that is, work to make the strategy explicit.

Teaching and Learning Strategies

Much of this chapter has highlighted the theoretical background to learning strategies and the practical implications they may have for the learner. As noted, such strategies often develop in a highly personalised way, but many of them are sufficiently broad to be used by a wide spectrum of learners. Recent years have seen increasing interest in the notion of *autonomy* in second language learning, as David Little will discuss in Chapter 2 (see also Gathercole, 1990; Page, 1992). This focus on the individual learner arises partly as a result of methodological disappointments, including communicative language teaching, but its increasing prominence can also be attributed to acceptance of a general conclusion of applied linguistic research: namely, that learners do develop at their own individual rate and follow some sort of broadly predictable sequence. The upshot of this realisation is that presenting learners with language elements too far ahead of their existing competence will simply lead to overload and prevent them from dealing with the language. In Vygotskyan terms, these elements lie outside their 'zone of proximal development' (Vygotsky 1978) and therefore cannot be brought under 'control'. It follows that teachers, no matter how sensitive to the needs of their learners, cannot know how each individual pupil is going to react to the language presented to them. The advocates of a more autonomous approach to second language learning believe that it is therefore better to let learners establish their own linguistic agenda. This happens anyway at a semi-conscious level, as we saw with the good language learner, so why not make it an explicit pedagogic fact?

'Autonomy' is consequently a term used in situations where learners themselves decide on the content of their learning and/or the means to work with it. Its definition is clearly quite broad and can accommodate a range of options, from total independence to limited choice. Its principled intent, however, is to introduce elements of autonomy and increase them as part of the learning process. In other words, autonomy – learner independence – becomes a central organising principle of language learning around which to base pedagogic activity. I shall not go into the details of how this might be achieved, since such a discussion would constitute another whole chapter. It is worth stating, though, that the principle of autonomy holds that language learners cannot be successful without operating to at least some degree in an independent linguistic manner. In other words, having language competence necessarily entails a measure of autonomy in language use. What does all this imply for classroom methodology and learning strategies?

In the earlier part of this chapter I described a archetypical modern languages classroom and noted the way the teacher prescribed language use and how it should be learnt. In a more autonomous classroom pupils will have a greater say in what they do and how they do it. This clearly does not mean that the teacher withdraws and leaves it all up to the pupils. In such a situation they will simply flounder and progress will be slow. Rather, the teacher provides the framework around which learning is organised and makes materials and resources available that will enable the pupils to carry out their tasks. Central to this methodological shift is a systematic dealing with the kinds of strategy to aid learning which are listed above. In other words, the National Curriculum *Programme of Study Part I* is unpacked to present a series and sequence of possible strategies that will cover the duration of a language-learning course. It is recognised that many of these learning skills are specific, so that a number of them must be presented, but it will finally be up to the pupils to decide which are of most use. Strategy instruction, as referred to above, will be one element in classroom organisation: this will provide opportunities for raising awareness of the importance of strategy use and encouraging learners to think about their learning. However, strategy instruction takes time. Teachers will also of course need to incorporate all this into their own view of the learning process over the short, medium and long term.

English primary schools are presently undergoing a revolution in the way they teach reading. Famously, a 'literacy hour' has been created, where pupils are required to follow a sequence of work for one hour a day. The hour itself is structured in a very specific way: 15 minutes on whole-class teaching on shared text work; 15 minutes on whole-class teaching on focused work; 20 minutes on group and independent work; and ten minutes on a plenary review of what has been learnt. Such a structure may not necessarily be suitable for a secondary school modern languages lesson, but it is important to realise that very soon primary school pupils used to this type of work will be going into secondary schools. They will have become accustomed to working together collaboratively and discussing language. Increased pupil independence is required and a prioritising of a strategic view of language and literacy teaching. Pupils will have a view of their first language of word, sentence, phrase and text level work. They will also be familiar with writing genres and the notion of audience (DfEE, 1998). Clearly modern languages teachers need to capitalise and build on this type of work. Fixed times need to be set aside and structured in a way which builds up an expectation on the part of the learner. Knowledge *about*, as well as of, language must be given prominence in the second language learning process. Shared meaning and experience both of and about language need to be present in language learning alongside experience in the language. This may mean a clearer distinction between literacy and oral/ aural skills. It is appropriate that reading, writing, speaking and listening have been given equal importance in curriculum and syllabus design, but we also know that communicative language teaching is often interpreted as prioritising oral and aural skills – so much so, that reading is often seen as an adjunct to learning and writing as mainly an expression of the spoken word. A clearer distinction between these two types of language and how they operate might open up opportunities for using reading and writing as a support to speaking and listening, by providing structures to help generate language and thought. A structured hour on a regular basis could put learners in a situation where they were expected to work both independently, on an individual basis, and collaboratively, as part of the group. In both cases the whole might be greater than the sum of the parts. Talking with a partner, working with each other, raises possibilities, makes knowledge explicit, and shares thinking about language in preparation for work in language; especially if backed up with whole-class plenaries, discussion and reviews which structure thinking and provide a scaffold on which all this work can be hung.

In 1996, possibly in search of a symbolic renaissance in the teaching and learning of second languages, the education committee of the Council for Cultural Co-operation (part of the Council of Europe) produced a *Common European Framework of Reference* for the teaching and learning of modern languages. It is true that we need some common European policy on the age at which languages are started, the content and methodology of approach in teaching languages, and which languages are to be taught. Moreover besides clear positions on each of these in our own national context, we need to be sure, in a world frequently dominated by American English, about what we ourselves envisage in terms of second language learning. The past decade has seen reform and yet further reform in secondary school second language learning. Diversification away from French as a second language has come and gone; the vision of 'languages for all' has proved to be something of a mirage. Faced with indecision and a lack of reform in second language learning at 16+, the examination boards have themselves profoundly changed their view of what constitutes an A-level in the major modern languages; so much so that it is often unclear what particular skills someone with this qualification may have. Will they be an astute literary critic, or vocationally adept?

The proliferation of undergraduate courses to cater for the spectrum of demand has created a similar doubt about our graduate linguists. Is it fair to expect the same proficiency from someone who has studied a second language along with history, sociology, economics, management and European studies as from another student who has focused exclusively on language competence? Clearly not. In primary schools the cessation of modern languages learning, following the Burstall report (Burstall *et al.*, 1974) on the 1960s experiment, has left lingering concerns about whether second language learning is even appropriate for this age range. Questions therefore remain about what should be taught at this age, and with what aims and objectives. Again, in the absence of clear pointers from those in control of curricula many schools have gone their own way and done their own thing in modern languages. The results are a proliferation of formats, some of which may seem idiosyncratic, and an unhelpful diversity of provision.

For those of us faced with these questions, the *Common European Framework* at least provides a structure within which we can formulate our response. Amongst its many lists concerning the types of social, linguistic and vocational skills and competencies we might expect from learners is the simple distinction between 'savoir-faire', 'savoir-être' and 'savoir-apprendre'. The first relates to the skills and 'know-how' of language learning; the second to the way individuals effect and are affected by their learning; and the third to pupils' ability to learn, in other words to learning strategies. We might feel that communicative language teaching as we know it has been too concerned with the first of these in recent years: how to get things done in the language, how to transact business. What we need is a greater sense of individuals developing and expressing themselves in the language. In early stages the practice of such an aim might be limited to simple expressions of pupils' likes and dislikes. However, and especially in the second part of secondary school modern languages lessons, pupils need to be presented with topics and issues which more closely match their intellectual maturity. Refined and grammatically more complex transactional dialogues simply do not engage the cognitive character of personal curiosity for a large proportion of our learners. The same argument might well be applied to languages at 16+. Greater recognition of the learner as an autonomous identity rather than as a linguistic *naïf* would provide a little relief from the tensions and strains inherent in being oneself in another language and the feeling and emotions necessarily evoked, but it could also give rise to greater involvement, motivation and more effective language learning.

All this, however, requires that a personal agenda be set and developed, and it is in that area that learning strategies have perhaps their most important part to play. As I have argued, the 'savoir-apprendre' of language learning starts as soon as learners are given some control over the decision process of language. It continues in group activity, which raises awareness and works collaboratively on knowledge about language and the means of working with it. And it results in learners with a greater sense of their own means for acquiring language in all skills in both public and pedagogic situations. Mostly, however, they develop their own repertoire of strategies to suit their own needs at that specific stage in their learning.

Such an approach and such a focus on strategy work requires a pedagogic shift on the part of teachers as well as learners. We know from research that teachers are reluctant to take on the job and to give up their traditional role of direct linguistic input and guidance. They feel there is enough to cover without having to deal with strategies as well. Teachers might also protest that, increasingly, their job is being defined as delivery of the prescribed syllabus. In this system there is little room for individual variation. Pupils' autonomy and the learning strategy work it entails therefore also imply teacher autonomy: that teachers have some control and power of decision-making over what is learned and how it is taught (for discussion of the professional development of modern languages teaching see Grenfell, 1997; 1998). Such a reorientation might lead to teaching strategies which are less focused on particular aspects of individual lessons and more concerned to take a long-term view of language learning, the stage learners are at, and how teaching approaches could match these underlying cognitive processes. Elsewhere (Grenfell, 1991) I have argued this position from a procedural view of language learning, suggesting that the five years of secondary school learning might best be viewed as three distinct but integrating 'cycles', each with their own characteristic strategic ends, aims and objectives.

The main message for the new millennium for modern languages learning and teaching from a strategic point of view, however, is that theory and practice can now be conceptually linked in a way which enjoins knowledge *of* language with knowledge *about* language; that pupil autonomy is a precondition to increasing successful learner linguistic competence; and that learning strategies represent one way of getting learners to work on their language by encouraging them to think more about what it is to learn a language and hence to know it. The pedagogic implications are enormous and it could be that much of what we traditionally accept for classroom use is rendered obsolete. Such a revolution in thinking and practice would require an alert and engaged teaching profession who had been given the time and space to let language happen with their learners. Teachers might gain from their own locally organised task forces or cluster groups in thinking through the issues raised by the strategic approach to language learning. Within these groups they would have the opportunity to develop their own knowledge about teaching and learning. Such meetings would have many of the characteristics of linguistic autonomy and strategic thought outlined above for the learner. To sum up: the study of modern languages needs to become less language learning, more learning to learn languages – a strategic as well as a communicative classroom for the twenty-first century.

Acknowledgements

I wish to thank Cheryl Hardy for reading through an earlier draft of this chapter and offering numerous comments which helped me develop my thinking and the style of what I have written.

I also wish to acknowledge my colleague Vee Harris. Much of my thinking on learning strategies has progressed through the work we have carried out together and the discussions and joint publications arising from it.

References

Burstall, C., Cohen, S., Hargreaves, M. and Jamieson, M. (1974) *Primary French in the Balance*. Slough: NFER.

Council for Cultural Co-operation, Education Committee (1996) *Modern Languages: Learning, Teaching and Assessment. A Common European Framework of Reference*. Strasbourg: Council of Europe.

Department for Education (DfE) (1995) *Modern Foreign Languages in the National Curriculum*. London: HMSO.

Department for Education and Employment (DfEE) (1998) *The National Literacy Strategy*. London: HMSO.

Gathercole, I. (ed.) (1990) *Autonomy in Language Learning*. London: CILT.

Grenfell, M. (1991) Communication: Sense and nonsense. *Language Learning Journal*

6–8.

Grenfell, M. (1997) Theory and practice in modern language teacher training. *Language Learning Journal* 16, 28–34.

Grenfell, M. (1998) *Training Teachers in Practice*. Clevedon: Multilingual Matters.

Grenfell, M. and Harris, V. (1993) How do pupils learn? (Part I). *Language Learning Journal* 8, 22–5.

Grenfell, M. and Harris, V. (1994) How do pupils learn? (Part II). *Language Learning Journal* 9, 7–11.

Grenfell, M. and Harris, V. (1995) Learning strategies and the advanced language learner. Paper given at 1995 conference of the British Association of Applied Linguistics, Southampton.

Grenfell, M. and Harris, V. (1999) *Modern Languages and Learning Strategies*. London: Routledge.

Habermas, J. (1984/1987) *Theory of Communicative Action* (2 vols). (T. McCarthy, trans.) Oxford: Polity Press.

Habermas, J. (1987) *Knowledge and Human Interests*. (J.J. Shapiro, trans.) Cambridge: Polity Press.

Naiman, N., Fröhlich, M., Stern, H.H. and Todesco, A. (1996/1978) *The Good Language Learner*. Clevedon: Multilingual Matters.

OFSTED (1995) *Modern Foreign Languages: A Review of Inspection Findings 1993/94*. London: HMSO.

Page, B. (ed.) (1992) *Letting Go, Taking Hold*. London: CILT.

Stern, H.H. (1975) What can we learn from the good language learner? *Canadian Modern Language Review* 31, 304–318.

Van Ek, J. (1975) *The Threshold Level*. Strasbourg: Council of Europe.

Vygotsky, L.S. (1978) *Mind in Society*. Cambridge, MA: Harvard University Press.

Vygotsky, L.S. (1962) *Thought and Language*. Cambridge, MA: MIT Press.

Wong-Fillmore, L. (1979) Individual differences in second language acquisition. In C.J. Fillmore, W.S.Y. Wang and D. Kempler (eds) *Individual Differences in Language Ability and Behaviour*. New York: Academic Press.

Chapter 2

Learner Autonomy: Why Foreign Languages Should Occupy a Central Role in the Curriculum

DAVID LITTLE

In formal educational contexts learners take their first steps towards autonomy when they begin to accept responsibility for their own learning. They exercise and gradually extend the range of their autonomy by sharing in the decisions and initiatives that give shape and direction to the learning process. And as they plan, monitor and evaluate their learning, they necessarily develop a capacity for reflective analysis.

Thus understood, the concept of learner autonomy – expressed, of course, in many different ways – has long been fundamental to liberal philosophies of education. But it has been a specific focus of debate in foreign language teaching only since 1979, when the Council of Europe published Henri Holec's *Autonomy and Foreign Language Learning* (Holec, 1981). At first learner autonomy was a minority interest, both as a theoretical preoccupation and as a guiding principle in classroom practice, but in the last few years it has been much more widely discussed, and at the end of the 1990s has much the same currency as 'communicative' and 'authentic' had in the 1980s. This is due partly to the influence of successful pedagogical experiments, but also to the fact that in the past decade curricular reforms in a number of European countries have highlighted the importance of developing learners' capacity for independent thought and critical reflection, of helping them to learn how to learn.

There is little evidence that this concern with autonomy has led to fundamental changes in the way foreign languages are taught. On the contrary, it is widely assumed that learner autonomy is a matter only of adding an extra dimension to what is done already – setting up a self-access centre, for example, or introducing strategy training. But learner autonomy, properly understood, involves a great deal more than the way in which we organise learning (self-access) or seek to develop our learners' metacognitive capacities (strategy training). As successful classroom experiments confirm, the

24

development of learner autonomy reveals profound truths about the ways in which human beings learn, and these ways of learning reveal profound truths about how human beings *are*. In other words, commitment to learner autonomy entails a readiness on the part of teachers and teacher trainers to explore what it is to be human and to rebuild pedagogy from first principles.

In this chapter I have two purposes. The first is to substantiate the claim I have just made, and the second is to show how learner autonomy, both as theoretical construct and as practical achievement, provides a powerful argument in favour of giving foreign languages a central role in general education. I begin with a practical example, a description of a successful experiment in learner autonomy and a commentary on its most prominent features. This is followed by two theoretical sections, the first concerned with learner autonomy and the second with the relation between learner autonomy and theories of pedagogy in general and foreign language teaching in particular. Finally, the fourth section considers some of the practical implications of my theoretical arguments.

Autonomy in Action: An Example

My example, based partly on a published account (Dam, 1995, Chap. 5) and partly on first-hand experience, is of an English class in a Danish middle school. The class comprises 21 learners aged 14 and 15. They are in their fourth year of learning English, so in school terms their level is intermediate. For two years now they have learned English chiefly by working in small groups on a succession of projects, each project cycle lasting four or five weeks.

The learners are half-way through a double lesson (90 minutes), and two weeks into their current project cycle. The lesson began with a brief plenary review of progress. This was conducted by the teacher with reference to a series of posters fixed to the classroom wall. These give basic information on each project – a title, the names of the group members, projected outcomes, and a brief action plan. The lesson will conclude with another brief plenary session in which groups will be able to ask questions and seek help of various kinds from the teacher and the other groups. For example they may have run into a problem that they do not know how to solve, or they may be unsure where to find textual material to support some aspect of their project. Before they leave the class all the learners will have engaged in at least a preliminary evaluation of today's learning, and they will know exactly what they must do for homework. In most cases this will be a matter of writing their own review of the class in their diary and working further on an aspect of the project for which they are personally responsible.

There are five tables in the classroom (for a diagram originally drawn by the learners themselves, see Dam, 1995: 73). At the first table Malene and Anders are making their own version of *Trivial Pursuit*. At the second table Martin, Louise, Rasmus and Sandra are writing a 'radio play' based on *Little Red Riding Hood*. Currently they are working on a script that in due course they will record on audio cassette. At the third table Betina, Morten, Rikke S. and Rikke P. are putting together a book – texts and pictures – about Australian marsupials. At the fourth table Klaus, Thomas and Jesper are compiling a book of poems (their own translations from Danish and English originals), while at the other end of the table Michael is working alone on a project entitled 'Games in English'. (Note that in this classroom individual work is the exception rather than the rule. It tends to occur when a new learner joins the class, when a learner who has been ill returns halfway through a project cycle, or when a learner's behaviour has caused him or her to be excluded from group work.) At the fifth table three groups are working: Anders and Maria are writing articles derived from newspaper reports on recent events in Romania (it is a matter of weeks since the fall of Ceausescu's dictatorship), Niklas and Helle are producing a book of anecdotes and jokes, and Camilla, Søren and Dennis are writing another 'radio play', this time based on the novel *Jaws*.

At the beginning of each project cycle the teacher invites ideas for possible projects, and groups form as ideas take shape. The learners themselves are responsible for taking the planning decisions that are summarised on the posters. It is also up to them to decide how to organise their work so as to bring their project to a successful conclusion. This is not necessarily a straightforward matter, especially if one or more members of the group contribute less to the project than they initially agreed to do, and it is sometimes necessary for a group to ask the teacher for help. Nevertheless it is clear that these learners are autonomous, in the fundamental sense that they set their own learning goals and select their own learning activities and materials.

The central role played by group work shows that autonomous learners are not isolated learners: in this environment learner autonomy is a matter of developing and exercising a capacity for independent learning behaviour in interaction with other learners. It is important to note that the ability to work autonomously in small groups is something these learners have gradually developed over several years. When they came to their first English lesson with this teacher, their classroom experience was entirely traditional: they were used to sitting in rows facing the teacher, and they had rarely been required to work with one or more other learners. They had to learn how to work collaboratively, first in pairs and then in small groups.

Their capacity for autonomous learning has developed gradually, in parallel with their proficiency in English, but from the beginning their English teacher has required them to be as autonomous as possible.

In this class there is no textbook; the only fixed support that these learners regularly refer to is a dictionary. What is more, the teacher has no list of grammar points that must at all costs be covered or communicative functions that must be drilled. This is not to say, however, that the class is working without regard to the curriculum. On the contrary: at the beginning of the school year the teacher explained the official curricular goals, and the learners are now working in ways that they believe will enable them to achieve those goals. Their belief is based largely on past experience: from their very first English class they have been encouraged to consider what is interesting and what is uninteresting, what is enjoyable and what is not enjoyable, what works and what does not work. So far from ignoring the curriculum, this class is dynamically engaged with the curriculum to an extent that is unknown in the majority of classrooms.

As one looks and listens, two things are immediately striking. First, although seven groups are working, and thus generating talk, in a relatively small space, the room is by no means noisy: these learners know how to communicate with other members of their group without disturbing the rest of the class. Second, the learners talk to one another for the most part in English. The teacher has insisted on this from the very beginning, for she knows that her learners will become proficient in English only by using the language for communicative purposes that matter to them. In this classroom learner autonomy is not an end in itself, but the means by which learners become more proficient in English than would otherwise be the case. Visitors from many different countries come here because they want to learn more about learner autonomy; interestingly, they tend to be impressed as much by the learners' readiness to communicate with one another in English and the fluency with which they do so, as by their collaborative working methods.

One also notices that these learners are fully absorbed in what they are doing. No doubt some of them, on this particular day as on any other, are more sharply focused and keenly motivated than others, and there are inevitable lapses in attention. But because they are working on projects that they have chosen, according to a plan that they have helped to negotiate, motivation is rarely a serious problem. When it does arise it can usually be traced to problems that the individual learner is having outside the classroom. Clearly, one of the most obvious benefits of transferring responsibility to the learners is that it goes a long way towards solving the motivational problem.

As they work the groups maintain a double focus: they are concerned at once with the task in hand and the language with which they perform the task. For example, the group working on the *Little Red Riding Hood* play must decide what the grandmother says next; but they must also attend to how she says it. 'Metatalk' (that is, talk about talk, or talk about language) is also fundamental to the way in which this class is organised at the most general level. The learners themselves are responsible for planning, reviewing and evaluating their learning, and none of these functions can be performed without recourse to metacognition and metalinguistic awareness. Many teachers who readily accept that their learners should perform communicative tasks in the target language nevertheless insist that it is impossible to use the target language for metatalk. This shows a serious misunderstanding of the nature of linguistic proficiency and communication: in most situations our capacity to talk is inseparable from our capacity for metatalk. Of course the learners in our example have had to learn how to engage in metatalk in their English class, but their teacher has treated it as just another aspect of learning to communicate in English.

I have already mentioned the posters on the classroom wall and the diaries in which individual learners keep track of their own learning, note down what they have agreed to contribute to the project in hand, evaluate their own and their group's performance, and so on. Writing is clearly one of the chief tools that these learners use in the exercise of their autonomy. They use it not only to maintain a personal record of the learning process, but also as a means of supporting the development of their spoken proficiency. Especially in the earlier stages of learning, they have been encouraged to use written prompts – key words, phrases and short texts – to support speaking activities.

These learners are generally comfortable communicating with one another in English. This is partly the result of habit, but it also has to do with the fact that they are continuously engaged in constructing an English-speaking culture rooted in their own Danish culture. They typically base their projects on authentic texts of one kind or another, but the texts are as often in Danish as in English. The groups writing plays based on *Little Red Riding Hood* and *Jaws*, for example, have derived their knowledge of these stories at least in part from Danish versions. In general, translation from Danish into English tends to figure prominently among these learners' preferred learning activities. This is only to be expected from an approach that encourages learners to work from their own preoccupations, interests and experience. Their method of working gives rise to a succession of intercultural encounters that take Danish as their starting point and move with growing fluency towards English. In this way, the learners' gradually developing proficiency in English is an authentic extension of their personal identity, which helps to explain their confidence in communication. They will never shed the cultural identity that they have acquired as Danes, but they are gradually becoming more proficient at being Danes in an English-speaking cultural environment.

What exactly does the teacher do in this classroom? As we have seen, she conducts a brief plenary session at the beginning and end of each lesson, and in this way maintains a sense of overall coherence. When the learners are working on their projects, she moves from group to group, sometimes observing, sometimes intervening with advice, sometimes answering learners' questions. At any time she may find it necessary to remind the learners of their short-term and long-term objectives, or challenge their working methods. She also takes in the learners' diaries on a regular basis so that she can monitor individual learning effort and progress. If learners have specific questions or problems, they write them in their diary and the teacher writes her response. In this way the diaries gradually develop a dialogic as well as a monologic dimension.

The teacher's own diary is the principal means by which she plans, monitors and evaluates her classes. In it she records the structure and content of each lesson and tracks the progress of the class (both groups and individuals) through the school year. The diary also serves the very necessary function of self-evaluation. The learners may be responsible for their own learning, but this does not absolve the teacher of responsibility for maintaining an appropriate learning environment and doing her best to ensure that as much learning as possible takes place. If it is appropriate for the learners to engage in regular self-scrutiny and self-evaluation, it is no less appropriate for the teacher to do the same. Stretching back across two and a half decades, this teacher's diaries are the rich deposit of a process of personal development that is still in train.

For more than 20 years this teacher's classrooms have provided inspiration for language teachers, teacher trainers and pedagogical theorists from many different countries. Perhaps more important, they have produced a steady stream of learners who are autonomous users of their target language. Inevitably, some learners are more proficient than others – have a more native-like pronunciation, a more sophisticated control of syntax, a more accurate grasp of morphology, a more wide-ranging vocabulary, and so on. But all learners can, to some extent, communicate in English. That is the peculiar and enviable triumph of this pedagogy oriented to the development of learner autonomy, and it surely represents a compelling argument in favour of giving foreign languages an obligatory role at the centre of general education.

Leni Dam's approach to the teaching of English is not standard practice in Danish schools. On the contrary, it remains a minority pursuit, though one that in recent years has begun to attract an increasing number of adherents. Nevertheless it is influenced in a number of ways by the environment in which it has developed. For example, average class size in Danish schools is significantly lower than in British and Irish schools. This does not mean that it is necessarily easier to organise group work in Danish than in British or Irish classrooms, but larger numbers may very well require different techniques. Also, in the Danish system pupils call teachers by their first names. No doubt in many cases this practice quickly fossilises into a meaningless routine, but its very existence implies a cultural readiness to share authority between teachers and learners. The same readiness is not usually apparent in the pragmatics governing communication between teachers and learners in British and Irish classrooms.

We must be aware likewise of important linguistic differences. For example, English is very much 'in the air' in Denmark, so that it is quite easy for learners to find authentic English materials for themselves. By contrast, French and German are not 'in the air' to the same extent in Britain and Ireland, which means that learners may find it more difficult to source their own materials. What is more, inflectional morphology is much simpler in English than it is in other European languages. The fact that Leni Dam's learners pay little explicit attention to the grammar of English seems not to disadvantage them, whereas to pay no attention to the grammar of French or German in British or Irish classrooms may be a recipe for disaster.

If we want to achieve the same kinds of effect as Leni Dam, then, we should not simply copy what she does. Rather we must seek the principles that underlie her success and consider how we can best apply them to our own situation. Accordingly my next two sections are theoretical rather than practical; they draw on work in a number of relevant areas, and in doing so, continue my commentary on Leni Dam's classroom.

Autonomy: A Natural Tendency in Human Behaviour

The behaviour of Leni Dam's learners coincides with seminal definitions of learner autonomy. For example, Holec (1981: 3) argues that autonomy is 'the ability to take charge of one's learning', which means:

> to have, and to hold, the responsibility for all the decisions concerning all aspects of this learning, i.e.:
>
> • determining the objectives;
> • defining the contents and progressions;

- selecting methods and techniques to be used;
- monitoring the procedure of acquisition properly speaking (rhythm, time, place, etc.);
- evaluating what has been acquired.

This is exactly how Leni Dam's learners exercise and develop their autonomy. And their behaviour similarly illustrates my own more general definition of learner autonomy as 'a *capacity* – for detachment, critical reflection, decision-making, and independent action' (Little, 1991: 4; italics in original). In developing this capacity learners achieve what has traditionally been one of the central goals of education; yet they do so in a way that makes it seem the most natural thing in the world. This is hardly surprising, however, for learner autonomy – the capacity for independent, self-managing behaviour in contexts of formal learning – is no more than a special case of a general behavioural capacity that seems to be fundamental to our human constitution.

For example, autonomy is at once the goal of developmental learning and a characteristic of its underlying dynamic. Consider the case of first language acquisition. In one sense we never stop learning our mother tongue – new words are constantly being coined, and at any time a change in our personal circumstances may require us to master a new terminology or a new style of speaking or writing. But in a more basic sense the learning process is completed early in life, at the age of 6 or 7; for by then children have acquired most of the structures of their mother tongue, a vocabulary that reflects their experience and the environment in which they live, and at least an implicit sense of the pragmatics of communication (when and how they are expected to speak in the different contexts they are familiar with). Clearly, then, one of the chief outcomes of first language acquisition is a capacity for autonomous language use. But this is not to say that children are non-autonomous during the acquisition process. On the contrary, they display a high degree of autonomy from the earliest stages, deciding, for example, when they do and when they do not want to communicate with those around them. Children do not first acquire their mother tongue in order then to become autonomous communicators – they are autonomous from the beginning, and the language they acquire serves merely to increase the range and scope of their autonomy.

Autonomy is similarly fundamental to the learning that we do informally in non-educational contexts. Such learning is driven by our personal needs and interests, which we pursue spontaneously, autonomously, and often without conscious awareness that learning is taking place. It draws on our intrinsic motivation, which is 'defined by our own personal interests':

> – the subject matter and activities we enjoy, the areas of knowledge we want to develop, the challenges we want to tackle, the skills we want to master. Intrinsically motivated learning is also contextualized learning, whereby skills are developed in their natural context of use through regular practice. Thus the intrinsically motivated learner will learn to paint by painting, to work with computers by working with computers, and to learn languages by using them. (Ushioda, 1998)

This helps to explain how we develop skills and amass knowledge simply by living; but it also helps to explain the success of Leni Dam's learners, who learn English by working on projects whose form and content are determined by their own interests.

The close link between autonomy, intrinsic motivation and the efficiency of developmental and experiential learning prompts the thought that all truly successful learners in any domain are autonomous learners. There is, however, a crucial difference between the child learning her mother tongue or the adult developing new skills through the practice of embroidery or carpentry on the one hand, and learners in formal educational contexts on the other. The autonomy that is an obligatory feature of developmental and out-of-school learning is something of which the individual may or may not be consciously aware, whereas in formal learning the exercise and development of autonomy are necessarily matters of conscious intention. This is because education is shaped by conscious intentions at every level: ministries elaborate curricula, teachers have their plans, and learners know that they go to school or college in order to learn. For this reason, metacognition and metatalk are in principle central to the educational enterprise, which should always be defined and shaped by what Bruner (1986: 125) calls 'the metalinguistic function, or turning around on one's use of language to examine or explicate it'. As we shall see, this thought is fundamental to the pedagogical theories on which I shall now draw to give further substance to the concept of learner autonomy.

Learner Autonomy and Pedagogical Theory

If learner autonomy is just a special case of a general human tendency, its development must be rooted in the knowledge, interests and perceived needs that learners bring to the learning situation. In other words, it must take its impetus from learners' intrinsic motivation. On the other hand, autonomy in contexts of formal learning entails the development of a reflective capacity that is underpinned by the steady growth of metacognitive and metalinguistic awareness. Again it is worth pointing out that this understanding of learner autonomy is entirely harmonious with traditional educational aspirations. After all, as Donaldson (1978: 123) has pointed out, the growth of intellect is closely associated with the growth of consciousness: 'If the intellectual powers are to develop, the child must gain a measure of control over his own thinking and he cannot control it while he remains unaware of it.'

According to this view, success in education arises when there is a sustained and fruitful interaction between 'school knowledge', which is formalised according to the conventions of educational and scientific culture, and 'action knowledge', which we acquire simply by living (these two terms were coined by Barnes, 1976). School knowledge demands conscious awareness and tends towards disembeddedness and abstraction, whereas action knowledge is context-bound and mostly acquired by implicit processes. Barnes (1976: 79f.) illustrates the relation between these two kinds of knowledge as follows:

> Imagine two children who have been learning about animals' diet and teeth. One child, if asked the right question, can tell you that some animals eat meat, some vegetable foods, and some both, and that this matches differences in their teeth. The other child has learnt that wild cats eat meat, knows that his own cat at home has a mixed diet, and wonders what effect this will have on his teeth. The first child in one sense 'knows' about diet and teeth but can only use it in the classroom; it is still 'school knowledge'. The other child is beginning to incorporate the information into the inner map of reality on which his actions are based, his 'action knowledge'.

The dominant tradition in pedagogy, what Barnes (1976: 142) calls the Transmission model, assumes that it is the teacher's task to transmit knowledge and to test whether the learners have received it. There is no doubt that some learners achieve autonomy within this tradition, but they do so randomly and often as a result of factors that lie outside the immediate educational environment. A pedagogy explicitly focused on the development of learner autonomy corresponds to what Barnes calls the Interpretation model: 'For the Interpretation teacher …the pupil's ability to re-interpret knowledge for himself is crucial to learning, and he sees this as depending on a productive dialogue between the pupil and himself.'

Much criticism of traditional pedagogy focuses precisely on learners' lack of involvement in the learning process (see, for example, Illich, 1971, 1979; Freire, 1972; Rogers, 1983; Tharp & Gallimore, 1988; Mayher, 1990).

This is at once a discoursal and a social problem. Learners can become more actively involved in their learning only by assuming a wider set of discourse roles than the traditional classroom allows them; but this will happen only if the traditional social structures of the classroom, and especially traditional power relationships, are relaxed. The problem is brought into especially sharp focus by the study of discourse and learning at home and at school carried out by Tizard and Hughes (1984). They identify five factors that facilitate learning in the home: the extensive range of activities in which the child is involved, the common experience she shares with her family, the degree of individual attention she receives, the fact that her learning is embedded in contexts that carry great meaning for her, and the fact that learning is supported by the closeness of family relationships (Tizard & Hughes, 1984: 250f.). Clearly, school is a very different environment, in which these factors are either absent or greatly attenuated. The difference is, of course, one of the reasons why we send children to school in the first place, but it does have an in-built tendency to generate varieties of talk in which children are assigned largely subordinate roles.

Anyone who reads a study like that carried out by Tizard and Hughes cannot fail to recognise that bridging the gap between home and school poses formidable problems. The example with which I began this chapter shows that the task is not beyond the abilities of the individual teacher; but in most educational systems it must be accomplished against the current. The difficulty of making widespread progress should not be underestimated, especially at a time when education is generally thought of as a commodity rather than a process. As Salmon (1995: 1) has written, 'underpinning the recent and unprecedented interference in schooling has been the metaphor of education as a supermarket'. The same metaphor encourages politicians to deride and condemn any pedagogical measures that strike them as experimental and (especially) learner-centred. In such circumstances the best we can do is refine our theoretical arguments by constantly measuring them against indisputably successful pedagogical practice.

It is clear that successful learning, and thus the development of learner autonomy, is promoted by some kinds of talk and not by others. This is not a matter of social or political preference; on the contrary, it arises from the very nature of the human organism. We are biological beings, born with a genetic inheritance that predisposes us to develop in particular ways; but we are also social beings, whose survival and growth depend on the support and stimulus that come to us from interaction with others. For example, naturally endowed children are pre-programmed to learn a mother tongue, but they will not do so if they grow up in isolation from other human beings. Our biological nature encompasses the things we have in common with one another, whereas our social nature accounts for the variety of human societies and cultures.

To the extent that it arises from interaction with others, human learning is a socio-cultural phenomenon. Indeed, the Soviet psychologist Lev Vygotsky argued that higher cognitive functions are internalised from social interaction:

> Every function in the child's cultural development appears twice: first, on the social level, and later, on the individual level; first, *between* people (*interpsychological*), and then *inside* the child (*intrapsychological*). This applies equally to voluntary attention, to logical memory, and to the formation of concepts. All the higher functions originate as actual relations between human individuals. (Vygotsky, 1978: 57; italics in original)

By this Vygotsky meant, for example, that children learn to pay attention to particular objects or events from the experience of shared attention that characterises their interactions with others. He formalised the role of social interaction in stimulating and guiding learning in his celebrated concept of the 'zone of proximal development', which he defined (1978: 86) as 'the distance between the actual developmental level as determined by independent problem solving and the level of potential development as determined through problem solving under adult guidance or in collaboration with more capable peers'.

According to Vygotsky, language plays a central role in learning because it is the symbolic tool that we use to guide problem-solving behaviour. Just as higher cognitive functions are internalised from social interaction, so our capacity for 'inner speech' – the thought clothed in language that we use to direct our actions – is internalised from 'social speech' via 'egocentric speech' (see for example Vygotsky, 1986: 86ff.) This process is summarised thus by Bershon (1992: 37):

> Speech used for problem-solving begins during social encounters involving communication and mutual regulation between children and adults or among children of varying capabilities. In this way, children build a lexicon of regulatory vocabulary that enables them to produce egocentric language to direct, control, and plan their activities during problem-solving. Finally, children internalize this language as inner speech, developing a vocabulary that they can draw on during task involvement to direct their actions.

Social, egocentric and inner speech all have a role to play in the exploratory talk that produces learning, but the pivotal function belongs to egocentric speech, which mediates between social–interactive and individual–cognitive processes. Any transcript of a successful learning interaction will confirm this: decisive moves tend to occur when one member of the group tries out an idea by thinking aloud, observing the interactive structure of the conversation, yet talking as much to himself as to the other members of the group.

Learner-directed group work plays a crucial role in the development of learner autonomy for three reasons. First, because learners come to the classroom with varying abilities, experience and interests, they are able to support one another in the performance of learning tasks; that is, they support one another in their respective zones of proximal development. Second, all forms of collaborative activity require that we make explicit to others, and thus to ourselves, what might otherwise remain implicit and thus unconscious. Participants in group work must maintain a shared understanding of the task they are engaged on, and contributions to the performance of the task must often be explained and justified. Third, the very fact that the group work is learner-directed guarantees that learners can share by negotiation the discourse roles they need to occupy in order to learn. In this regard it is worth noting the example of 'reciprocal teaching', a technique originally devised to teach reading and listening comprehension. Based on the strategies of questioning, summarising, clarifying and predicting , reciprocal teaching requires that 'students and teachers take turns leading discussions about shared text' (Palincsar *et al.*, 1993: 43). The success of experiments in reciprocal teaching seems to depend not only on making learners explicitly aware of strategies they previously lacked; as Wertsch (1998: 28) puts it, 'the level of engagement and the power and authority given to students in reciprocal teaching seem to be crucial'. In successful learning, in other words, the cognitive is never easy to separate from the affective, which brings us back to the two-way relation between intrinsic motivation and the development of learner autonomy.

Each successive element in the argument of this section so far echoes at a theoretical level one or another aspect of the practical example with which I began. Yet the argument is one that claims general pedagogical validity: in principle it is as relevant to the teaching of history or science as to the teaching of foreign languages. It is now necessary to extend the argument to take account of specific issues that arise in teaching a foreign language.

In my example two of the techniques employed are specific to language learning: the learners all communicate with one another in English, and writing the target language is no less important than speaking. The first of these techniques coincides with a growing body of empirical research findings in second language acquisition, as well as with commonsense intuition: there is only one sure way of learning to speak a foreign language, and that is by speaking it. The second technique is perhaps less obvious, not least because many so-called communicative classrooms continue to follow audiolingual orthodoxy in postponing the introduction of writing until basic speaking skills have been established. As I shall show, however, both techniques are the inevitable outcome of applying our theoretical principles to foreign language learning, and they serve to reinforce one another.

Barnes (1976) reports on research that he and his colleagues undertook to enable them to place teachers in relation to the Transmission and Interpretation views of learning. Perhaps predictably, they found a great deal of variation among the teachers of particular subjects; nevertheless, on a continuum stretching from extreme Transmission to extreme Interpretation views, specialist teachers arranged themselves in this order: science, foreign languages, domestic science, geography and history, religious education, English (as mother tongue). Barnes interprets this finding as follows (1976: 143f.):

> In both science and languages most teachers perceive themselves to have access to coherent and public bodies of knowledge which their pupils' everyday experience does not give them access to. Most English teachers do not believe themselves to hold a unique body of knowledge which is out of their pupils' reach, but see themselves as helping pupils to extend and refine the knowledge and skills which they use in everyday life.

In other words, in science and foreign language classrooms school knowledge is not easily brought into interaction with learners' action knowledge, whereas in the mother-tongue classroom action knowledge is inevitably implicated at every turn, because the mother tongue itself is a key part of the identity the learners bring to the classroom. Although the position of Barnes's foreign language teachers on the Transmission–Interpretation scale is easy to understand, it is clearly at odds with the ostensible communicative purpose of most foreign language teaching, which entails that learners should be able to express meanings rooted in their individual identity and shaped by their action knowledge.

Now, learners' action knowledge can be exploited in the foreign language classroom only on the basis of translation. For much of the present century the grammar/translation approach dominated foreign language teaching in our schools (for obvious reasons, it was much less common in environments where teacher and learners typically did not share the same

mother tongue). But if the use of teacher-selected translation, especially
from the mother tongue into the target language, has been largely discred-
ited as the chief weapon in language teachers' armoury, that should not
blind us to the fact that we necessarily experience a foreign language
through the prism of our mother tongue. This is a matter not of learner per-
versity but of psycholinguistic inevitability (for a summary of research into
the phenomenon of language transfer, see Odlin, 1989). Vygotsky (1986:
159f.) put the matter thus:

> While learning a foreign language, we use word meanings that are al-
> ready well developed in the native language, and only translate them ...
> The acquisition of a foreign language differs from the acquisition of the
> native one precisely because it uses the semantics of the native lan-
> guage as its foundation.

In other words, translation – equivalence and contrast between the target
language and the mother tongue – is the inevitable starting-point and an
obligatory travelling companion in any process of foreign language learning.

One of the first things Leni Dam requires her learners to do is to write a
simple description of themselves in English (see Dam, 1995, Chap. 2). In order to perform this task, they must first assemble an appropriate stock of
English words and phrases. This she provides in a whole-class activity in
which individual learners call out in Danish the things they want to be able
to say about themselves and she writes the English equivalents on posters.
In this way learners begin to develop a sense of how not just their own, but
also other learners' identities translate into English. Having been provided
with the necessary raw materials, Leni Dam's learners then write their self-
descriptions for homework. In the next lesson some of the descriptions are
read aloud to the class, and all of them can be used as the basis for speaking
English in pairs and small groups.

Two things should be noted about this simple technique for helping
learners to get launched on the process of speaking English to one another.
First, the meanings they are encouraged to express come from within themselves; they are not those that a textbook writer believes beginners in
English should be introduced to. Thus the activity takes an essential first
step towards involving the learners' action knowledge in their foreign language learning and rooting their gradually developing proficiency in their
personal identity. Second, writing plays a central role in the process. When
children learn to read and write in their mother tongue, they usually do so
on the basis of well-developed oral proficiency; essentially, their task is to
learn how to map the sounds of the mother tongue on to its writing system.

The development of literacy generally produces significant growth in the child's vocabulary (reading opens up areas of experience to which the child does not have immediate, physical access). It also has cognitive consequences, at least potentially, in that it provides the means by which thought and speech can be detached from the flow of time and subjected to analysis and questioning; in other words, it is the very basis of the educational process (for seminal discussion of the cognitive consequences of literacy, see Bruner *et al.*, 1966; Scribner, 1997; Olson, 1991). When foreign language learning begins after the learners have at least begun to master literacy skills in their mother tongue, reading and writing can be used to support the development of speaking. Learners can construct their own meanings 'off-line' and then use their written texts as prompts for speaking activities. Besides helping learners to overcome the problem of 'cognitive overload' as they try to speak English (having already decided what they want to say, they can then concentrate their processing capacity on how they say it – on pronunciation and intonation), this use of writing should help them to develop an early sensitivity to grammatical forms in the target language. For as Olson (1991) has pointed out, there is a sense in which literacy *is* metalinguistic (that is, grammatical) awareness, since it makes language visible and enables us to examine and manipulate words and phrases as though they were physical objects. In this way, the foreign language should gradually supplement the mother tongue as a tool by which learners exercise and explore the 'metalinguistic function' (Bruner 1986: 125) that is fundamental to our educational purpose.

Implications for Pedagogical Practice

The theoretical argument I have just developed can be summarised as follows. In education generally, success depends on bringing school knowledge into appropriate and fruitful interaction with the learners' action knowledge. This entails processes of explicit negotiation and exploration in which the learners should be involved as equal partners. In this way they begin to accept responsibility for their learning and take their first steps towards autonomy. At the same time, negotiation and exploration necessarily engage the 'metalinguistic function' that analyses, questions and evaluates. When the focus of learning is a foreign language, learners' action knowledge is engaged by involving them in activities that arise from their interests and preoccupations. This must involve translation from their mother tongue into the target language and vice versa, and sustained interaction between their own and the target-language culture. By using the technology of literacy to help learners develop their speaking skills, teachers draw attention to the forms of the target language and thus make it possible for learners to develop a dual focus: expressing their own meanings, but at the same time learning to adopt an analytic approach to linguistic form. In order to integrate this analysis with the larger process of language learning, it is essential that learners use the target language to plan, monitor and evaluate their learning as well as to perform learning tasks; indeed, they will not get far in their use of the target language for collaborative learning unless they do so.

What are the practical implications of this theoretical position? In the space available to me I shall briefly address the curriculum, examinations and assessment, the organisation and content of learning, and teacher training.

As Leni Dam's example shows, curricula laid down by educational authorities are not in themselves a bar to the development of learner autonomy. On the contrary, they provide the starting-point and necessary framework for the negotiation and exploration that are fundamental to the process. As I noted in my introduction, curricular reforms of the past decade or so have increasingly tended to emphasise the importance of developing learners' capacity for critical and independent thinking (in other words, learner autonomy). No doubt they could do more to recognise the essentially dialogic nature of language and learning and the crucial role that is played by learner empowerment. But no amount of curricular reform can ensure the more widespread achievement of autonomy in foreign language classrooms.

If autonomous learners are by definition successful learners, it might seem irrelevant to concern ourselves with forms of assessment: surely autonomous learners should be able to take examinations in their stride. But this begs two questions. First, it is by no means clear that existing forms of assessment are appropriate to the evaluation of learning that goes on in autonomous classrooms; and second, it ignores the washback effect that forms of assessment inevitably have on classroom practice. If we wish to promote a foreign language pedagogy that is explicitly oriented to the development of learner autonomy, we may need to make adjustments to the ways in which foreign language learning and its outcomes are assessed.

In an ideal world, the assessment of foreign language proficiency in autonomous classrooms would combine the auditing of project work produced in the classroom with examinations designed to test the skills, capacities and knowledge of individual learners; it would also take account of learning process as well as learning outcome. Work produced in the classroom, including group work, might comprise three elements: the target-language product – a written, audio- or video-recorded text; the learners' account of the process that underlay the product; and their evaluation of both process and product. The assessment of such project work could usefully include an interview in the target language between the examiner and the group of learners. This would enable the examiner to evaluate the learners invidually; and as a communicative event it would make a great deal more sense than most traditional tests of oral proficiency. Written examinations appropriate to the autonomous classroom should be task-based, since that corresponds to the way in which learning proceeds. In judging learner performance, priority should be given to how well the task has been performed in terms of completeness, content, and communicative efficiency and effectiveness. Only when the learner's performance has been judged, at least provisionally, according to these criteria is it appropriate to pay attention to matters of formal accuracy. In accordance with the central role played by reflection and analysis in the autonomous classroom, tasks should be constructed in such a way that the examiner is provided with evidence of process – in the form of plans and commentaries – as well as the product that represents completion of the task. These assessment instruments are by no means novel, but they have not yet been brought together as an explicit means of encouraging the development of learner autonomy.

Of course, however much pressure is exerted from outside, by curricula and examinations, what really matters is what goes on in the classroom. This is a matter not only of pedagogical procedure but of learning materials and resources. We have seen that in Leni Dam's classroom the learners do not use a textbook. We have also seen that, although Danish learners of English have relatively easy access to materials in English, much of their learning arises from Danish sources that in one sense or another they translate into English. In other words, although British or Irish learners may find it relatively difficult to access their own language-learning materials, that may not be as great a problem as one might at first suppose. In any case, there are commercially available alternatives to the textbook – for example, the Authentik newspapers and cassettes. Relatively few foreign language teachers work without a textbook, however – in too many cases, teaching is little more than a matter of taking the learners through the textbook page by page, with results that it is not necessary to dwell on. If the teacher decides to dispense with a textbook, she must construct the ongoing learning dialogue in negotiation with her learners. But then, that is the very essence of a pedagogy designed to foster the development of learner autonomy. Any textbook is a potential obstacle to the development of learner autonomy because it presents a ready-made learning dialogue in which the most that is required of learners is that they speak someone else's lines. There are undoubtedly ways of using a textbook that subordinate it to a learning dialogue negotiated between teacher and learners and allow it to be supplemented – or perhaps framed – by learning activities and materials chosen by the learners. But it is arguably easier to dispense with a textbook altogether than to use it in this way.

It is probably true to say that most language classrooms make less use than they might of the resources offered by media technologies. Of course, the inclusion of listening comprehension in public examinations ensures that audio recordings are used, at least to give learners practice at doing listening tests. But language laboratories have always been a minority enthusiasm, especially since the effective demise of the audiolingual method of which they are an electronic embodiment; video has largely been bypassed; and in many schools the computer network is the preserve of mathematicians and scientists. This is a pity, for there are two ways in which the computer can play a central role in the development of language learners' autonomy. On the one hand, it can be used as a tool for processing language: for example, Legenhausen and Wolff (1991) have shown that using a computer for group writing activities has a number of clear advantages over the traditional pencil-and-paper method. On the other hand, a computer connected to the Internet can be used as a channel of communication with the target-language community and culture. Learners can use e-mail to communicate with native speakers of their target language – this is especially beneficial within a framework of tandem learning (where, for example, English-speaking learners of French form learning partnerships with French-speaking learners of English; see Little & Brammerts, 1996); and the Internet provides immediate access to authentic texts in print, audio and video. (For a fuller discussion of the use of information systems and information technologies to promote the development of autonomy in foreign language learning, see Little, 1996.)

Above all, of course, the more widespread and effective pursuit of autonomy in foreign language learning depends on teacher training. Teachers are notoriously impatient of theory, though their impatience mostly arises from a false understanding of the relation between theory and practice. They need to be better equipped than they usually are with theoretical understanding; but their teaching practice also needs to involve them explicitly in the practical exploration of theoretical issues. They should understand, for example, the theoretical reasons for giving group work a central role in their classrooms; but they should also be given the opportunity to explore how best to implement group work in their own particular educational environment. Similarly, it is not enough to arm teachers with theoretical arguments in favour of using the target language as the preferred medium of classroom communication from the very first lesson. They must also explore in practice what exactly that means and how it is to be done. Most important of all, programmes of pre- and in-service teacher training should be designed and implemented so as to provide teachers themselves with an experience of autonomous learning. The example of reciprocal teaching shows that it is not enough to draw learners' attention to appropriate strategies: learners must discover the effectiveness of the strategies for themselves in processes of interaction that they control in collaboration with their teacher. In the same way, it is not enough to lecture teachers in training about the virtues of learner autonomy. They must experience those virtues for themselves through reflective and critical involvement in the planning, monitoring and evaluation of their training (for a discussion of the relation between learner autonomy and teacher autonomy, see Little 1995).

Conclusion

When pedagogy is not specially focused on the development of autonomy, some learners achieve it but the majority do not. On the other hand, when the development of learner autonomy is a central pedagogical goal, as in the example with which I began this chapter, it turns out that all learners are capable of becoming autonomous within the limits of their ability. When the focus of learning is a foreign language, autonomous learners become confident communicators in that language (again within the limits of their ability); and when the foreign language is the channel through which their autonomy is developed, it effects a genuine expansion of their identity, carrying them beyond the communicative, cultural and self-reflective confines of their mother tongue. This is a much more powerful argument for giving foreign languages a central role in the curriculum than any argument from utility.

More than 20 years ago, Douglas Barnes wrote:

> In making the ethical decision to prepare pupils for choice and responsibility, teachers implicitly choose also an Interpretation view of learning. What is of practical interest is that a large proportion of teachers who would publicly assert their ends to be a world of self-responsible and flexible people do not in fact will the means that are required. (Barnes, 1976: 143)

These words are as true now as they were in the mid-1970s. What is more, they apply not only to teachers but to teacher trainers, curriculum designers, educational administrators and politicians. As I hope I have shown, the development of learner autonomy in foreign language classrooms involves a great deal more than enhancing current provision with a few extra techniques or facilities. There is no doubt that the theory I have elaborated can be converted into successful practice, but this will happen on a large scale only as a result of sustained political as well as educational effort: precisely the kind of effort that the beginning of a new millennium seems to call for.

References

Barnes, D. (1976) *From Communication to Curriculum*. Harmondsworth: Penguin.

Bershon, B.L. (1992) Co-operative problem solving: A link to inner speech. In R. Hertz-Lazarowitz and N. Miller (eds) *Interaction in Co-operative Groups: The Theoretical Anatomy of Group Learning* (pp. 36–48). Cambridge: Cambridge University Press.

Bruner, J. (1986) The language of education. In J. Bruner (ed.) *Actual Minds, Possible Worlds* (pp. 121–33). Cambridge, MA: Harvard University Press.

Bruner, J.S., Olver, R. and Greenfield, P. (1966) *Studies in Cognitive Growth*. New York: Wiley.

Dam, L. (1995) *Learner Autonomy 3: From Theory to Classroom Practice*. Dublin: Authentik.

Donaldson, M. (1978) *Children's Minds*. London: Fontana.

Freire, P. (1972) *Pedagogy of the Oppressed*. Harmondsworth: Penguin.

Holec, H. (1981) *Autonomy and Foreign Language Learning*. Oxford: Pergamon. (First published 1979, Strasbourg: Council of Europe.)

Illich, I. (1979) *Deschooling Society*. Harmondsworth: Penguin. (First published 1971, New York: Harper and Row.)

Legenhausen, L. and Wolff, D. (1991) Der Micro-Computer als Hilfsmittel beim Sprachenlernen: Schreiben als Gruppenaktivität, *PRAXIS des neusprachlichen Unterrichts* 38, 346–56.

Little, D. (1991) *Learner Autonomy 1: Definitions, Issues and Problems*. Dublin: Authentik.

Little, D. (1995) Learning as dialogue: The dependence of learner autonomy on teacher autonomy. *System* 23 (2), 175–81.

Little, D. (1996) Freedom to learn and compulsion to interact: Promoting learner autonomy through the use of information systems and information technologies. In R. Pemberton, E.S.L. Li, W.W.F. Or and H.D. Pierson (eds) *Taking Control: Autonomy in Language Learning* (pp. 203–18). Hong Kong: Hong Kong University Press.

Little, D. and Brammerts, H. (1996) A guide to language learning in tandem via the Internet. CLCS Occasional Paper No. 46. Dublin: Trinity College, Centre for Language and Communication Studies.

Mayher, J.S. (1990) *Uncommon Sense: Theoretical Practice in Language Education*. Portsmouth, NH: Boynton/Cook.

Odlin, T. (1989) *Language Transfer: Cross-linguistic Influence in Language Learning*. Cambridge: Cambridge University Press.

Olson, D.R. (1991) Literacy as metalinguistic activity. In D.R. Olson and N. Torrance (eds) *Literacy and Orality* (pp. 251–70). Cambridge: Cambridge University Press.

Palincsar, A.S., Brown, A.L. and Campione, J.C. (1993) First-grade dialogues for knowledge acquisition and use. In E.A. Forman, N. Minick and C.A. Stone (eds) *Contexts for Learning: Sociocultural Dynamics in Children's Development* (pp. 43–57). New York: Oxford University Press.

Rogers, C. (1983) *Freedom to Learn for the 80s*. New York: Merrill.

Salmon, P. (1995) *Psychology in the Classroom*. London: Cassell.

Scribner, S. (1997) The cognitive consequences of literacy. In E. Tobach, R. Joffe Falmagne, M. Brown Parlee, L.M.W. Martin and A.S. Kapelman (eds) *Mind and Social Practice: Selected Writings of Silvia Scribner* (pp. 160–89). Cambridge: Cambridge University Press.

Tharp, R. and Gallimore, R. (1988) *Rousing Minds to Life*. Cambridge: Cambridge University Press.

Tizard, B. and Hughes, M. (1984) *Young Children Learning: Talking and Thinking at Home and at School*. London: Fontana.

Ushioda, E. (1998) Tandem language learning via e-mail: From motivation to autonomy. Paper presented at the 5th CERCLES International Conference, Bergamo, 17–19 September.

Vygotsky, L.S. (1978) *Mind in Society: The Development of Higher Psychological Processes*. Cambridge, MA: Harvard University Press.

Vygotsky, L.S. (1986) *Thought and Language*. Cambridge, MA: MIT Press.

Wertsch, J.V. (1998) *Mind as Action*. New York and Oxford: Oxford University Press.

Chapter 3

Motivation and the Learners of Modern Languages

GARY CHAMBERS

This chapter presents some of the findings of a study on pupils' perceptions of the in-school foreign language learning experience. This represents one area of a larger, accelerated, longitudinal study on the motivational perspectives of secondary school pupils learning German. What experience of foreign language learning do pupils bring to the secondary school? What are the factors which influence their views of what goes on in the classroom? What are their likes and dislikes? How do they feel the in-school experience could be enhanced? Can this help identify what it is that leads to the apparent diminution in their enthusiasm for learning (languages, specifically) between the ages of 11 and 13?

The chapter also has a comparative dimension, as the same questions are asked in relation to the English-learning experience of comprehensive school pupils of the same age in Schleswig-Holstein in northern Germany. From these findings, can anything be learned which may have a beneficial influence on how languages are taught?

Characteristics of the 'Demotivated' or 'Disaffected' Pupil

At the time of writing Wayne, Chris, Hannah and Norman are in Year 9 of a coeducational comprehensive school and have been learning German as a second foreign language for a year and a half.

Wayne is gregarious, affable and usually full of *joie de vivre.* He enjoys a good chat with his classmates. When asked to be quiet he apologises, remains silent for all of two minutes and then sets off talking again. This pattern is repeated again and again until the teacher either explodes in frustration or simply capitulates. Wayne, with the best will in the world, seems incapable of following the instruction. He does not rate German very highly. He does not rate school very highly. His father has a fishmonger's stall in the local market and Wayne intends to join the family business as soon as he leaves school. He claims that his father left school at age 15 without any qualifications and is doing very well, thank you. 'Why do I need to learn German?' he asks. 'There aren't any Germans in our market. I don't need no [sic] German!'

Chris hates school. He hates German. The only thing in school which he regards as worthwhile and enjoyable is football. He has a very short fuse. He hurls books across the room in anger and frustration. Even though the teacher and 29 classmates see him do it, he claims innocence. He maintains that teachers pick on him. His mother believes he is right. She cannot see the point in his learning German. 'Why can't he do something useful instead, like more maths or English?'

Hannah has the face of an angel. She is not disruptive or rude. She does not speak out of turn. In fact she does not really speak much at all. Her handwriting is almost illegible. Homework is rarely handed in on time; when it is, it is either incomplete or of very poor quality. Her mother never comes to parents' evenings. She does not respond to letters. It is hard to tell whether Hannah enjoys German or not. Communication is usually limited to a shrug of the shoulders.

Norman is a 'loner'. He hates school. He hates German. He hates life. He bursts into tears for what appears to be no reason at all. The girls in the class feel sorry for him and try to protect and comfort him. The boys call him a 'big fat poof'.

If you are teachers you may recognise some of these pupils from your own experience. You may not necessarily have a Wayne, a Chris, a Hannah or a Norman in your class but you may have pupils who display some of their characteristics and indeed other behaviours. Not all the characteristics of the category of pupil who may be labelled 'disaffected', 'demotivated', 'disenchanted' or 'switched off' are featured in the four descriptions. Such pupils may have poor concentration, low self-esteem, make little or no effort to learn, reflect the 'what's the use?' syndrome, fail to respond to praise (or respond only in a negative fashion), distract other pupils, shout out, fail to bring materials to lessons or claim to have lost them (see Alison, 1993.) This list is by no means exhaustive.

'Demotivated' and 'disaffected' pupils are not an invention of the 1990s, but have occupied classrooms for as long as formal schooling has been a concept. Hargreaves (1982: 102) paints a disheartening picture of the 'indifferent' pupil with whom we may all be all too familiar:

> 'It's boring, sir' is their most common complaint. They display a persistent lack of enthusiasm to most of what the school offers, though a skilful teacher or carefully planned lesson may capture their imagination and attention, for a moment. Whilst exams and other incentives

tend to be ineffective with them, they show little active resentment or opposition. They seem to be overwhelmed by lethargy, lacking the energy to praise or condemn. They drift through their schooldays. In consequence, whilst they avoid anything more serious than a half-hearted, game-like resistance to teachers, they are nevertheless not easy to teach. Quite often they worry their parents as much as their teachers for their lifelessness and lack of initiative.

Lack of motivation can also manifest itself in a manner which is much less passive but nevertheless equally challenging and arguably more disturbing for the teacher. Hargreaves describes pupils who react in a more overtly aggressive way as 'oppositionals':

They turn in overt and sometimes powerful resistance to school and to teachers. Antagonism is overt, pronounced and prolonged. They become defined, individually and collectively, as a "discipline problem" for teachers – and sometimes for their parents.

Stradling *et al.* (1991: 25) provide a synopsis of the behaviours of pupils like Wayne, Chris, Hannah and Norman, as well as Hargreaves' 'indifferents' and 'oppositionals', in an effort to define what they term the 'reluctant learner':

- non-completion of assignments;
- lack of persistence and expectation of failure when attempting new tasks;
- high level of dependency on sympathetic teachers (needing constant attention, direction, supervision and reassurance);
- signs of anxiety, frustration and defensive behaviour;
- disruptive or withdrawn behaviour;
- apathetic non-participation in the classroom;
- non-attendance and poor attendance;
- frequent expression of view that school is boring and irrelevant.

What are the factors which lead to pupils joining the category of 'reluctant learners'? The media would have us believe that it is the fault of the teachers (*Daily Telegraph*, 25 January 1995: 'Do your job, teachers !'; 23 September 1995: 'What emerges most clearly from the reports of Inspectors of Schools is that the pupils most likely to behave badly are those who have been badly taught.'). Stradling *et al.* seem to share this view, but they also recognise other possible contributory factors beyond the beleaguered teacher, the classroom and the school (1991: 27):

- low expectations by teachers;
- not being sufficiently 'stretched' in lessons;
- unrealistic demands on learners;
- too many teachers, too many subjects, too little time;
- insufficient reinforcement of learning;
- timetable and course structures too inflexible to permit learners to work at own pace and thus finish assignments;
- lack of short-term learning targets to reinforce learning;
- course content and teaching methods which are insufficiently stimulating or relevant to pupils' needs;
- insufficient attention given by some teachers to individual learning difficulties;
- lack of external motivation and incentive to learn (e.g. through broader accreditation schemes, job, further education and training prospects etc.);
- lack of parental support and encouragement;
- peer group pressure to conform to a norm of non-achievement;
- fear of success (especially among some adolescent girls);
- social disadvantage and deprivation.

Who would be a teacher? Rather than keeping a multitude of plates in the air, it appears their job requires them to juggle with something akin to hedgehogs. Who, moreover, would be a teacher of modern foreign languages? As well as meeting all the challenges listed above, they have to cope with the low status accorded to their subject by pupils (Stables and Wikeley (1997) found that Year 9 students placed French and German equal bottom in their league table of 'liked' subjects); the high currency of English (the language of interaction of most of their pupils) across the world; the problem of teaching the target language in an English-speaking environment; having to teach in a foreign code ...The list provided by the besieged teacher of foreign languages could go on and on.

The Research

In the market-driven society in which we live, the perceptions of consumers (in this case, pupils learning foreign languages) are, for better or worse, of paramount importance. In the context of modern languages this must surely be for the better; a view supported by Rudduck (1996):

If we want to enhance pupils' achievement, why don't we take our agenda for school improvement from their accounts of learning – what helps them to work hard, what switches them off, what kinds of teaching do they value and what kind of support do they need? They are, after all, our 'expert witnesses'.

So what do 13- to 15-year-old pupils think of their in-school experience? What can we learn from their views? And teachers may also be a valuable source of information – though how reliable is open to question: they may have a perception of the level of a pupil's motivation, but without much insight into the factors behind it. As Crookes and Schmidt (1991: 480) find:

> When teachers say that a student is motivated, they are not usually concerning themselves with the student's reason for studying, but are observing that the student does study, or at least engage in teacher-desired behavior in the classroom and possibly outside it.

This chapter will therefore focus on the views of pupils rather than those of their teachers and will investigate their motivational perspectives towards learning foreign languages (with special reference to German) in the National Curriculum era. Not that pupils' views have been neglected hitherto. The work of the Assessment of Performance Unit (DES/DENI/WO, 1985, 1986, 1987) provides useful insights into pupils' likes and dislikes in the foreign language learning classroom. They liked 'listening to French on the tape-recorder' but disliked 'answering the teacher's questions in French about a tape' they had listened to. They liked 'talking to the French assistant', although over half the pupils surveyed had never had such an opportunity. The most unpopular of any of the speaking and reading activities was 'reading aloud in French to the class' (DES/DENI/WO, 1984: 221–2). (This still goes on!) (1)

The 1985 report (DES/DENI/WO, 1987: 63–4) drew up tables for the top three most-liked and most-disliked activities.

Table 3.1 Most-liked activities

	Boys (%)	Girls (%)	All (%)
Playing games or doing puzzles	46	42	44
Drawing pictures, maps, diagrams	44	32	39
Watching a film, slides about France	26	16	22

Table 3.2 Most-disliked activities

	Boys (%)	Girls (%)	All (%)

Learning verbs	30	38	34
Reading aloud in French to the class	26	30	28
Learning lists of French words	19	25	22

This report also reveals interesting insights into potentially useful and enjoyable activities which pupils claim not to experience in French.

Table 3.3 Activities not perceived by pupils as part of formal lessons, with % responding 'Not done'

Talking to the French assistant	58
Making a recording of yourself speaking French	54
Doing a project on France	45
Watching a television or video programme in French	38
Singing French songs	37
Reading French magazines or storybooks by yourself	36
Talking in English about a French story you have read	30
Watching a film or slides about France	30
Writing in French about something you did	29
Writing a made-up story in French	28
Writing a letter in French	27

What can be learned from the Germans?

There exists a popular perception that motivation to learn foreign languages is a greater problem for the British than it is for other nationalities, not least the Scandinavians, Dutch and Germans. Hooley and Newcombe (1988: 400) describe the British attitude to foreign language learning as 'cultural myopia' and contrast this with the positive, need-driven attitude of the Germans. Other comparative studies have led to similar conclusions – see, for example, the work of Stewart-Smith et al. (1996) on a comparative study of 14-year-olds in north-east England and St Petersburg in Russia.

Do German pupils' perceptions of their learning experience differ very much from those of their UK counterparts? Piepho (1983: 119ff.) worked with 1700 pupils of all abilities in Years 7 to 9 (12- to 14-year-olds) in order to ascertain their likes and dislikes and which aspects of English-learning influenced motivation. He found the majority of pupils keen to learn. Problems were caused, however, by unimaginative approaches to introducing vocabulary, the exploitation of texts and grammar drills. Boring, unattractive worksheets, uninteresting texts, meaningless oral exercises and disappointing test results were also identified by pupils as doing little to enhance their enjoyment of learning English.

It is reassuring perhaps for the frustrated teacher of foreign languages in the UK that pupils in Germany have complaints too. The difference in outcome, however, remains disconcerting. Some German pupils find aspects of language learning boring but still appear to reach a level of competence which seems so much higher than that attained by UK learners of French and German. In a comparative study by Milton and Meara (1998) 187 14-to15-year-old foreign language learners in Britain, Germany and Greece were tested using versions of Meara's (1995) LLEX Lingua vocabulary tests. The results are summarised in Table 3.4.

Table 3.4 Vocabulary scores from LLEX Lingua vocabulary tests

	Mean %	_Mean (words)_	_SD_
Greek students learning English (63)	70	1680	290
German students learning English (80)	50	1200	440
British students learning French (54)	30	660	310
British students learning German (8)	41	984	156

Milton's and Meara's findings reflect not only the greater knowledge of vocabulary of both Greek and German English-learners over their British French- and German-learning peers, but also the greater length of time spent on foreign languages (see Table 3.10) and the greater demands made on the Greeks and Germans in English examinations in comparison to GCSE.

The research described below also had a comparative dimension in that it included pupils of the same age in similar schools in Kiel, Schleswig-Holstein. It was thought that much could be learned from the examination of attitudinal and motivational similarities and contrasts regarding their learning of English. It is recognised that the range of variables makes a direct comparison impracticable but, at the same time, if conclusions are to be drawn about influences on motivation in one country, some sort of baseline from another country is needed.

Pupils from four Leeds and two Kiel comprehensive schools or _Gesamtschulen_ were surveyed in 1992 and again in 1994. This accessed not only their consciously held views on each of the two occasions but also provided insight into any development or change in these views. A 10% sample was interviewed after the survey, reflecting an equal balance of pupils with positive, neutral and negative motivational perspectives, based on their answers to a range of motivational and attitudinal questions. Pupils' perceptions on a wide range of variables were targeted. This chapter concentrates exclusively, however, on the following:

- pupils' evaluation of previous foreign language learning experience; and

- pupils' perception of the classroom experience.

Pupils' evaluation of previous foreign language learning experience.

What, if any, experience of French or German or Spanish do newcomers to secondary school bring to foreign language classes? Do they come full of enthusiasm? Do they come full of fear and dread? If any learning experience they may have had at primary school has been positive, perhaps they come full of excitement at the prospect of yet further enjoyment. If they have not had any experience of foreign language learning, are they fearful about this new subject area, or attracted by the novelty value and the promise of a fresh start on an equal footing with most other pupils?

Eleven-year-old English pupils filled out a questionnaire on the very threshold of their Leeds secondary school experience in the first week of September 1992. This presented an opportunity to access the attitudes and motivations which pupils brought with them to Key Stage 3 foreign language learning, before they were influenced by the teacher, the teaching, experience of success or failure and any other factors. How did they view the prospect of setting out on their odyssey towards French or German competence? In addition, how much experience of French and German had these pupils had prior to transferring to secondary school?

The responses of the Leeds pupils revealed that 63.9% claimed to have had some foreign language tuition, in 91.1% of these cases French. Only 1.6% claimed to have learned some German. The predominance of French is hardly surprising given the position it has traditionally occupied as first foreign language on the vast majority of English secondary school timetables. In a survey of 1140 maintained and independent secondary schools conducted by the Centre for Information on Language Teaching and Research (CILT, 1995a) it was found that 96.6% offered French, 33% German, 10.2% Spanish and 0.7% Italian. Where primary school teachers enjoy foreign language competence this is more likely than not to be in French. A primary school-focused CILT survey (1995b) confirmed that an early start to foreign language learning in primary schools really meant an early start to French (in 93.5% of primary schools offering foreign languages) rather than any other language.

The duration of the foreign language experience varied between one (48.3%) and two years (46.7%). How intensive the experience may have been is not known, although anecdotal evidence suggests that it is likely to have taken the form of a taster course. There are areas of the UK, for example Scotland (Tierney, 1998) and North Yorkshire (Geoghegan, 1995), where despite National Curriculum pressures foreign languages still form a constituent part of the primary school diet, but that was not the case with our Leeds-based sample.

Extent of enjoyment of previous foreign language learning experience

When asked how much they enjoyed the foreign language learning experience, pupils' general response was positive, with 85.3% scoring it 3 or above on a scale of 1–5, ranging from 'I did not enjoy it' through 'It was OK' to 'I enjoyed it very much'. Whilst 46.6% of the sample of 11-year-olds opted for the top scores of 4 and 5, a median of 3 (37.7%) and a mean of 3.57 suggest however that the experience was by no means exclusively positive but rather tempered in some cases.

Table 3.5 Percentages of Year 7 Leeds pupils in 1992 responding to the question 'Did you enjoy learning the foreign language?'

Not at all →		It was OK →		Very much			
1	2	3	4	5	Sample	Mean	SD
8.2	6.6	37.7	15.6	32.0	122	3.57	1.23

What were the reasons for pupils' enjoyment or lack of enjoyment of any previous foreign language learning experience they may have had? When asked in open questions to justify their response, only 65.5% of 11-year-old beginners chose to do so. Of this number, 45.8% identified the influence of the teachers and their teaching, 30% providing overtly positive, and 16.6% overtly negative comments; 21.2% also referred to enjoying learning a foreign language because it was something new and quite different to other subjects in their experience so far: 'I enjoy it because there are a lot of funny words in it like "Farter" [*sic*] which means "father".'

Anticipation of German, French and other subjects

How did the English pupils feel about the prospect of learning foreign languages at secondary school? They were not asked about German or French in isolation but as subjects amongst a number of others which were to form part of their school timetable. There was little to be learned from their claim to absolutely adore or loathe French when this might also apply to all other subjects. More was to be gained from a picture of their perceptions of a given subject (in this case French and/or German) within a context of their perceptions of learning in general (i.e. the other subjects taken in Year 7).

When asked, 'How much are you looking forward to taking each of the following subjects at secondary school?' the Year 7 pupils adopted a generally positive outlook across most curriculum subjects. Pupils bring with them an enthusiasm for school and for learning. There is some evidence to suggest a specific enthusiasm for German and French, as these occupied laudable fourth and sixth places respectively of the 'most looked forward to subjects', behind art, PE and technology and split by science.

When asked how they felt about the prospect of learning a foreign language, again the response was positive, with 81.6% either 'excited' at the prospect or 'quite looking forward to it'. Only 11.6% were indifferent; just 6.9% were either not looking forward to learning a foreign language or hated the thought of it. The picture of general enthusiasm for languages in Year 7 was corroborated.

The data were analysed for gender difference. Previous research had revealed that in general boys show greater enthusiasm for science than do girls (Whyte, 1981) and that with regard to modern languages (Clark & Trafford, 1995; Powell & Batters, 1985; Powell & Littlewood, 1983; Buckby et al., 1981; Burstall et al., 1974) girls feel more positively inclined towards French than do boys. It is particularly interesting in relation to this study that no significant gender difference is apparent except for German, where boys show more enthusiasm. To what can this male enthusiasm be attributed? It must be remembered that they have, in all likelihood, very little experience of German on which to base their positive response. Are they influenced by comics and war films (O'Sullivan, 1990), the success of German sports stars and teams, contact with German visitors?

The general enthusiasm for foreign languages, German in particular, is confirmed in pupils' responses to questions relating to which subjects they were looking forward to/dreading most of all.

Table 3.6 Percentages of Year 7 Leeds pupils in 1992 responding to the questions 'Which subject are you looking forward to most of all?' and 'Which subject are you dreading most of all?'

Subject	% (n = 194) Looking forward to	% (n = 194) Dreading
Art	23.7	4.6
PE	16.5	7.2

German	15.5	5.2
Maths	9.3	21.6
Technology	8.2	0.5
English	5.2	1.5
French	5.2	6.2
Science	4.6	4.1

Again it is hard to explain the very healthy response to German. Is it the novelty value? Pupils are unlikely to be attracted by the mellifluous flow of the language, by any predominance of German songs in the pop charts (they were too young to remember Kraftwerk's 'Auf der Autobahn' or Nena with her '99 Luftballons') or by German-speaking role models. They were given the opportunity to give reasons for their answers in an open question. In terms of both the subject they were most looking forward to and the subject they were most dreading, there appear to be two categories of justification for their choice: first, the novelty of a new subject ('I couldn't wait to learn a foreign language as I didn't do anything like this in junior and infant school'; 'I'd never done a language before and my older friends could talk a language and it sounded really good'; 'I couldn't wait to get a French homework'); and second, the influence of previous experience (both positive – 'I like singing French songs' – and negative – 'It's boring'). Not having done foreign languages before was seen by 13.8% in a positive light, whilst 10.5% took the opposite view; 12.8% claimed always to have wanted to learn a foreign language, and 14.6% and 11.4% respectively saw the utility of foreign language competence in terms of talking to people and going on holiday. Those with little enthusiasm at the prospect of learning a foreign language based this response on previous negative experience where they had felt they were 'no good at it' (9.5%) or were 'bored' (4.9%).

Table 3.7 Percentages of Year 7 Leeds pupils in 1992 responding to the question 'How do you feel about the prospect of learning a foreign language? Explain why.'

Reason	% (n = 194)
I like languages	13.4
Ability to talk to other people	9.3
I always wanted to learn languages	8.2
Holidays	8.2
I've never done it before (positive)	8.8
I've never done it before (negative)	6.7

I'm no good at languages	6.1
I don't like languages	3.1
Other	25.9
No response	10.3

As for German, it appears that the subject may have profited from pupils' lack of experience of it in advance of coming to secondary school. They seemed to be looking forward to something new. The expectation was exciting. In this case ignorance may have been bliss. It might also be argued that pupils' perception of German may have been positively influenced by their experience of French at primary school; if this was positive it may have induced a positive attitude towards learning foreign languages in general; if negative, pupils may have been looking forward to learning a completely different language instead.

In order to get closer to the existence of any relationship between the extent to which pupils looked forward to learning German and whether or not they had already had experience of foreign language learning, these two variables were examined more closely.

It seemed that 11-year-olds looked forward to learning German whether or not they had previous language-learning experience. There was a difference, however, in the level of enthusiasm displayed between those with and those without this experience. Those with experience of foreign language learning were less likely to opt for the top end of the scale, whilst those without were prepared to show extreme enthusiasm. This may be an indication of the difference between the expectation of learning a new language and the reality of what such learning entails.

Taking the pre-secondary school foreign language learning experience a stage further, was there any relationship between the level of pupils' enjoyment of the experience and the extent to which they claimed to be looking forward to learning German?

The research confirmed that pupils are generally enthusiastic at the prospect of learning German, regardless of their previous learning experience. Of the 17 who claim not to have enjoyed their previous learning experience, only three are unenthusiastic about their forthcoming German experience. Whilst not confirming the 'fresh start theory', these data may provide some tentative, evidential underpinning. It would be erroneous to jump to any conclusions, taking the data in isolation, however.

Summary of pupils' perceptions

Given that modern foreign languages do not form part of the National

Curriculum for Key Stages 1 and 2, it may come as something of a surprise that almost 64% of 11-year-olds in this 1992 study claimed to have had some experience of learning a foreign language. It is arguably all the more surprising given that at the time of the survey the National Curriculum was in the early stages of its introduction in primary schools, and teachers were already voicing concern at the lack of space available on the timetable to meet its requirements (Pollard *et al.*, 1994; Campbell & Neil, 1994).

It comes as less of a surprise that almost all of these pupils claimed that their foreign language experience at primary school was of French. This almost certainly reflects the traditional dominance of French in UK secondary schools. In the exceptional event of a primary school teacher having competence in a language other than French, however, she (2) should not be misled by the idea that because pupils are more likely than not to be learning French at secondary school, they should therefore learn French at primary school. There is evidence (for example Burstall *et al.*, 1974) to suggest that pupils with experience of French at primary school have to cover the same ground again at the beginning of the secondary school French course and lose some enthusiasm as a result. Hawkins (1997: 4) sees foreign language learning at school as an 'apprenticeship in learning how to learn language'. If this is so, it matters little which language is taught/learned.

Most pupils appear to have found their first taste of foreign language learning a reasonably positive experience, 46% scoring it 4–5 on a scale of 1–5, although 38% were not prepared to commit themselves to the positive or negative side of the 3. When these data were cross-tabulated with variables relating to how much pupils were looking forward to German, some interesting trends were revealed. Whether or not 11-year-old pupils have had a foreign language experience, they look forward to learning German.

Whither all that enthusiasm?

The general picture provided by the Leeds sample of Year 7 pupils is of the majority of 11-year-olds entering their foreign language learning classes for the first time full of enthusiasm and eager to learn. Does the picture remain the same after two years of the course? Is the level of enthusiasm maintained? Are the expectations of Year 7 met by the learning reality? Two years later the same pupils, now in Year 9, were asked to assess their school subjects in terms of how these measured against their expectations.

As far as modern languages were concerned, especially German, the picture did not appear at first to be quite as bright as it had been in Year 7. The research suggested that pupils in the main had had their generally positive expectations just about met by German. For those who had had positive expectations this might present a positive response. For those who had been less than positive in their expectations it was a less than encouraging result. The response for French was slightly more positive. Given that there were nine subjects in all to which pupils gave a positive rating, indicating expectations bettered to varying degrees, it might arguably be concluded that their enthusiasm for German was not what it had been in Year 7.

The 13-year-olds were given the opportunity in an open question to explain their feelings regarding German. The majority of answers do not provide much useful insight ('I like it': 55.7%; 'I don't like it': 22.7%). In so far as other explanations are provided in numbers of any significance, teachers and their teaching appear to be important influences, both positive and negative, for some pupils (around 11%): 'The teacher goes too fast'; 'I'm scared of getting shouted at if I can't do it'; 'We've had too many different teachers'.

Interview responses suggest that pupils who enjoy German do so because they appreciate its novelty as a new subject. Those who do not enjoy the subject tend to blame the teacher ('Teachers shout at you when you don't understand'; 'The teacher complains about my writing – you should see her worksheets'; 'When the teacher says, "I thought we went over this in class" it makes me mad'), or the degree of difficulty ('I am slow at learning and it's too hard'; 'It's hard to pronounce'; 'You don't understand what foreign people are saying').

Enjoyment of activities in German lessons

Pupils were asked to consider a range of foreign language learning activities and rate them on a scale of 1–5 (see Table 3.8 on page 60). They were also given the opportunity in open questions and interviews to add to and justify their responses.

In six out of the seven categories in which answers were provided in both years there was a drop in the mean. When the paired samples t-test (3) was applied it was found that in four of the categories the difference was statistically significant:

group work: $t = 2.71$, df $= 78$, $p < 0.05$
writing: $t = 3.88$, df $= 112$, $p < 0.001$
reading: $t = 2.86$, df $= 93$, $p < 0.05$
speaking: $t = 3.68$, df $= 113$, $p < 0.001$

It is interesting that these should include three out of the four basic skills or 'attainment targets' (ATs) (listening and responding; speaking; reading and responding; writing). Whether pupils' experience of German learning

Table 3.8 Percentage of Leeds pupils in 1992 and 1994 responding to the question 'How much do you enjoy the following activities in German lessons?

Activity	Age/yr	Not at all → Quite → A lot					Not done*	Sample	Mean**	SD**
		1	2	3	4	5				
Computer	13/92	0.9	3.5	0.9	3.5	7.9	83.3	114	3.84	1.39
	15/94	1.7	1.7	0.9	1.7	5.2	88.7	115	3.61	1.61
Pair work	13/92	0.0	6.1	15.7	31.3	43.5	3.5	115	4.16	0.92
	15/94	0.0	0.0	20.9	38.3	40.0	0.9	115	4.19	0.76
Group work	13/92	0.0	4.4	19.3	28.1	32.5	15.8	114	4.05	0.91
	15/94	1.7	5.2	29.6	22.6	24.3	16.5	115	3.75	1.02
Project work/	13/92	5.3	5.3	11.4	8.8	1.8	67.5	114	2.89	1.15
Coursework***	15/94									
Speaking	13/92	7.0	10.5	34.2	24.6	23.7	0.0	114	3.47	1.17
	15/94	10.4	15.7	44.3	22.6	7.0	0.0	115	3.00	1.04
Reading	13/92	3.5	9.6	35.1	24.6	13.2	14.0	114	3.40	1.01
	15/94	7.0	14.9	43.0	21.9	4.4	8.8	114	3.02	0.96
Listening exercise	13/92	9.6	17.5	41.2	21.1	10.5	0.0	114	3.05	1.10
	15/94	11.3	20.9	43.5	20.9	3.5	0.0	115	2.84	0.10
Writing exercise	13/92	6.2	8.8	40.7	30.1	14.2	0.0	113	3.37	1.04
	15/94	9.6	12.2	53.9	20.0	4.4	0.0	115	2.97	0.94

* 'Not done' indicates activities in which pupils feel they do not engage in class.
** Includes only those pupils who claim to participate in activities, i.e. excludes those under 'Not done'.
*** In 1992 13-year-olds were not asked about project-/coursework, as this was not considered to be part of their language-learning experience. It is included two years later as the result of greater emphasis on a modular approach and on flexible and independent learning.

becomes less enjoyable or whether they become more critically aware as they get older is open to question.

Immediately striking is that among the most enjoyed activities are those which for a substantial number of pupils form no part of their German-learning experience. (This is also reflected in Table 3.3.) The figures in the 'Not done' column for computer-related activities (83.3% and 88.7%) are particularly disturbing, not least in the light of the emphasis placed on these in the National Curriculum for modern foreign languages (DES/WO, 1991; DFEE/WO, 1995). (See also *The Times*, 22 July 1996, 'British schools lead the world in teaching information technology'.) The very few pupils who claimed to have had the experience of computer-based learning in foreign language lessons indicated that they thoroughly enjoyed the experience. It is disconcerting that access has been provided to such small numbers.

Results for project- and coursework (this applies only to the pupils in 1994, at 15) are also quite alarming, but for different reasons. Such work appears to be done by comparatively few pupils (32.5%), in spite of the opportunity it provides for them to engage in teamwork, to learn autonomously and to work at their own pace with short-term objectives and rewards. These are some of the transferable 'life skills' sought by employers (see the *Independent*, 11 July 1996, 'A range of skills will pave the way to a job'; *Guardian Higher*, 15 July 1997, 'Mastering the basics'.) In contrast to computer work, however, the few who had had this experience did not seem to have enjoyed it very much, the mean score for it being 2.89.

Of the activities which form part of the 'standard' German lesson, pair work ('You don't have to work – I let my partner do it all'; 'You learn from each other'; 'You don't get embarrassed') and group work ('We have the chance to chat about other things'; 'Your friends understand your problems better') were the most popular, although not all pupils engaged in the latter (see Littlejohn, 1983; Long & Porter, 1985). The other activities, including work on the four ATs, got a mixed review, with some pupils giving a positive response and others negative. Speaking, listening and, in so far as it was done at all, reading, were popular activities with some pupils and less so with others. Thirteen-year-olds in 1992 gave reasonably high mean scores for speaking (3.47), reading (3.40) and writing (3.37), but speaking could be a source of embarrassment for some pupils: 'I feel scared to answer – if I make a mess, people laugh at me'. (See Keller, 1983 on the human need for 'affiliation', the need to be successful and establish links with other people.) And those who did not enjoy writing sometimes failed to see the point of it all: 'We just copy and copy and copy'; 'Sometimes all we seem to do is copy out things we do not understand'.

These 13-year-olds were less enthusiastic about listening exercises, giving them a mean score of 3.05. Pupils complained of unclear recordings, defective equipment, foreigners speaking too fast and inappropriate tasks. One pupil's response suggests that video-recordings might be more helpful than audiotapes: 'I can't watch their lips.' One 13-year-old, however, was less concerned about the enjoyment of activities than the outcome: 'I'm not bothered what the teacher does to learn [sic] us; it onestly [sic] dosent [sic] matter how he does it as long as we learn it.' (13-year-old)

As 15-year-olds in 1994 the pupils seemed to enjoy the four ATs rather less (in three out of the four, significantly less), giving them a mean of just over three or under.

Data relating to Kiel pupils

Pupils in Kiel were asked to address the same issue. Would their language-learning experience and their reaction to it be different to that of their Leeds counterparts?

It transpired that the extent of the differences in perceptions was not big enough as to justify the presentation here of a full table of Kiel results. As was the case for Leeds, pair work and group work were much enjoyed in English lessons in Kiel and were identified as the most popular activities. Computer work was done as rarely in Kiel as it was in Leeds (13/92: 83.2%; 15/94: 82.0%; n=139 in each case). A reason for this may be the absence of hard- and software: 'The ratio of computers to children in secondary schools (10–18 years) is only 1:1200 – and many schools have no computers.' (Cohen, 1997) Those who had had this experience shared the enthusiasm of their Leeds peers. Apart from speaking (fourth most popular of the eight activities), the four skills – one cannot refer to ATs in the German context – did not score terribly well, especially writing (least popular). Listening not only featured towards the bottom of the enjoyment table (second least popular) but was claimed not to be done by 18% of learners of English at age 13 and 24.6% at age 15. Given the nature of this skill and its basic importance, these appear disturbingly high percentages; they may result from a teaching methodology which is largely based on comprehension of written texts and discussion/question and answer in the target language, which could be thought to preclude the need for formal listening comprehension exercises. (See Mreschar, 1991 and Chambers, 1991 who criticise a 'sterile' and 'unimaginative' approach to the teaching of English in Germany.)

It is interesting to note that a small number of pupils took the opportunity in the open questions to raise objections to the target-language approach: 'Englisch finde ich schlecht – die Lehrerin redet nur Englisch' (*'I don't like English – the teacher only speaks English'*) (15-year-old). Projectwork and coursework in English lessons were experienced by few, and enjoyed by some but not by others.

Other influential factors in German/English lessons

There may well have been other extrinsic factors affecting pupils' motivation to learn German (or in the case of Kiel, English). Pupils were questioned on what these might be and the extent of their influence. Both sets of pupils were in agreement as to the most important factors contributing to a positive view of their foreign language learning experience. These were:

- the teacher;
- the textbook;
- the equipment;
- teacher-made materials.

That the teacher should top the list of important factors in foreign language lessons should come as little surprise. Interview comments and responses to open questions relating to a range of aspects of the learning experience tend to focus on the negative; compare the results of a MORI study into pupils' perceptions of the most common obstacles to learning at school: these were poor teaching (77%), and teachers who do not understand how children learn (72%) (Sutcliffe, 1998).

The textbook is second on the list for Leeds, though 'most of the pictures are from the 60s and boring' (13-year-old – this seems surprising, given the attractive, colourful publications currently on the market; see O'Sullivan, 1990 and Shirey & Reynolds, 1988 on the role of teaching materials in motivation) – as it is for Kiel. The mean score is higher in the latter, however; in the case of the 15-year-olds, significantly so. Anecdotal evidence combined with the outcomes of the question on enjoyment suggest that work in English lessons in Kiel tends to be much more textbook-based than is usually the case in German classes in Leeds (Mreschar, 1991; Chambers, 1991). It is interesting that Kiel pupils should attach importance to equipment, for example cassette-recorders or listening-posts, given that they appear to use little of it. Teacher-made materials are possibly given importance because pupils may see them as an attempt to get away from the textbook and introduce more variety.

As for the remaining factors, low scores indicate that Leeds learners of German, like Kiel learners of English, attach little importance to computers (since they claim to use them so little, it is perhaps predictable that they view them as unimportant), the way their classroom is furnished, or pen-pals.

Pen-pals are clearly not as popular in Germany or the UK as they once were. This is regrettable, given the opportunities they provide for authentic writing and reading tasks (see *The Times Educational Supplement*, 7 March 1997, 'Répondez s'il vous plaît'), quite apart from the establishing of international contacts and relationships. There is some evidence to suggest, however, that with the spread of e-mail in schools the pendulum may swing back and such contacts become popular again (see *The Times Educational Supplement*, 7 March 1997, 'Cross-cultural collaborators').

The only areas which provided a significant difference between Leeds and Kiel 13-year-olds in 1992 were:

(1) the number of pupils in the class. Kiel pupils view the number of pupils in a class as important, increasingly so as they get older; Leeds pupils seem less concerned with this, though two 13-year-olds observed: 'I can't learn German because the group is too big'; and 'We should have a bigger room and two teachers'. Generally class size tends to be smaller in Germany than is the case in Leeds. This is a topical issue both in Germany (Chambers, 1995) and in the UK (see, for example, 'Revealed: how 10,000 teachers disappeared' in the *Independent*, 28 September 1995; 'Class sizes up again' in *The Times Educational Supplement*, 5 July 1996), as budget cuts demand more pupils per class and fewer teachers per school.

(2) the exchange. In contrast to Kiel pupils, Leeds pupils tended not to regard the influence of exchanges as important. This may come as some surprise given that an exchange visit represents an opportunity to target a short-term goal and put into practice what has been learnt.

Two years later the picture changes. At age 15 there were significant differences between the indifferent responses of Leeds and the more assertive responses of Kiel pupils in almost all areas: teacher: textbook, teacher-made materials, equipment, computers, number of pupils in the class, exchange. The only areas in which there was no significant difference were the classroom and pen-pals. Why there should be this difference in response between pupils at ages 13 and 15 is difficult to explain. One possibility, admittedly difficult to prove, may be that Leeds pupils have the opportunity to drop foreign language learning after GCSE (and the majority take advantage of this) whilst their Kiel peers are obliged to continue with English. As a result they may take the above considerations rather more seriously. This view may be supported by the importance Kiel pupils attach to English-learning generally, which is reflected in their response to the question on what they would do if English were not taught at school. Leeds pupils were asked the same question but relating to German.

There appears to be a clear distinction between the more proactive reaction of Kiel and the rather apathetic response of Leeds. Up to 77.3% of Leeds pupils opting not to bother with learning German at all seems to suggest that they rather struggle to appreciate any real relevance or importance the language may have. The contrast with the reaction of Kiel pupils (in terms

Table 3.9 Percentages of Leeds and Kiel pupils responding to the request to complete with the phrase most applicable to them the statement: 'If German/English were not taught in the school, I would probably ...'.

	Age/Year	% Leeds (n =)	% Kiel (n =)
not bother learning German/English at all	13/94	77.3 (185)	33.3 (198)
	13/92	54.9 (113)	30.9 (139)
	15/94	70.4 (115)	27.0 (137)
	15/92	61.5 (13)	32.8 (58)
	17/94	69.2 (13)	11.9 (59)
try to get lessons in German/English somewhere else	13/94	13.0 (185)	43.4 (198)
	13/92	22.1 (113)	33.8 (139)
	15/94	13.0 (115)	43.1 (137)
	15/92	30.8 (13)	29.3 (58)
	17/94	23.1 (13)	40.7 (59)
pick up German/English in everyday situations (books, magazines, newspapers etc.)	13/94	4.9 (185)	21.7 (198)
	13/92	10.6 (113)	33.1 (139)
	15/94	10.4 (115)	24.1 (137)
	15/92	7.7 (13)	29.3 (58)
	17/94	7.7 (13)	35.6 (59)

of English) is striking. More than two-thirds of German pupils claimed that they would make an effort to learn English elsewhere or in other ways. This may indicate an awareness of English competence as an important life skill.

Similarly when Leeds pupils were asked to comment on the usefulness of the subjects on their timetable, mathematics, English and science came out on top. Foreign languages were generally not perceived as useful. The Kiel pupils regarded mathematics, English and German as the three most useful subjects.

Pupils' views on how German/English learning could be enhanced

Pupils were given the opportunity to suggest ways in which German learning could be enhanced. Up to 70% of Leeds pupils in the 13–15 cohort opted not to answer this question. Does this indicate general apathy? Is it an indicator of the 'anti-achievement culture' which allegedly exists in our schools and some parts of society? According to a survey conducted by Keele University (Whitehead, 1996) 82% of pupils (n = 30,000) said that classmates who worked hard were 'ridiculed'. Perhaps it is more an indication of pupils' struggle to identify and articulate what they really want and need. The few who did respond suggested that there should be no change (13/92: 16.5%; 15/94: 17.4%). It is open to speculation whether this reflects general satisfaction, or an appreciation of a need for change but an inability to identify what that change should be. For those pupils who had suggestions, the proposal that 'more interesting teaching methods' should be adopted attracted the support of 30.4% of 13-year-olds in 1992. Perhaps this advice was accepted, as two years later this percentage drops to 7.8%. More exchange visits (13/92: 8.7%; 15/94: 3.5%) and a change of teacher (13/92: 7.8%; 15/94: 10.4%) were other suggestions represented.

The trends for Leeds 13–15 cohorts were broadly replicated in the responses of Kiel learners of English. Where any changes were suggested, the emphasis appeared to be on greater attention given to activities relating to oral work. (Emphasis is placed on oral activities in the UK, but it can be argued that this is not reflected in the quality of oral performance; see Milton & Meara, 1998.) It is interesting to note that 25% of 13-year-old Kiel pupils interviewed in 1992 suggested a reduction in the amount of scolding might enhance the perception of English lessons: 'Manche Lehrer flippen schnell aus.' (*Lots of teachers quickly lose their cool.*') One 15-year-old (1994) appealed for a calmer approach: 'mehr Zeit, Geduld und Ruhe' – '*more time, patience and quiet*'. Another appeared critical of the teacher's English competence and suggested the requirement for all teachers of English to spend a year in an English-speaking country: 'Alle Englischlehrer müßten ein Jahr oder mehr im englischsprachigen Ausland verbringen, um "lebendiges Englisch" zu lernen.' (*'All English teachers should have to spend a year in an English-speaking country in order to learn up-to-date English.'*)

Responding to diminishing enthusiasm

On the basis of this sample, there is some evidence to suggest a lessening of enthusiasm for the in-school experience of German learning between Years 9 and 11. The data for Kiel pupils are not so very different.

To what may this apparent diminution be attributable? Two possibilities are evident from the Leeds/Kiel study: only a few activities can be said to be enjoyed, and there is also the rather disturbing tendency of pupils to regard as enjoyable those activities to which they claim to get little or no access; computer-based tasks, for example, are experienced by relatively small numbers. Project work is rarely done. Why is this so? The data relating to the four attainment targets are disturbing, too.

Computer-based tasks

Much of the National Curriculum documentation stresses the importance and benefits of the implementation of information and communication technology (ICT) in the foreign languages classroom. This includes word-processing, e-mail, software packages relating to creative writing, learning of vocabulary, practising of grammar and other exercises. ICT gives pupils the opportunity to work with a medium which many of them have at home and enjoy, to work independently and at their own pace and to create documents which can be corrected neatly without the need for the teacher's dreaded red pen. Much has been written about its potential for motivating pupils, especially the less able (Atkinson, 1992; White & Wacha, 1992; Martin & Hampson, 1991; Brown, 1993). Research by West *et al.* (1997) suggests that 7-year-olds like working on computers better than anything else they do at school. In spite of this, however, in excess of 80% of pupils in the Leeds 13–15 cohort studied claimed not to experience computers as part of their German-learning reality. The few pupils who had had the experience claimed to enjoy it enormously (see also Clark & Trafford, 1995: 321).

Why should so few pupils have had this experience? Poor access to hardware (Chambers & Higham, 1993; OFSTED, 1995) is a major problem. In most schools other subject areas, such as business studies, computer studies and mathematics, tend to block-book the computer room. The typical modern languages department has just one or two computers on a trolley which can be used by groups of up to three pupils at a time. This limits the computer to being used as part of a carousel of other activities. Under such conditions it is hardly surprising that teachers do not often feel inclined to make the considerable effort needed, if ICT is to become part of regular German learning and teaching provision.

A common problem is the tendency for teachers to feel they lack the necessary ICT competence (Chambers & Higham, 1993; OFSTED, 1995; Gunn, 1998). A certain degree of confidence in one's own ability and familiarity with the hard- and software are necessary before basing a lesson for up to 30 pupils on an ICT package. As a result of these and other difficulties it must often seem less trouble for teachers to stick to the methodology which they feel works and with which they are familiar, rather than introduce a medium which they may perceive as having the potential to create more problems than it solves.

Project-work/autonomous and flexible learning

Autonomous and flexible approaches to learning were born of an effort to meet the diverse needs of the range of pupils within a class, including the 'disaffected'. They give pupils the opportunity to set short-term, achievable goals, to work at the pace which best suits them and to work independently, as part of a pair or of a group. This has the potential not only to enhance the subject-specific learning experience, whether the subject is

German or any other, but also of giving the pupils access to life skills much demanded by employers (Schofield, 1996).

As is the case with ICT, however, experience of project- and coursework, which may form part of a flexible/autonomous learning package, appears to be the exception rather than the rule in the German-learning classroom. Here again, teachers may have various justifications for not adopting the flexible/autonomous approach. Evans (1993) poses pertinent questions:

> How is the teacher who has always adopted a didactic and serial mode of teaching to elicit this kind of autonomy from his or her pupils? It will surely not be enough to rely on the occasional session of group work to nurture this kind of competence. What systematic ways are there of monitoring independence, and how can a teacher balance a necessary diet of centrally directed 'teaching' with structured access and use of multiple resources allowing for increased pupil independence in the work scheme for a given class?

In addition, the autonomous approach is relatively new and comparatively untried and teachers may feel uncomfortable with a concept which gives pupils responsibility for their own learning. They may harbour fears that pupils will not set themselves targets which are demanding enough and worry about the implications of this in an age of 'league tables' for schools. A flexible/autonomous approach demands much of a teacher in terms of preparation. If pupils are to work independently with any degree of success, then the teacher has to provide an adequate stock of appropriately differentiated materials. Assessment also poses a challenge in that not all pupils will be ready to submit themselves for tests at the same time and at the same level. Having an accurate grasp on who is doing what is a source of concern for some teachers. They may fear that they simply do not have the capacity to retain an overview of up to 30 or more pupils striving to meet their own targets.

The four attainment targets

Listening and responding (AT1), speaking (AT2), reading and responding (AT3) and writing (AT4) get a mixed review from pupils. Some reasons for this are revealed in their responses in the interviews and open questions. Should consideration be given to an adjustment to teaching methodology to meet needs common to many pupils? (For articles dealing with teaching the four ATs see, for example, Elston, 1991; Fawkes, 1993; Klapper, 1992a; 1992b; 1993; Mitchell & Swarbrick, 1994.)

AT1 (listening and responding) and AT3 (reading and responding) cover the 'receptive skills'. Considerations for teachers might include:

- To what extent are listening and reading activities *testing* rather than *learning* experiences? (Chambers, 1996; Klapper, 1993.)

- Are pupils given the opportunity to infer and predict – skills which they apply in their mother tongue?

- How much effort is made to establish overtly what learners *know*, as in for example 'Underline all the words you understand' – a positive, success-oriented approach – rather than what they *don't know*, as in 'Underline all the words you don't understand' – a negative, failure-oriented approach?

- Is enough care taken with choice of texts and preparatory activities to allow pupils to read fluently, for example by arousing their curiosity (Crookes & Schmidt, 1991: 488), establishing the context, their knowledge of language, their knowledge of the world? (See also Council of Europe, 1996: 37.)

- How often are pupils given a *real* reason to read (Turner, 1997) or to listen (Chambers, 1996), such as access to needed information; interest; enjoyment? How often are target-language speakers or the class link with the school in Germany/France/Spain exploited for this purpose? As Wringe (1994) laments: 'the field of reading ...is now often limited to scanning for information and skimming for the phrase that will enable the fumble-fingered editorial assistant to match up the magazine readers' letters with the agony aunt's replies.'

- Concerning listening: how often do teachers over-use the pause-button, trying to help their pupils but in the process denying them the opportunity to hear enough known language to be able to contextualise and infer unknown language? (Chambers, 1996.) Are pupils given adequate opportunities to control the number of times they hear the text, both in its totality and/or in parts? 'Every time I press the play-back button in front of the class, I am condemning the whole class to work at an identical speed' (Elston, 1992).

- Concerning reading: how often are pupils given the opportunity to read for pleasure and/or choose what they wish to read? How much *real* reading do pupils do in preparation for GCSE? Are they offered no more than 'an odd mixture of signs and snippets' (Turner, 1998), as opposed to texts of any real substance? 'If we have no purpose in meaning (as often happens in the foreign languages classroom), we can bring no understanding to the text and it will therefore be meaningless' (Klapper, 1992).

- How much reading of any kind is done in the classroom of the 'communicative era'? Should reading not be more than a required adjunct as the GCSE examination approaches? (Turner, 1998.)
- How often do teachers give pupils the opportunity to discuss their own strategies for working out the meaning of unknown words?

With regard to AT2 (speaking) and AT4 (writing), the 'productive skills', teachers might like to consider:

- How often are castles built in the sand? How often do teachers expect the language to come out before it has been properly put in, implying inadequate presentation and practice? Wringe (1994) notes the consequences of this in the context of a survey on birthdays:
  > Having started off amid great enthusiasm, the activity may quite quickly fall apart because numbers have not been revised beforehand, or those above 20 not even taught.
- How often are role-plays and writing tasks set up without pupils being given enough models upon which to base their production?
- How often are pupils given a *real* reason to speak (an authentic audience) and write (an authentic readership)?

Conclusions

Of all the factors which may contribute to a pupil's positive or negative evaluation of a subject, the teacher comes out on top for all cohorts in Leeds and Kiel. (This was also found in Filmer-Sankey's studies for OXPROD, 1989, 1991, and Sutcliffe's for MORI, 1998. See too Clark & Trafford, 1995: 318, 321.) The quality of the teacher is a factor which permeates almost every issue investigated in the survey relating to pupils' feelings about learning German/English and 'in-school' issues. The responses to the open questions where pupils have the opportunity to explain their views are particularly revealing. Again and again the teacher is named as the reason why, for example, they like/dislike German/English; why their learning experience has improved/deteriorated; how German/English could be improved, and so on. The teaching methodology, the textbook, the computers available count for little if the teacher–pupil relationship is lacking. The teacher carries an enormous burden of responsibility.

How often it seems that teachers in the UK are made to feel inferior to their colleagues abroad. Contrary, however, to the glowing picture painted in the UK media, in which all things German are held up as a model of excellence (cf. Channel Four Television, 1993; Green & Steedman, 1993; MacLeod, 1995), Mreschar (1991) reports that pupils there have their complaints, too. He claims that German pupils generally have a low opinion of their teachers, especially with regard to their poor level of communicative competence and their inability to bring relevance to the real world into their lessons.

The position of English as a 'Weltsprache' (world language or lingua franca) must, however, contribute to making the lives of teachers of English in Germany so much easier than is the case for their German-teaching counterparts in England. Of the 72 Kiel pupils interviewed only one claimed not to regard foreign language competence as important. The interviewees appreciated the application of foreign languages in the world of work and in practical communication. All but two thought English to be the most important of all foreign languages. The work of Milton and Meara (1998) shows how other countries attach much greater importance to the teaching and learning of English than we do to French and German here in Britain. This is reflected in the following table from their study relating to the approximate number of hours of foreign language tuition received by 14- and 15-year-olds.

Table 3.10 Approximate hours of foreign language tuition received by subjects

British students learning French	210
British students learning German	80
German students learning English	400
Greek students learning English	660

Heuer (1983: 104ff.) conducted research into motivation and the learning of English with Year 7 pupils (12-year-olds) in the *Hauptschule*, roughly the equivalent of the secondary modern school in Britain. He found that of the 845 pupils involved, 81.9% recognised the value of English for travel and future career and had used it in some way, usually in connection with television, records, reading, interaction with tourists and travel; 33.3% had read an English newspaper or magazine.

A similar study was conducted with pupils in Years 5 to 9 (10- to 14-year-olds) by Fengler and Fischer (1983: 112ff.). In response to the question 'Why learn English?' the 310 pupils responded as follows:

33.3% – because it is a compulsory subject

68.7% – travel

67.1% – career

As many as 72.4% of the boys and 59.7% of girls claimed to come from families with English-speaking competence.

The foreign language teaching situation in Germany, at least in terms of pupil reaction to provision, seems little different to that in the UK. The major difference appears to lie in the area of perceived relevance. German learners apparently attach considerably more importance to foreign language learning than do their British peers and as a result are prepared to tolerate a teaching approach which they may find less than inspiring.

Keller (1983), in his education-oriented theory of motivation, regards 'instrumental' needs as the most basic determinants. (See also Gardner & Lambert, 1972.) Such needs are met when the content of the lesson matches what the learners feel they need to learn. For reasons which lie beyond the classroom, for example the low status of foreign language learning in the UK, the absence of role models with foreign language competence, the dominance of Euroscepticism in the media (Young, 1993: 115, 120), there is often a mismatch between what the teacher provides and pupils' perceptions of what their needs are.

The Leeds/UK teacher is up against it. She continues to play a key role in motivation. Her support, enthusiasm and positive approach in providing a learning experience which has practical application, vocational value and is enjoyable and fulfilling are key motivational components. She is constantly walking a tightrope, endeavouring to strike a balance between pupils' ability and the amount of challenge in lesson content: 'When the level of challenge is perceived as higher than the individual's level of ability, the result is anxiety; and when the level of challenge is perceived as lower than the individual's ability, the result is boredom' (Crookes & Schmidt, 1991: 488).

It is important that teachers access their pupils' views on their learning experience in order to provide for their varying needs. If these needs are to be met and if teachers are to compete with their Kiel/German counterparts on a level playing-field, as surely they must, they have to be provided with, amongst other things, the necessary in-service training (for example in information technology and autonomous/flexible approaches to learning), the necessary resources (such as computers and adequate teaching space, preferably in the form of smaller classes), time (to properly plan and prepare lessons), and support (classroom assistants and, in the increasingly technological world of modern languages teaching and learning, technicians; why should technicians be limited to the support of science and technology teachers?).

This chapter merely touches upon one tiny part of what is a vast motivational carpet made up of legion interlocking threads. There remains much to be done in the area of pupils' motivational perspectives of the foreign language learning experience. Crookes and Schmidt (1991: 499–500) rightly identify the need for research into motivation from the teacher's point of view and the issue of long-term reward. Only when these and other related areas become the focus of attention, via a range of methodologies beyond mere questionnaire and follow-up interview, can the problem of motivation in the UK foreign language-learning classroom context be tackled with any seriousness, and with any hope for some degree of resolution.

Notes

1. The author in a teacher educator and advisory role observes many classes in a range of schools. Reading aloud remains part of the staple language-learning diet of a significant number of pupils. When asked for their views on the experience, pupils said, first, that they dislike reading aloud because other pupils make fun of them, and second, that they don't like listening to the others reading because it is so boring. The author has also noted that in this phase of the lesson pupils often become restless and display disruptive behaviours.
2. The feminine pronoun is adopted because most primary school teachers and foreign language teachers in the UK are women.
3. A non-parametric test was applied in the first instance, since the assumption of equal interval data is questionable. It was thought however that, given the large sample, a parametric test would be adequately robust. It was found that both the parametric and non-parametric approaches led to precisely the same conclusions.

References

Alison, J. (1993) *Not Bothered? Motivating Reluctant Learners in Key Stage 4*. London: CILT.

Atkinson, T. (1992) 'Le hamster a mangé mon pneu': Creative writing and IT. *Language Learning Journal* 6, 68–70.

Brown, R. (1993) Developing IT in modern languages. *Language Learning Journal* 8, 51–3

Buckby, M. *et al.* (1981) *Graded Objectives and Tests for Modern Languages*. London: Schools Council.

Burstall, C., Cohen, S., Hargreaves, M. and Jamieson, M. (1974) *Primary French in the Balance*. Slough: NFER.

Campbell, J. and Neil, S. (1994) *Curriculum Reform at Key Stage 1*. London: Longman.

Chambers, G. (1991) A win in anyone's language. *Guardian*, 30 July.

Chambers, G. (1993) Taking the 'de' out of demotivation. *Language Learning Journal* 7, 13–16.

Chambers, G. (1994) A snapshot in motivation at 10+, 13+ and 16+. _Language Learning Journal_ 9, 14–18.

Chambers, G. (1995) Binational problem-solving. _German Teaching_ 11, 14–17.

Chambers, G. (1996) Listening. Why? How? _Language Learning Journal_ 14, 19–22.

Chambers, G. (1996) Motivational perspectives of secondary school pupils taking German. Unpublished PhD thesis, University of Leeds.

Chambers, G. and Higham, J. (1993) Information technology: The school dimension. _Information Technology in Initial Teacher Education: The Modern Languages Perspective_. University of York: National Council for Educational Technology.

Channel Four Television (1993) _Dispatches: All Our Futures_. London: Channel Four Television Publications.

CILT (1995a) _The TES/CILT Modern Languages Survey of Secondary Schools: An Outline of Preliminary Findings_. London: CILT

CILT (1995b) _Modern Languages in Primary Schools: CILT Report_. London: CILT.

Clark, A. and Trafford, J. (1995) Boys into modern languages: An investigation of the discrepancy in attitudes and performance between boys and girls in modern languages. _Gender and Education_ 7 (3), 315–25.

Cohen, M. (1997) Germans play game of catchup on the Net. _Guardian Education_, 6 May.

Council of Europe (1996) _Common European Framework of Reference for Language Learning and Teaching_. Strasbourg: Council of Europe.

Crookes, G. and Schmidt R. (1991) Motivation: Reopening the research agenda. _Language Learning_ 41 (4), 469–512.

DES/DENI/WO (1985) _Foreign Language Performance in Schools: A Report on the 1983 Survey of French_. London: HMSO, APU.

DES/DENI/WO (1986) _Foreign Language Performance in Schools: A Report on the 1984 Survey of French, German and Spanish_. London: HMSO, APU.

DES/DENI/WO (1987) _Foreign Language Performance in Schools: A Report on the 1985 Survey of French, German and Spanish_. London: HMSO, APU.

DES/WO (1991) _Modern Languages in the National Curriculum_. London: HMSO.

DFEE/WO (1995) _Modern Languages in the National Curriculum_. London: HMSO.

Elston, T. (1991) Are your students good listeners? _Francophonie_ 4, 13–14.

Elston, T. (1992) In one ear ..._The Times Educational Supplement_, 3 April.

Evans, M. (1993) Flexible learning and modern languages teaching. _Language Learning Journal_ 8, 17–21.

Fawkes, S. (1993) Reading for pleasure and the National Curriculum. _Francophonie_ 8, 41–3.

Fengler, A. and Fischer, A. (1983) Wie sehen Schüler den Englischunterricht? Eine Nachuntersuchung zur Motivation im Englischunterricht. In G. Solmecke (ed.) _Motivation und Motivieren im Fremdsprachenunterricht_. Paderborn: Schöningh.

Filmer-Sankey, C. (1989) _A Study of First-year Pupils' Attitudes towards French, German and Spanish_. Oxford: OXPROD, University of Oxford, Department of Educational Studies.

Filmer-Sankey, C. (1991) _A Study of Second-year Pupils' Attitudes towards French, German and Spanish_. Oxford: OXPROD, University of Oxford, Department of Educational Studies.

Gardner, R. and Lambert, W. (1972) _Attitudes and Motivation in Secondary Language Learning_. Rowley, MA: Newbury House.

Geoghegan, R. (1995) _Modern Languages in North Yorkshire_. North Yorkshire County

Council.
Green, A. and Steedman, H. (1993) *Educational Provision, Educational Attainment and the Needs of Industry: A Review of Research for Germany, France, Japan, the USA and Britain.* London: National Institute of Economic and Social Research.
Gunn, O. (1998) Excellence for all children: Meeting special educational needs. *Teaching Today* 19.
Hargreaves, D. (1982) *The Challenge for the Comprehensive School.* London: Routledge Kegan Paul.
Hawkins, E. (1997) *30 Years of Language Teaching.* London: CILT.
Heuer, H. (1983) Zur Motivation im Englischunterricht. In G. Solmecke (ed.) *Motivation und Motivieren im Fremdsprachenunterricht.* Paderborn: Schöningh.
Hooley, G.J. and Newcombe, J.R. (1988) Ailing British exports: Symptoms, causes and cures. In M.J. Thomas and N.E. Waite (eds) *The Marketing Digest* (pp.397–410). London: Heinemann.
Keller, J. (1983) Motivational design of instruction. In C. Reigeluth (ed.) *Instructional Design Theories and Models* (pp. 386-433). Hillsdale, NJ: Erlbaum.
Klapper, J. (1992a) Reading in a foreign language: Theoretical issues. *Language Learning Journal* 5, 27–30.
Klapper, J. (1992b) Preliminary considerations for the teaching of FL reading. *Language Learning Journal* 6, 53–6.
Klapper, J. (1993) Practicable skills and practical constraints in FL reading. *Language Learning Journal* 7, 50–4.
Littlejohn, A. (1983) Increasing learner involvement in course management. *TESOL Quarterly* 17, 595–608.
Long, M. and Porter, P. (1985) Group work, interlanguage talk, and second language acquisition. *TESOL Quarterly* 19, 207–28.
MacLeod, D. (1995) Hands across the sea. *Guardian Education,* 30 May.
Martin, G. and Hampson, E. (1991) Using the concept keyboard in modern languages. *Language Learning Journal* 3, 59–60.
Meara, P. (1995) *LLEX Lingua Vocabulary Tests.* Swansea: CALS.
Milton, J. and Meara, P. (1998) Are the British really bad at learning foreign languages? *Language Learning Journal* 17.
Mitchell, I. and Swarbrick, A. (1994) *Developing Skills for Independent Reading.* Pathfinder No. 22. London: CILT.
Mreschar, R. (1991) Was Schüler von der Schule halten. *Kultur Chronik* Vol.4 in *Langenscheidts Sprach-Illustrierte* Heft 3.
O'Connor, M. (1994) The voice of the pupil is heard. *The Times Educational Supplement,* 14 January.
OFSTED (1995) *Modern Foreign Languages: A Review of Inspection Findings 1993/94.* London: HMSO.
O'Sullivan, A. (1990) The foreign language coursebook: A study of its role in learner motivation. Unpublished PhD dissertation, University of London, Institute of Education.
O'Sullivan, E. (1990) *Friend and Foe: The Image of Germany and the Germans in British Children's Fiction from 1870 to the Present.* Tübingen: G. Narr Verlag.
Phillips, D. and Clark, G. (1988) *Attitudes towards Diversification.* Oxford: OXPROD, Oxford University Department of Educational Studies.
Phillips, D. and Geatches, H. (1989) *Diversification and 'Transfers-in'.* Oxford: OXPROD, Oxford University Department of Educational Studies.

Piepho, H. (1983) Englischunterricht aus der Schülerperspektive. Ermittlungen zu Erwartungshaltungen und Urteilsstrukturen als Voraussetzung schülerischer Curriculumentwicklung. In G. Solmecke (ed.) *Motivation und Motivieren im Fremdsprachenunterricht.* Paderborn: Schöningh.

Pollard, A., Broadfoot, P., Croll, P., Osborn, M. and Abbott, D. (1994) *Changing English Primary Schools?* London: Cassell.

Powell, R. and Batters, J. (1985) Pupils' perceptions of foreign language learning at 12+: Some gender differences. *Educational Studies* 11 (1), 11–23.

Powell, R. and Littlewood, P. (1983) Why choose French? Boys' and girls' attitudes at the option stage. *British Journal of Language Teaching* 21 (1), 37.

Rudduck, J. (1996) Testimony of the expert witnesses. *The Times Educational Supplement*, 28 June.

Schofield, P. (1996) A range of skills will pave the way to a job. *Independent*, 11 July.

Shirey, L. and Reynolds, R. (1988) Effect of interest on attention and learning. *Journal of Educational Psychology* 80, 159–66.

Solmecke, G. (ed.) (1983) *Motivation und Motivieren im Fremdsprachenunterricht.* Paderborn: Schöningh.

Stables, A. and Wikeley, F. (1997) Changes in preference for and perceptions of relative importance of subjects during a period of educational reform. *Educational Studies* 23 (3), 393–403.

Stewart-Smith, Y., Elliott, J. and Hildreth, A. (1996) Attitude is what gives Russians the edge. *The Times Educational Supplement*, 13 December.

Stradling, R., Saunders, L. and Weston, P. (1991) *Differentiation in Action: A Whole-School Approach for Raising Attainment.* London: NFER and DES.

Sutcliffe, J. (1998) Pupils give voice to their criticisms. *The Times Educational Supplement*, 15 May.

Swarbrick, A. (ed.) (1994) *Teaching Modern Languages.* London: Routledge.

Tierney, D. (1998) Modern languages in the primary school (MLPS) in Scotland: 10 years on. *Language Learning Journal* 18.

Turner, K. (1998) Reading: Meeting the demands of the National Curriculum. *Language Learning Journal* 17, 8–13.

West, A., Hailes, J. and Sammons, P. (1997) Children's attitudes to the National Curriculum at Key Stage 1. *British Educational Research Journal* 23.

White, C., and Wacha, H. (1992) Information technology and modern langauges. *Language Learning Journal* 5, 40–3.

Whitehead, M. (1996) Hard to keep the customers satisfied. *The Times Educational Supplement*, 5 March.

Whyte, J. (1981) Sex typing in schools. In A. Kelly (ed.) *The Missing Half: Girls and Science Education.* Manchester: Manchester University Press.

Wringe, C. (1994) Ineffective lessons: Reasons and remedies: Jottings from the tutor's note-pad. *Language Learning Journal* 10, 11–15.

Young, A. (1993) Peer and parental pressure within the sociolinguistic environment: An Anglo-French comparative study of teenage foreign language learners. *Language in a Changing Europe: British Studies in Applied Linguistics* 9, 112–22.

Chapter 4
The Primary Sector

ANN GREGORY

As long ago as 1977, the Hoy report, *The Early Teaching of Modern Languages*, advised of the importance of aims and objectives, of building on known and necessary conditions for success. It underlined the need for appropriately qualified teachers and a clear definition of short- and long-term teaching and learning goals. These basic requirements for the introduction of modern foreign languages into the primary curriculum are no less relevant now than then, and in fact are perhaps even more pressing.The 1990s have seen a rapid growth in the Early Teaching of Modern Languages (ETML) throughout Britain, but little evidence of clear planning. Apart from Scotland and a select number of local education authorities (LEAs) in the rest of the country, most initiatives depend on the enthusiasm and/or linguistic competence of individual teachers, working in isolation and with varying degrees of success. Although the Centre for Information on Language Teaching (CILT) survey of 1995 showed that between 5% and 7% of primary pupils in the state sector were learning a foreign language at that time, as well as an additional estimated 6.5% in the private sector and thousands more through private language clubs, no national policy has emerged.In most other European countries a modern foreign language is an established part of the primary curriculum.

The negative side of the story

On the surface, the picture is gloomy not just at the primary level in particular but for foreign languages in general. One might highlight recent reports on the dwindling number of students taking modern foreign languages as A-level options, concerns expressed by the Department for Trade and Industry about the shortage of linguists, a wealth of unfilled places on degree programmes involving foreign languages in the 1997 UCAS clearing period, a shortage of applicants for PGCE foreign language courses, and a reduction in the number of Higher Education Institutions (HEIs) offering primary teacher training with a specialism in French. The various factors responsible for these related situations may include the perceived difficulty of A-level foreign language courses by comparison with 'new' subjects such as psychology and media studies, the status of English as a world language, media reports of teacher stress and a lack of positive publicity about the successes of language graduates in employment.

Because of the shortage of foreign language teachers in secondary schools and the financial implications of introducing foreign languages into all primary schools, governments have been reluctant to support a national ETML initiative. In spite of pledges by the previous Conservative government, statements of intent in the Labour party pre-election manifesto, declarations by the Council of Europe, support from the Association for Language Learning (ALL) and the National Association of Head Teachers (NAHT) and specific reference to foreign language possibilities in the Dearing report (1995), there have been few signs of practical support at a national level. The result has been a lack of cohesion and co-ordination, and a continuation of many of the problems identified by Clare Burstall *et al.* in 1974.

The positive side of the story

Despite apparent lack of action at government level, there have been several indicators which give rise to a certain level of optimism in the ETML supporters' camp. As the CILT report on ETML (1995) concluded: 'It is there and it is growing.' The report showed that some schools which had introduced foreign languages in the 1960s and 1970s as part of the Nuffield project had continued to teach them. In areas where middle schools existed, French had been retained for the younger children as well as for those over 11. With the advent of 1992 and the introduction of European Awareness in the national curriculum, a sort of European fever developed and more schools started to take another look at foreign languages. As travel became easier, more and more parents had come to see the real values of being able to communicate in a foreign language. Indeed, ETML became a customer-driven activity, and schools in competition with each other for pupils often succumbed to parental demand and introduced a foreign language. Modern technology also played a part in the revival, as pupils began to be able to link up with schools abroad. Even though British children are still not exposed to foreign languages through television programmes and pop songs the way their counterparts are on the Continent, young children are now becoming more aware of other languages. A significant step forward was made when the BBC took the decision to introduce children's programmes aimed at supporting foreign language learning.

In terms of planning foreign language initiatives, Scotland set the lead in their pilot scheme entitled 'Modern Languages at Primary School' (MLPS).

In England, initiatives such as the Tameside scheme, later 'transferred' to the Isle of Man, and projects such as those in Surrey, Kent, Birmingham and Yorkshire were developed. On the whole the foreign language taught was French, as this was the language most commonly spoken by the primary teachers. However some projects reflected the diversification of the secondary schools' curriculum; for example, German was introduced in some primary schools in Cornwall and West Sussex. At this point it should not be forgotten that Welsh has been taught both as a foreign language and as mother tongue in primary schools in Wales for many years.

Realising that foreign languages in primary schools were expanding, publishers began to follow the example of the BBC. Pilot projects initiated by LEAs engendered their own teaching support materials, such as *Pilote*, born of the Kent project, and *C'est facile comme bonjour* in the London borough of Richmond. Inevitably foreign publishers also sought to get a corner of the market and several thick pedagogical guides appeared on the bookshelves. High street bookshops started to sell games, audio cassettes of songs and rhymes and publications of the 'teach your child a foreign language' type. Sadly many of these were written by those with little experience of foreign language teaching and even less of the primary pupil, with the result that the children's linguistic progress and accuracy were not very evident. More successful were the home-produced materials, developed by primary teachers and therefore appropriate to the young child's age and educational development. Once again, Scotland set the scene with an emphasis on 'embedding' the foreign language into the curriculum, using materials and situations with which the young child was familiar, such as story-telling and topic work.

Although many schools started lunch-time and after-school foreign language clubs it was clear that these excluded some children, and in many schools headteachers gradually moved the foreign language into the normal timetable, taught in the ideal situation by the class teacher. It became apparent that 'little and often' was more beneficial than long lessons of French, and even more effective was the move to use practical activities, emphasising oral and aural skills. Children were less anxious and therefore more likely to respond.

Demand for training and in-service courses increased, although the fact that foreign languages were not a National Curriculum subject below Key Stage 3 meant that individual schools, particularly small schools, were reluctant to devote funds to this area. However some LEAs dedicated funding to both linguistic and methodological training , and others bid for Lingua assistance, or sought sponsorship, as was the case in York and Basingstoke. Some HEIs organised accreditation for Inset courses, and organisations such as CILT and ALL set up conferences and workshops to support the demand. At the annual Language World conference, primary languages became a regular focus in the programme, and the Primary Languages Show, organised by CILT and first held in Manchester in 1997, promoted unprecedented interest. Awareness grew of ETML developments in Europe and as far afield as Australia, and there was increasing research activity into issues relating to the particular problems of young learners. European Lingua funding supported intensive programmes centred on areas such as teaching foreign languages through practical activities, involving students and trainers from England, France, Denmark and Norway.

The National Primary Languages Network, in existence for over ten years and now meeting twice a year at CILT, London, has provided a focus for the campaign to introduce foreign language teaching into the primary curriculum in a co-ordinated and planned fashion. It consists of a group of 'expert' advisers, inspectors, trainers and teachers, as well as representatives from other groups involved in ETML such as ALL, the Goethe-Institut and the Central Bureau, and trainers from Scotland and Northern Ireland. One of the group's most challenging tasks was to draft a proposal for the national introduction of foreign languages into the primary schools, considering not only the content and structure , but also issues such as language awareness, progression, languages-other-than-French, and the difficult subject of teacher training. This latter included a possible framework for initial teacher training (ITT), specialist teacher training, and in-service provision. One of the proposals of the document was the inclusion of a GCSE foreign language entry requirement to ITT programmes. This would result in a less costly exercise, as only methodological training would then be required for new entrants to the profession. Experiences in Scotland would serve as a guide for realistic planning and practical implementation.

So what next?

It is evident from the success of the Scottish pilot scheme and from reports reflecting the work that has gone on all over the country, that far from quashing it, the time is in fact ripe to develop ETML. As Keith Sharpe (1991) suggested, it is 'more phoenix than dodo now'.

The conference organised by the Schools Curriculum and Assessment Authority (SCAA) in 1996 on 'Modern Foreign Languages in the Primary Curriculum' was heavily over-subscribed. Although the conference report reflected the groundswell of support for ETML, it also indicated a note of caution: SCAA and the Teacher Training Agency (TTA) were considering the issues, but there were more pressing educational priorities. There had indeed been a period of stability when no further changes were being made to the National Curriculum, but the feeling of members of the National Primary Languages Network was that at the next point when changes were implemented, serious consideration should be given to the case for ETML. A spokesman for the DFEE's National Curriculum and Assessment Division, Clive Griffiths, wrote to the National Primary Languages Network in 1997: '[The TTA's] immediate priority is to address the problem of the supply of MFL teachers in secondary schools .. the debate about the teaching of modern foreign languages in primary schools is still very much alive.'

Despite this reserve at government level, at the chalkface ETML continued to mushroom. One example of the growing number of projects was a well-planned initiative co-ordinated and led by a secondary school in the East Riding. Here the seven feeder primary schools met regularly to plan a programme which would allow them to introduce French in a co-ordinated way, so that the experiences of all Year 7 pupils were the same. For some of the primary teachers this necessitated extra French lessons, and revision classes were set up at the local FE college. The LEA adviser provided further support, and a training day focusing on methodology and appropriate materials was delivered by the University College of Ripon and York Saint John. This example of a pyramid or cluster approach to the inter-phase transfer situation demonstrates what can be achieved with limited resources but a strong team spirit.

Sadly, the findings of the Burstall report are reflected in several areas by the problem of Year 7 pupils arriving with different levels of French, or none at all. One school in North Yorkshire, albeit in an unusual situation as it serves as the secondary school for the whole diocese, receives pupils in Year 7 from over 50 primary schools. Here the head of modern languages expects his staff to build on previous knowledge and the ethos of the school encourages pupils to be sympathetic to individual needs and to help each other, but it is still clear that pupils who have achieved a high level of French after up to four years in primary schools are going to experience a degree of repetition and possibly boredom. Sometimes these pupils are advised to start a different language in Year 7 and then take up French again in Year 8. This raises inevitable questions of continuity and progression which continue to stimulate interesting debate on both sides. There is certainly scope here for more research.

If it is impossible for practical reasons to put Year 7 pupils into classes according to their previous language-learning experiences – something that is frequently dismissed on social grounds, as it is felt desirable for classes to reflect a mix of feeder schools – then the minimum requirement should be some record of 'previous linguistic achievement'. Many secondary school transfer forms allow no space for reports on foreign languages; even more sadly, modern languages teachers themselves have no access to this relevant information. One primary school teacher near York has overcome this difficulty by starting a language project with her pupils which they will work on over the summer, and complete in their first few weeks at the secondary school.

For primary pupils in Year 6 waiting to transfer to secondary schools it is possible to provide an extra sense of success and motivation to further study by arranging special events which bring together groups of pupils with similar experiences. In some areas primary schools studying French in relatively isolated situations, and not even necessarily 'feeding' the same secondary school, have organised 'French afternoons' where all pupils become aware of their common purpose and achievement. These celebrations have been held in HEIs, planned and organised by teacher training students of French, or in large sports halls, sponsored by local businesses and involving sixth-form pupils on work experience. They may involve each school group providing some part of the entertainment, or a carousel of different 'fun' activities in the target language, and of course the inevitable French café where pupils can buy refreshments using plastic French coins.

The Europa Centre in Havering operates commercially but offers the same sort of opportunity for pupils to be immersed in an 'authentic' foreign situation without the problems of crossing the Channel – buying food and souvenirs, asking the way, and completing activities whilst surrounded by the target language. When pupils from small schools are exposed to this kind of experience their self-confidence and self-esteem increase, and by encountering others who can communicate in the same code they appreciate the value of learning a foreign language. Even more motivating, as Burstall *et al.* discovered in 1974, is a visit to the foreign country. Inevitably schools in the south of England find this easier to arrange and finance. Those in the Kent project being particularly close to France are able to benefit from a stay at education centres in the Pas-de-Calais from where they can also spend some time with their partner school pen-friends without losing the reassurance of the familiar faces of their teachers.

Even for pupils living in the north of England exchanges with foreign partner schools can be arranged. One small village school in the East Riding regularly organises exchange visits with France, and a school in Hexham, Northumberland has taken mixed groups of German and English pupils on outdoor pursuit weeks in both countries.

Even without exchange visits other possibilities exist, and for primary pupils living further from Channel Tunnel links or ports, modern technology has provided a means of communicating through e-mail or faxes, video exchanges and audio-recordings. One useful tool which features prominently in most primary classrooms is the computer. It has been suggested that the government's initiative to introduce more computers into schools could encourage linking with primary schools abroad. A wide range of useful computer programs designed for the primary age group now exist to support foreign language teaching and learning. In Middlesbrough a project to support primary foreign language learning through computer-assisted programmes has been set up by Jim McElwee, but is still at an early stage.

Uses of modern technology in this way bring the foreign language right into the classroom, with an immediacy which has not previously been available. Video-conferencing is another way in which pupils learning a foreign language can be linked together. Several small schools in the Whitby area of North Yorkshire have benefited from a British Telecom-sponsored project, where one French teacher is able to teach pupils in several other schools. In a primary classroom the best way to introduce a foreign language is recognised to be the class teacher teaching his or her own class, but in small schools with mixed-age class groups this is often difficult to manage, and video-conferencing may be the way for one specialist language teacher to support a group of class teachers who are less confident or competent.

Of course the best way to eliminate the problems of inter-phase transfer and continuity would be the creation of a national programme which aimed to cover the first two levels of the National Curriculum modern foreign languages attainment targets in Key Stage 2. Pupils would work towards achieving a certificate or statement of achievement, with the assessment based not on pencil and paper tests but on teacher observation. This could then form the basis of the differentiation in teaching in Year 7. One might glibly suggest that if differentiation is required in mathematics, why not in foreign languages?

How can changes be implemented?

The recently formed Qualifications and Curriculum Authority (QCA) and the TTA are already considering the possibilities of introducing a modern foreign language into the primary curriculum. The Scottish model was founded on a substantial pilot scheme, and it may not be necessary to repeat this exercise south of the border. However, certain differences between England and Scotland should be considered. On the whole Scotland operates a system of cluster schools, where it is easier to identify feeder primary schools. In English inner cities, in particular, the situation of ethnic minority languages must be considered. A limited number of pilot areas, building on existing schemes and expertise, could study any regional differences or problems before launching a national scheme. Much has been learnt already about the practical and financial implications of introducing foreign languages, and a modified version of the Scottish model might be introduced without too much delay.

Before any national scheme can be introduced, however, several fundamental questions must be answered. One issue is the age factor. Many nursery schools have already successfully introduced a foreign language through games, songs and stories, but the problem of teacher supply will be exacerbated if a national scheme includes pupils in Key Stage 1. There has been much debate around the optimum age at which to start learning a foreign language. Recent experience in Hungary and Spain would suggest that nine is appropriate from the point of view of both linguistic and mental maturity. Eric Hawkins (1991) supports this view, suggesting that this is also the age when children's attitudes to foreigners, foreign languages and cultures are most open: foreign is 'different' and 'interesting', not 'bad' or 'wrong'. If ETML were to be introduced on a national scale, starting in Year 5 would allow two further years for negotiating and planning the necessary changes in the secondary school. These might include reviews of resources and textbooks – publishers are already considering this scenario – and also the introduction of a second foreign language. Introducing a language at primary level would allow more time overall for foreign language study, and according to early research on Scottish MLPS pupils reaching Standard Grade examination, should result in higher achievement(Johnstone, 1996). It should also encourage secondary schools to rethink the existing decline in second foreign language provision, perhaps introducing a second language for all pupils in Year 7. This could then have an effect on the number of students taking two languages at GCSE, one possibly accelerated, which might encourage a healthier uptake at A-level, which in turn would hopefully be reflected in increased applications to higher education courses.

Another question to be answered is that of whether the aim of ETML is language awareness, or language acquisition. Eric Hawkins (1981) argued the case for an 'education of the ear', giving pupils a grounding in the patterns and forms of language as a basis for future language learning. Several schools have adopted this approach, which may include introducing limited phrases in several languages, often as part of European Awareness sessions. In Scotland, although language awareness forms a part of the primary pupils' experience, the main purpose of introducing modern foreign languages is to encourage linguistic competence. Progression and continuity are important aspects of the scheme, which aims to give pupils a sense of achievement: Success hopefully breeds success.

The effect of an early start on pupil attitudes has already been mentioned. Introducing pupils at an early age to foreign languages and cultures has been shown to mean they also retain more positive attitudes in their teenage years. If a pupil's first language-learning experience has been a happy and successful one, the challenge of learning another foreign language in later life will be less daunting. No one can be sure which foreign language may be needed in the future, whether for employment, travel, holidays or personal pleasure, and it is incumbent on schools to foster the positive attitudes which will encourage a life-long language-learning process. Many of the factors necessary for creating positive attitudes already exist in the primary situation, such as close teacher–pupil relationships, an anxiety-free environment, parental involvement, and opportunities for 'fun' and creative activities linked to language learning. It has been shown that there is space within the curriculum to include a language, and that other subjects do not suffer when one is introduced. In fact studies in Italy suggest that development in the mother tongue is enhanced by introducing a foreign language.

Pupil attitudes are not the only key to the introduction of ETML. Parental attitudes have also influenced the campaign to start foreign language learning earlier in the school career. We live in an age of parental choice and pressure groups and the voices of parents demanding opportunities for their children which they themselves were often denied are now beginning to be heard. The spectacular growth of private clubs such as La Jolie Ronde and Le Club Français, which grew to an international organisation with 30,000 members in 1994, serves to illustrate this point. An in-depth study of attitudes to primary French in two schools in North Yorkshire showed that 94% of the parents interviewed were in favour of primary French. The main reason given was that they felt it would help pupils at secondary school. Many parents had been abroad and felt that learning a language was important. They said that primary children were less inhibited about making mistakes than secondary pupils, and that children who had started a language at primary school were much more self-confident in the secondary school. They cited special educational needs (SEN) children whose self-esteem had risen in the oral/aural/practical foreign language situations, and they were also very aware that the English were lagging behind the rest of Europe in foreign language abilities. Parental pressure is certainly a force to be dealt with, and may well play an important role in persuading those in power to make a commitment to ETML.

The question of which language to introduce is a vexed one. At a meeting hosted by the ALL at the 1997 Language World, one speaker suggested that if any government was to consider funding a national ETML project, the decision about which language to introduce would be more influenced by economic considerations relating to parity, quality control, and the cost-efficiency of a single-subject training programme than by moral or philosophical debates about minority or less commonly taught languages. Even under the careful planning of the Scottish scheme, some of the non-French primary schools have reverted to French because of administrative problems and the difficulties of teacher supply. It remains the case that in England French is still the most widely taught and spoken language, and that HEIs offering honours degree modern languages courses with Qualified Teacher Status for the primary sector have been restricted by CATE regulations to French. For individual primary schools it has to be a brave headteacher who endorses a decision to introduce other languages.

This is not to say that other languages are excluded at primary level, and there have been successful projects funded by the Goethe-Institut for teachers in some schools in Cornwall and West Sussex, as well as a project involving non-linguist primary teacher training students at York. Sheffield's 'multilingual city' initiative has led to the inclusion of ethnic minority languages, thus valuing the cultural and linguistic diversity of today's society. In other areas individual schools have benefited from the foreign language skills of individual staff, parents or friends to introduce other languages. It is just that when asked 'Which language?' many of those in advisory roles feel that realistically it is better to concentrate on one language at primary level, with no more than brief encounters with other languages through European Awareness topics or links with language awareness. It would seem preferable to leave the choice of language in the hands of the LEAs, which would allow for initiatives in languages other than French in areas where this could be supported and sustained.

If it is not possible to continue in Year 7 with the language started in the primary school, it is important that the primary foreign language programme should achieve its aims and that the 'package' delivered should stand as a unit which is capable of forming the basis for further study, whether as a GCSE option, a sixth-form or university short course, part of a vocational qualification, through independent or distance learning (for example via the BBC or Open University), in evening and recreational classes, or for personal satisfaction on holidays and for travelling. Life-long learning starts early.

If the primary foreign language is to be continued in the secondary school, much of what has been stated above will also apply, but there must be more liaison and contact with the receiving secondary school. One of the key reasons for the failure of the 1960s primary French project was an inability to recognise the needs of those pupils who had done French in primary school, particularly if they were in classes alongside those with no prior French. The cluster French project in the East Riding of Yorkshire already mentioned is unusual in that the project is being supported and coordinated by the secondary school's Head of Languages. Headteachers are in the best position to make sure that the channels of communication between the primary feeder schools and their associated secondaries are effective, and in areas where several secondary schools are involved the LEA modern languages adviser has an important role to play. It quickly becomes apparent that, if not yet a national policy, then a whole-LEA policy is needed if the transfer from Year 6 to Year 7 is to be smooth and progress in the language continuous.

Before a primary school starts to introduce a foreign language its headteacher would be well advised to meet with the secondary headteacher and the head of modern languages to establish what might be achieved by the early start, and also what repercussions this might have on the secondary school's foreign language teaching and organisation. It might be that the secondary foreign language staff would be very keen to offer advice and support, or that sixth-form students of languages might be available to take part in work experience projects in the primary foreign language lessons. There might be a possibility of sharing resources and materials; or the foreign language assistant might be employed by the primary school for a few hours each week. One Training Day might involve colleagues from both phases, and eventually a plan for ETML might emerge which threatened no one, but rather led to closer collaboration and trust.

The writer was personally involved in such a close team of professional teachers, who agreed to swop classes for a term and share the teaching across the whole 9–18 age range. For primary colleagues it was a chance to see some former pupils in a sixth-form environment, to follow the progress of slow developers or of those with special talents, to review teaching practices and methods, but above all to feel valued by secondary colleagues. Secondary teachers were surprised to see the 'little sponges', as they called the nine-year-olds, whose insatiable curiosity and boundless enthusiasm was a treat after the self-conscious teenagers at the 'big' school. They marvelled at the display work and the flexibility and creativity available in the primary curriculum, and they saw at first hand the contribution that primary teachers were making to forming a sound and planned base on which they would later build. One early result of this collaborative project was the decision to offer the possibility of a second foreign language to all pupils aged 13, rather than only to the highest achievers. This had long been an area of concern for the average achievers, and it had the secondary effect of increasing the number of applicants to the GCSE language courses at the option stage. In fact one special needs pupil felt so confident in his foreign language lessons that he challenged the system by opting for Latin! This was one of the unexpected results of close liaison with the secondary school.

Once decisions have been made about the starting age, the aims, the structure, the language to be taught, questions of continuity, liaison and progression, it is necessary to tackle the specific objectives of the programme. Is the foreign language going to be delivered in an integrated way and 'embedded' into the primary curriculum? Is it intended to emphasise oral and listening skills, and are reading and writing to be introduced? Experience in Scotland would suggest that to tackle the foreign language through class or school topics, to use the foreign language to take the register, to count the numbers for packed lunch, to line up for lunch, to make and do and sing and cook are objectives which can be achieved within the primary context. Of course there must also be periods of 'serious' work, as pupils do not expect school subjects to be easy, and are prepared to work at them if they can be motivated to see a purpose. There will be points in the programme where new structures or vocabulary must be taught, usually by the teacher in a whole-class situation. There is also a place for reinforcing sums and tables, for listening to stories in a foreign language, for using drama and role play as a medium for the foreign language, for using the computer. The overriding aim should be to include experiences and methods of teaching which are appropriate to the age group, employing communicative methodology and using the target language as much as possible. As primary teachers are on the whole less confident linguistically than their secondary colleagues they need to be taught how to maximise the language they are comfortable with, so that with elaborate gestures, flashcards, and their accepted ability to simplify and break things down into small steps, they can maintain the foreign language for most of the time. Once this initial hurdle has been cleared, primary teachers see many more opportunities for reinforcing the language than might be imagined, and their own self-confidence grows.

Should all the lessons be oral/aural? There was a fashion in the 1970s for putting off reading and writing in the foreign language in the secondary school situation, and it seemed that a teacher's credibility among his or her peers increased the longer she or he could hold out. In some cases teachers managed to maintain exclusively oral/aural lessons for up to six months. This is no longer the fashion in secondary schools, and one of the things which primary pupils look forward to on transfer to Year 7 is to do some 'proper' work, i.e. reading and writing. At the moment there are as many different approaches to teaching primary languages as there are schools and teachers. Although the accepted order for teaching the four skills is 'listen then speak then read then write', many primary teachers have not received sufficient methodological training and tend to introduce reading and writing before pupils are confident with the sound of the spoken word. On the other hand, an early introduction of the written form can act to reinforce what is being taught and create links for pupils with their concurrent development in the mother tongue. Nor is there anything wicked about labelling the different items in the classroom, or places in the school, or copying and labelling key vocabulary, or having a French library-book corner where pupils can browse through books in the target language, or asking pen-friends to write in their own language and handwriting. The consensus would seem to be that when a pupil is starting to read and write in their own language, this is the appropriate time for introducing reading and writing in the foreign language. The two activities can be mutually supportive as long as there is a 'décalage'; this means that a pupil is not expected to write 'Je m'appelle Jane' before she can confidently write 'My name is Jane'. Looking at the written form in the foreign language can in itself be an interesting exercise in language awareness. In many cases it is pupils themselves who request to see what particular words or phrases look like, and for this reason a supply of colourful dictionaries and reference books is an essential part of the foreign language corner.

For SEN pupils it is particularly important in the primary school situation that the success achieved in an oral/aural situation is not lost by introducing the more difficult tasks of reading and writing. At this point the primary teacher is usually well versed in the skills of differentiation and individualisation, and there tend to be more adult helpers, either parents or Non-Teaching Assistants (NTAs), in the primary school than in secondary situations. One of the arguments expressed against the introduction of primary foreign languages is that if the child can't even write in his or her own language, why start another? The counter arguments are those which apply to all SEN pupils, relating to equality of opportunity, as well as indications that progress in the mother tongue is enhanced by learning a foreign language.

The final question to be answered in relation to a national programme of primary foreign language teaching is what the content of the course should be. Most of the schemes and guidelines produced by LEAs or groups of schools have a common core. These are based on themes or topics, many of which are covered in the early stages of published secondary coursebooks. They include such topics as 'myself', pets and animals, 'my home', the weather, and numbers. In terms of linguistic progression pupils and teachers are expected to extend the length and complexity of the language used, so that they move from a one-word response to creating new dialogues by recycling words and phrases that they have learnt previously. This approach to a 'syllabus', rather than being over-prescriptive allows the necessary flexibility in the primary classroom or school for incorporating the foreign language into plans for special themes or events. In a primary school class teachers are in the ideal position for seizing the opportunity, being less restricted by timetables and bells, and as they know their pupils well they are often able to take a language situation one step further, or alternatively on occasion to cut an unsuccessful session short.

The question of training

If a national scheme is to be introduced in England, the logistics of planning and delivering the necessary training and retraining programme are enormous and therefore likely to be costly. A political decision to launch pilot schemes in selected areas only, however, will find much expertise already available; lessons can certainly be learned from the Scottish scheme. In order to expand such pilot schemes to a national project, plans must be laid now to ensure that there are enough trainers and specialist teachers on hand to deliver a nationally recognised and accredited training programme. Once again, Scotland has already devised courses, videos and support materials which may be appropriate with little amendment, and several existing training agencies could be expanded to meet the increased demand.

There are two distinct training needs, linguistic and methodological. As a starting-point, all entrants to all initial primary teacher training programmes should be required to have GCSE grade C or above, or equivalent, in a modern foreign language. As the majority of applicants to the ITT programmes in 1997 have followed the National Curriculum, most of them already comply with this proposal. Within the initial teacher training programme for intending primary teachers, provision should be made for methodological training as well as opportunities for further improving linguistic competence. 'Languages for All' schemes should be developed more widely in HEIs and universities and students should gain accreditation for their successful completion. As there are two routes to primary teaching, three- and four-year programmes with Qualified Teacher Status as well as one-year PGCE programmes, different training needs exist. Similarly there will continue to be a need for specialist primary teachers with a high level of language competence, for whom a substantial period of study abroad would continue to be a requirement. Efforts should be made to increase the number of institutions offering these key programmes, perhaps encouraging applicants with some financial incentive as is the case at present with one-year PGCE foreign language courses for secondary teachers. For intending generalist primary teachers further study of the language should be available, alongside opportunities for a shorter study period abroad. All the language courses should be supported by distance and open learning.

All intending teachers would require methodological training. As in the case of the linguistic training, these courses should be accredited. They should include elements of cultural and language awareness, emphasise the communicative approach and use of the target language, and draw on appropriate primary practice. The initial aim would be to place one expert foreign language teacher in each primary school, as was the initial aim in Scotland. It is anticipated that this training programme would represent a maximum of 240 hours of taught sessions for those with no prior language skills.

Apart from the need to train intending primary teachers, a programme will be required for existing teachers who are willing to introduce a foreign language. For them the same needs apply as for the student teachers, and both methodological and linguistic training will need to be delivered. Finally there will be a need for regular refresher and in-service courses, and opportunities to study abroad.

Conclusion

Optimistic readers will support the view that current developments in the primary phase are encouraging. They will also recognise that if foreign languages are introduced into the primary curriculum, media coverage and increased visibility for all language courses will follow. Once a political decision has been made and funding secured, other benefits accrue. Pupils need teachers and teachers need appropriate training, but for those teenagers with a foreign language there are now opportunities for a training and a job and the future begins to look rosy. Soon secondary teachers struggling to motivate disaffected pupils will be teaching pupils with positive attitudes towards foreign languages, cultures and peoples, because they have started learning a language in their primary years.

There is strong parental demand for access to foreign language learning for all children. Among educationalists in the primary field, this feeling seems to indicate a belief that English pupils should no longer be disadvantaged compared to their European neighbours. Politicians appear to agree – the Labour manifesto 'Excellence for everyone' (1997) stated: 'Labour will develop the teaching of foreign languages in primary schools to boost children's linguistic skills'

The Council of Europe spoke about the birthright of all young children to learn a foreign language. The policies of the Association for Language Learning and the National Association of Head Teachers both include support for an expansion of foreign language teaching into primary schools. The BBC has invested large sums of money in its foreign language programmes for younger pupils. SCAA and the TTA have stated that they are considering the issue and have produced a conference report. The National Primary Languages Network has identified appropriate aims and training needs for a national project. And personally, I am sure it will happen.

Bibliography

Association of Language Learning and National Association of Head Teachers (1992) *Joint Report on the Coventry Conference*.
Burstall, C. (1968) *French from Eight*. Slough: NFER.
Burstall, C. (1969) The evaluation of the primary French pilot scheme in Great Britain. In H.H. Stern (ed.) *Languages and the Young School Child*. Oxford: Oxford University Press.
Burstall, C. (1970) *French in the Primary School*. Slough: NFER.
Burstall, C., Cohen, S., Hargreaves, M. and Jamieson, M. (1974) *Primary French in the Balance*. Slough: NFER.
Channel Four Television (1993) *Little Englanders*. March.
CILT (1995) *Modern Languages in Primary Schools (CILT Report)*. London: CILT.
Dearing, R. (1995) *The National Curriculum and its Assessment*. London: Schools Curriculum and Assessment Authority.
DES, Welsh Office (1985) *Modern Foreign Languages in the National Curriculum*. London: HMSO.
Fernandez, S. (1992) *Room for Two*. East Melbourne: National Languages and Literacy Institute of Australia.
Gamble, C.and Smalley, A. (1975) 'Primary French in the balance' – Were the scales accurate? *Modern Languages* 6, 190–201.
Geogeghan, R. (1995) *Modern Languages in North Yorkshire*. North Yorkshire County Council.
Harris, J. (1992) Foreign languages in Irish primary schools: Weighing the evidence. *Teangeolas*.
Hawkins, E. (1981) *Modern Languages in the Curriculum*. Cambridge: Cambridge University Press.
Hawkins, E. (ed.) (1996) *30 years of Language Teaching*. London: CILT.
Hickman, P. (1991a) National Primary Languages Network. Unpublished report.
Hickman, P. (1991b) Modern languages in the primary curriculum: A renaissance. La Sainte Union College of Higher Education: unpublished report.
Hood, P. (1992) Primary foreign languages project newsletter. Birmingham City Council Education Department.
Hood, P. (1994) Primary foreign languages – the integration model: Some parameters for research. *Curriculum Journal* 5 (2), 235–47.
House of Lords Select Committee on the European Communities, Session 1989–90 (1990) European schools and language learning in UK schools, with evidence. Paper 48, paras 65–8.
Hoy, P. (1997) *The Early Teaching of Modern Languages*. London: Nuffield Foundation.

Isle of Man Department of Education (1991) *French in the Primary School*. Video.

Johnstone, R. (1994) *Teaching Modern Languages in the Primary School. Approaches and Implications*. Fort William: Scottish Council for Research in Education.

Johnstone, R. (1996) The Scottish Initiatives. In E. Hawkins (ed.) *30 Years of Language Teaching*. London: CILT.

Low, L., Brown S., Johnstone, R. and Pirrie, A. (1995) *Foreign Languages in Primary Schools. Evaluation of the Scottish Pilot Projects 1993-1995*. Final Report. Stirling: Scottish CILT.

Low, L., Duffield, J., Brown, S. and Johnstone, R. (1993) *Evaluating Foreign Languages in Primary Schools*. Stirling: Scottish CILT.

Luc, C. (1992) Intervention. Conference paper, 8 April. Paris: INRP.

Mitchell, R., Martin, C., Grenfell, M. (1992) Evaluation of the Basingstoke language awareness project 1990–1, final report. Occasional Paper No. 7, Centre for Language in Education.

NAHT (1992) *Modern Languages in the Primary School*. Haywards Heath: NAHT.

National Primary Languages Network (1992–8) Minutes. London: CILT.

NFER (1997) *The Early Teaching of Modern Languages*. Windsor: NFER.

Poole, B. and Roberts, T. (1995) Primary school modern language teaching: Some unanswered questions. Occasional Paper No. 1. London: Institute of Education.

Rapaport, B. and Westgate, D. (1974) *Children's Learning and French*. London: Methuen.

Rumley, G. (1992) An evaluation of the Kent primary French project, 1990–2. Kent County Council.

Satchwell, P. (1996) The present position in England. In E. Hawkins (ed.) *30 Years of Language Teaching*. London: CILT.

Satchwell, P. and de Silva, J. (1995) *Catching Them Young*. London: CILT.

Schools Council (1996) Working Paper 8: French in the primary school. London: HMSO.

Sharpe, K. (1991) Primary French: More phoenix than dodo now. *Education* 3 (13), 49–53.

Sharpe, K. (1995) The primacy of pedagogy: Some notes on training teachers for the early teaching of modern languages. *Language Learning Journal* 12, 40–4.

Singleton, D. (1989) *Language Acquisition: The Age Factor*. Clevedon: Multilingual Matters.

Stern, H.H. (1969) *Languages and the Young School Child*. Oxford: Oxford University Press.

Tierney, D. (1995) Modern languages in the primary school: The national training programme in Scotland. *Links* 12, 111–12.

White, R. (1994) *Guidelines for Early Foreign Language Learning in Primary Schools*. Surrey County Council.

Wilson, A. (1994) Evaluation of the PRISM Scheme (Primary into Secondary Modern Languages). MEd thesis, Manchester University.

Chapter 5

Modern Languages within a Policy for Language in Education

CHRISTOPHER BRUMFIT

The National Curriculum

In 1988 the Education Reform Act established the most sweeping range of changes seen in British education since this was first established as a major state concern in 1870. Among these changes, for the first time the government laid down a 'national curriculum' for all learners between the ages of 5 and 16 in England and Wales (for historical reasons Scotland and Northern Ireland had similar but independent provision, which resulted in significant differences in detail and sometimes in general approach). Previously the main constraint on the curriculum had been the similarity between syllabuses for external examinations.

In principle the National Curriculum had the power to provide an important impetus towards equal provision for all learners, for it implied an entitlement for all. Dissatisfaction with the quality of British education, first signalled by prime minister James Callaghan's Ruskin speech of 1976, gradually led to a determination among civil servants and politicians (actively supported by many journalists) to intervene more directly than ever before in the professional activities of teachers and teacher educators. The emphasis shifted from an education system which identified learners who worked hardest or most effectively to one which offered learners certain specific entitlements. The National Curriculum became a description of what all learners were entitled to receive, laid down by the authorities who paid out of taxes for the education service.

This shift could have been liberating, and perhaps in due course will prove to have been so. But at the time it was introduced at great speed, wholesale and from the top down, without any of the implications being carefully considered. Conservative politicians in the late 1980s were in a hurry; they needed to show their successes before the next election. 'Consultation' was rapid and perfunctory, successive working parties met shorter and shorter deadlines and there was little time for examination in detail of the strengths and weaknesses of provision in other countries, or of learning theory for particular subject areas. The education service was turned upside-down, and – among many other un-anticipated results – the National Curriculum established a *de facto* language policy in British education by laying down which languages should be centrally available in different regions of the country.

However, as the policy was not created deliberately but on the back of these wider reforms, and as it was not accompanied by substantial discussion of its implications for learning, it contains inconsistencies, and has never yet been subject to coherent analysis as a package within the government agencies which have to implement it. It arose by accident, in the course of laying down guidelines for the teaching of all subjects, and as the century ends it urgently needs to be reviewed.

The 1988 Education Reform Act was only the beginning of a flurry of legislation on the curriculum, for difficulties in implementing the rushed and ill-thought-through policy led to a succession of revisions. Thus curriculum reform dominated the latter years of the Conservative regime that was led successively by Margaret Thatcher and John Major, even though it was only a small part of the massive revision of all aspects of British education. Linguistic issues had been addressed seriously in the 1970s, most notably in the Bullock Report (1975) on the teaching of English, while foreign languages had seen *Modern Languages in the Comprehensive School* in 1977 followed under the new Conservative government by *Foreign Languages in the School Curriculum: A Consultative Paper* in 1983. Also relevant to language teaching was the last of the major reports, from a working group set up before the Thatcher government was elected, *Education for All* (also known as the Swann Report) on the education of ethnic minorities, published in 1985. This last raises a large number of language-teaching concerns, picking up some of the issues relating to bilingual learners briefly addressed in the Bullock Report.

The later period of Conservative legislation was dominated by an urgent desire for change in education, as we noted above. Dissatisfaction with the performance of all sectors led to an increasing demand for centralisation and close control by ministers and senior civil servants. Speed of change became more important than either careful monitoring of the effects of reforms or identifying a considered research base as justification for the types of change advocated. For foreign languages alone, major policy documents were published in 1986, 1987, 1988, 1989, 1990 (2), 1991 and 1992. These were additional to the major Education Act of 1988 and general changes to curriculum and assessment practices which affected modern languages along with all other subjects.

Against this background it has been difficult for academics and commentators to maintain a principled position. This is partly because of the sheer speed of change, and partly because anyone with relevant expertise has been not only bound up in the administration of the changes themselves but has also indeed been likely, in the confrontational atmosphere that led to the desire for change in the first place, to be perceived as reactionary opposition that must be marginalised or overridden if necessary alterations are to be implemented. But it is possible to produce a principled position which is compatible with National Curriculum legislation, and – since the structure of the curriculum is in a state of permanent review and revision – such a position is very important, if revisions are not to be simply the prey of fashion or the latest whim of the civil servants or politicians who have the power. The more centralised the system, the more important well-argued principles become.

In the following section I shall try to present key principles that could underlie the teaching and learning of language within British education. These have been developed over the years through the work of the Centre for Language in Education at the University of Southampton, and are based partly on interpretation of international research on processes of language learning and teaching, and partly on work in Britain. In Southampton, studies of learners and teachers of English mother tongue, foreign languages, ethnic minority languages, as well as investigations of teachers in training all support the general position outlined below.

A policy for language, not policies for languages

Language provision in schools cannot helpfully be broken down into disconnected compartments. Although learners understandably perceive separate language classes as offering separate activities, research into the psychological bases of language acquisition show learners developing an ever-extending linguistic repertoire through interaction with their social environment. Schools can assist and guide this process, and can help it to be more effective than it would be unassisted – but the process continues with or without schools. And foreign languages can be as much part of this process as the languages spoken in home and school. While major differences undoubtedly exist in the conditions of language learning at different ages, there is never a clear-cut boundary between one type of learning and another. Many people who live in environments where different languages coexist cross linguistic boundaries all the time; after the earliest years, there are no circumstances where explicit and conscious learning may not be combined with implicit and unconscious acquisition. Moving from the intimate language of the home to the more public discourses of the school, or from the improvisation of speech to the more controlled environment of reading and writing, is not a permanent shift where one mode is left behind and another adopted. We move to and fro all the time, in and out of different styles and different dialects and – to varying degrees – across different languages. In contemporary Britain (as the analysis of one evening's viewing on a single television channel makes abundantly clear) stylistic, dialectal and linguistic variation is an unavoidable fact of our environment, and as language users we all participate in creating that environment. So because language is so central to processes of learning and processes of socialisation, and because we live in such a rich and potentially fluid environment, thinking about one part of the language curriculum in isolation from other parts makes very little sense. Drawing the separate parts together is sensible because of the ways in which we learn languages, because of the ways we use them, and because of the nature of our linguistic environment.

Thus Panjabi speakers mix languages and cross easily between Panjabi and English both in school and at home, sometimes speaking Panjabi to grandparents, a mixture to parents, and varying in their choice with brothers and sisters; so too do children of mixed linguistic parentage where (for example) one parent uses French and another English, and so do most advanced learners of foreign languages, whether at university or home, if the conditions favour such mixing of codes.

The fact of English

In the United Kingdom any coherent language policy for foreign languages must start with the central fact of the British situation – that English is the main language and that, because of the dominance of the United States, it is the language of world economic power. The majority of fluent English users in the world are non-native speakers. This is true of no other language, and because this is true, learning foreign languages in the UK poses problems for teachers that are not found in more multilingual countries, or in those where the economic pull of English as a foreign language provides strong motivation to learn. A language policy for Britain must recognise the implications of this fact, and at the same time be sensitive to the negative effects it may have. These vary from individual weaknesses such as complacency about the need to learn other languages, to institutional risks such as an arrogance about the nature of the English language which can itself lead to racism and xenophobia in organised attitudes to those who resist the domination of English. But even more important than these, because less obvious and more subtly damaging, is the implicit assumption than monolingualism is the norm. This can imperceptibly shift into an assumption that not just monolingualism but mono*dialectalism* is the norm, especially for 'educated' people – a damaging view, not just because it causes its adherents to be insensitive to the wide variation of linguistic styles that make up any rich dialect, however educated, but also because it is predicated on a restricted understanding of the role of language in enabling different cultural groups to express themselves in varied ways, both by communicating and by refusing to communicate with others. Language conceals as well as reveals, and it is the interplay between these processes that makes linguistic communities active changing and living entities. To start with the current fact of the linguistic hegemony of English is realistic; to *rely* on it for a curriculum is to misunderstand the nature of language and of communication.

Bilingual learners

Any language policy which is to command widespread acceptance by the monolingual majority must simultaneously be responsive to the complexities of the British linguistic context for bilingual learners. A language policy must be just to all learners, and at the same time accept the needs of typical learners. There are, it is appalling to state, no reliable figures on bilingual speakers in Britain, so planning takes place in a relative vacuum – but Alladina and Edwards (1991) report on 32 separate and active speech communities within the UK, and the 1987 Inner London Education Authority reported 172 languages active in London schools. In the Southampton area alone more than 70 minority language maintenance classes have been active through the 1990s, and 26 different new languages can be learnt from scratch in adult education classes. Further, these figures disregard those who, while being native English speakers, regularly read, write or speak other languages as part of their work. If the policy is to be an entitlement policy, it cannot helpfully differentiate between English and other languages as the starting-point at birth, although of course any curriculum has to distinguish certain end-points as more important than others. Recognition of all languages active within Britain is a necessary precondition for starting the process of language learning. But just as effective use of the language(s) of work, public life and government are essential end-points for participation in democratic processes, so English and, in some areas, other languages are necessary as minimum conditions for adult life.

The functions of language

Broadly, language can be said to perform three main roles. It has a pragmatic function as a means of getting things done in the world ('Please shut the door'). It has a learning and conceptualising function, as a means of understanding the world, of making sense of ideas and evidence ('If we examine T.S. Eliot's work in relation to that of a French poet he greatly admired such as Laforgue, what influences do we find?'). And it has an archive function, as a means of storing understandings from the past ('The rules of chess', 'The works of Shakespeare', etc.). Different languages will provide bases for different kinds of experience. Some (and particularly the major languages of national and international communication, including English) will provide a basis for action in the world, as well as for learning and conceptualising. Some (and particularly mother tongues in the early years) will be crucial at particular stages as the major means by which learning takes place. Some (particularly classical languages and those with strong literary, religious and scientific traditions) will have a major role to play in reinforcing understanding of heritage – a result of the archive function. All may have some role to play in relation to each function, but how these roles operate for particular speech communities at particular times will vary.

Language and identity

Language use will be closely bound up with individuals' and groups' identities. In so far as those are contested because of particular social or political frameworks, language may be a symbol of independence or of subservience, and language issues may become central to debates about power and cultural autonomy. Thus the privileged status of Welsh in British education, compared with – say – Panjabi or Cantonese, is largely a product of assumptions about the political role and social coherence of Wales (see discussion in the Introduction to Alladina & Edwards, 1991).

The Language Charter

What, then, do such principles imply for all learners in schools? If we assume that a specification of entitlement is what is required, what could that look like? We have tried to encapsulate a proposal for an agreed agenda in the form of a charter for all language learners. This Charter offers an agenda to define what – subject as always to resource limitations – we should be trying to provide as an entitlement (see Brumfit, 1986 for the first outline of the charter idea, and Brumfit, 1995 for a development of the ideas in relation to National Curriculum provision).

Bases for a language charter

The fundamental requirement is for an equality of provision. As far as resources permit, and subject to local demand and needs, we should aim to provide for all learners what is outlined in the following Charter.

Language Charter

It is the policy of

(insert name of institution or authority)

to enable all learners, to the maximum extent possible within available legislation and resources

(i)   to develop their own mother tongue or dialect to maximum confident and effective use;

(ii)   to develop competence in a range of styles of English for educational, work-based, social and public-life purposes;

(iii)   to develop their knowledge of how language operates in a multilingual society (ideally including basic experience of languages other than their own that are significant either in education or the local community);

(iv)   to develop as extensive as possible a practical competence in at least one foreign language.

It is our belief that the development of these four strands in combination will contribute to an effective language curriculum for Britain in the twenty-first century more than emphasis on any one of them separately at the expense of the others.

Signed:

Date:

For foreign languages to thrive in schools, they should be systematically linked to provision under each of the first three of these headings. Why?

Very briefly, they should be linked to (i) because there is convincing research evidence that people learn second languages well when they are confident language users, and that they develop that initial confidence through their mother tongues. And further, as their repertoire extends, the standard language, the languages of literacy, and eventually foreign languages all have the potential to grow out of that confident language use.

They should be linked to (ii) because English is the dominant language of education and public life, hence competence in foreign languages should accept and relate to the competences that are required in English. Further, translation, interpreting, mixed English/foreign-language activity, cross-referring to activities taking place in English – all these will help to overcome the distance between English and foreign languages that is so distinctive a feature of UK culture. The link between grammar and descriptive work in English and that required in foreign language learning needs to be made clear, too.

They should be linked to (iii) because unless all learners understand what it is to be part of a multilingual country in a multilingual continent, in a multilingual world, the point of foreign language learning will be lost. And knowledge about language helps effective language learning.

Implications of a language charter for the curriculum

Language is a vehicle for a wide range of activities and, as we have argued above, is closely bound up with personal development, concept formation and identity, simultaneously tied in to both public and private communication processes. The language curriculum must therefore reflect a range of activities with different purposes. Drawing upon our discussion of the functions of language, we can define these broadly for the Charter as follows, together with their operational consequences. Most language work should incorporate aspects of all three of these.

Table 5.1 Functions and operational consequences of language

Function	Operational consequence
Developmental and concept-creating	Helping learners to become confident users for purposes of their own choosing, to become creative and imaginative, to be willing to think about and reflect on their own language practices
Understanding heritage	Making sense through language of past achievements and traditions
Functional	Enabling learners to operate with the conventions demanded by society

Furthermore, enabling such incorporation to happen requires the curriculum to draw upon institutionalised language practices: within language work specifically, literature, drama, and media understanding may be significant elements; within other subject areas, understanding the genres of scientific or historical writing (for example) become important. Implementation of the Language Charter requires integration of all these activities, though the ways in which this will happen will vary at different levels of education, and with different language groupings.

The Charter proposal is based on views of social justice. It is entirely compatible with National Curriculum requirements, but it provides a coherence and a focus on learners' entitlement which is more specific than offered there. It could also be translated into any level of education, for it can be adapted to pre-school, community, further and higher education as well as mainstream schooling and provides a rationale for language-teacher education.

Specifying its implications with greater delicacy for particular groups is a task primarily for practitioners. I shall offer two examples below: implications for, first, conventional foreign language learners, and second, bilingual learners (drawing on Mitchell & Brumfit, 1997).

Implications for the foreign language curriculum

The Charter's four elements are ordered in the most logical form for the majority of British learners. They imply:

from the Charter's first requirement:

- a recognition by foreign language teachers that second language use is not a replacement for, but an extension of mother-tongue activity, and that this should affect the pedagogical strategies adopted; and
- a willingness by teachers to acknowledge the bi- and multilingual skills brought by learners with mother tongues other than English, and to incorporate this awareness into pedagogy wherever appropriate;

from the Charter's second requirement:

- systematic curriculum links between work in foreign languages and in English classes, either by liaison where appropriate on multilingual activities/tasks crossing subject boundaries, or by exploiting and following development in the English curriculum by related activities of a simpler kind in the foreign language class;

from the Charter's third requirement:

- systematic use of cross-reference between the multilingual/ multidialectal characteristics of the target-language world communities, and those of the English-speaking world (and where appropriate of other language groups); and
- constant recognition of the target language as a code used in specific social contexts, with learning related to all the functions of language identified in earlier discussion;

from the Charter's fourth requirement:

- consistent pressure to ensure that the foreign language curriculum is genuinely made accessible in appropriate ways to *all* learners.

Implications for bilingual learners

For certain groups some reordering would make sense, as particular details of the Charter's implications are spelt out. Refinement of the Charter's minimum requirements to provide full equality of opportunity for bilingual learners in the British context would imply:

from the Charter's second requirement:

- development of full proficiency in spoken and written English, with command of a variety of styles appropriate to the needs of public, vocational and private life; and
- development of parallel proficiency in the mother tongue (and where appropriate in a related written language variety), in the range of styles necessary for fullest participation in the life of the relevant speech community;

from the Charter's fourth requirement:

- the opportunity to learn at least one further foreign language to an advanced level;

from the Charter's first requirement:

- the right and opportunity to use both the national standard language and the mother tongue/heritage language as media for learning across the curriculum wherever practicable and appropriate;
- multilingual home–school communication, as needed, to facilitate contact with families etc.; and
- a teaching methodology by all language teachers which is hospitable to diversity and responsive to multilingualism in the classroom;

from the Charter's third requirement:

- a 'knowledge about language' curriculum strand for all learners, incorporating understanding of language variation and multilingualism, information about English as an international, national and local language, as well as understanding about other local heritage languages and speech communities, and their roles, national, international and local, inside and outside the UK;

from the Charter as a whole, for provision within a general entitlement curriculum:

- the opportunity to enter relevant public examinations in English, heritage language(s) and foreign language(s); and
- full access to all non-language strands of the school curriculum.

Clearly such a specification is a statement of what a well-resourced school could aim for if it was embedded in a community or communities with substantial numbers of speakers of particular languages. But the existence of the basic elements of the Language Charter allow for discussion which is not haphazard but which enables us to develop principles applicable with adaptation to any situation within schools in Britain. Thus the implications for foreign language teaching operate mainly at the level of pedagogy.

Finally, the implications for the teaching of English as a mother tongue would relate most obviously to the confident development of individuals' dialects, to their use of English for public life purposes, and to the basic understanding of language – but there would also be an obligation for a systematic relationship with foreign language work to be developed.

And it would, of course, be easy to outline further extensions – for higher education or for further education, using the basic school provision as the starting point, and seeing purpose-specific enrichment programmes moving on from this. Such development could probably proceed from existing National Curriculum provision. But the advantage of this proposal over the present National Curriculum is that it centres on the learning process and the individual entitlement within it. From the individual language of home develops both the advanced literacy and the publicly required confident use of English, on the one hand, and eventually the foreign language provision, on the other. Everyone becomes entitled to develop the linguistic resources they bring to education, while keeping central the national requirement for capacity to participate in British democratic life and in the multilingual world of which Britain is a part.

Furthermore, this part of the curriculum can thus be finely tuned to the needs of particular regions, towns or individual institutions, without constant debates about the conflict between centralised policy and local need. This means that language provision in education will become more principled, more attuned to research evidence, and more accountable.

Given the problems of foreign language learning that arise from the strength of English, such a policy seems worth attempting. At the very least it might provide a means of overcoming our inherited weakness in foreign language learning, for this may be partly attributable to the traditional compartmentalisation of languages into separate and unrelated subjects.

References

Alladina, S. and Edwards, V. (1991) *Multilingualism in the British Isles* (2 vols). Harlow: Longman.

Brumfit, C.J. (1989) Towards a language policy for multilingual secondary schools. In J. Geach (ed.) *Coherence in Diversity*. London: CILT. Originally a lecture given in 1986; developed at book length in: Brumfit, C.J. (ed.) (1995) *Language Education in the National Curriculum*. Oxford: Blackwell.

Mitchell, R.F. and Brumfit, C.J. (1997) The National Curriculum experience of bilingual learners. *Educational Review* 49 (2), 159–80.

Chapter 6
Higher Education

ANTHONY LODGE

Speech-communities across the world all experience language problems of one sort or another. Some communities in the developing world have to cope with difficulties of language standardisation, others with obstacles raised by multidialectalism and multilingualism; most countries nowadays face the task of acquiring adequate competence in English in order to participate in international affairs. In Britain, however, the central language problem takes a different and rather special form: it lies in people's (and especially men's) reluctance to learn any language other than their own.

The causes of this particular British disease are obvious and well known: a population surrounded by sea rather than by speakers of other languages, blessed with possession of a world-wide lingua franca as its mother tongue and sharing its language with the world's lead economy (the USA) is not going to be pushed into foreign language learning by any sense of urgent economic need. So it is not at all surprising when we find that at secondary school level in Britain, the language teacher's most intractable problem is one of learner motivation.

By the time learners reach higher education the terms of the language problem have altered, but the root cause remains the same. Post-secondary learners, having developed a wider awareness of the world in which they live, usually recognise very belatedly that foreign languages are not a dispensable part of their intellectual baggage; but by this stage both they and their institutions are having to reconcile foreign language learning with other more pressing educational objectives.

The term 'modern languages' is commonly used as though it had a single, agreed meaning. When we look at it in the context of higher education, however, we discover that it is in fact an umbrella term covering differing, and often conflicting, sets of ideas. For most outsiders the label denotes first and foremost 'the teaching of practical skills in a particular foreign language' (language as instrument); for many insiders, on the other hand, it implies above all some sort of discipline in its own right, of which language teaching forms only a minor part (language as discipline).

Tension between instrumentality and disciplinarity in modern languages is considerable. By 'instrumentality' I understand study of the language for largely practical purposes, for the accomplishment of specific communicative tasks. By 'disciplinarity' I mean study of the language as part of an overall intellectual discipline, referred to traditionally as 'French studies', 'German studies' etc. Analogous tensions exist in a number of university subjects, notably between pure and applied science, but in the arts and humanities no subject has had to confront this tension in such an acute form as has modern languages. Therein lies both our strength and our weakness.

If there has been a constant pattern in the development of modern languages in higher education over the past 30 years, it has been a shift in the overall balance from discipline to instrument. Universities have striven to increase their language teaching capacity so as to equip young people with the language skills required in an economy where markets have expanded from the county, to the 'nation', to the continent, and now to the entire globe. But where has this promotion of modern languages the instrument left modern languages the discipline? Not only are students increasingly coming to modern languages with purely instrumental objectives – to exacerbate the problem, consensus among modern linguists about what constitutes the discipline of modern languages has almost disappeared. The subject is fragmenting into numerous sub-disciplines: literary studies, cultural studies, area studies, language studies, and so on. Are we then witnessing the end of languages as a university discipline, or is there some new prescription which might help them maintain coherence and enhance their position in the educational world?

In what follows I will offer a brief description of the changed institutional framework (the universities, the students, the degree structures), before focusing the bulk of my remarks on the content and coherence of the modern languages discipline.

The Changed Institutional Setting

With the Europeanisation and indeed the globalisation of the British economy over the past 30 years, patterns of provision in modern languages education at tertiary level have had to change radically. The number and range of institutions offering languages in the university sector has increased fourfold, the number and range of students requiring access to modern languages within them has expanded in an even greater proportion. The structure of degree courses involving languages has had to become much more flexible. Homogeneity and stability in the system have been replaced by a strong tendency to diversity and change.

The pattern of universities

The provision of modern languages in British universities today is strikingly different from what it was a generation ago. Describing the state of modern languages in British universities in the early 1960s was a relatively simple affair. The number of universities offering degree programmes in languages stood at between 20 and 30: Oxford, Cambridge and London, together with the four ancient Scottish universities, were flanked by the big civics which had developed in the nineteenth-century industrial cities. The students were for the most part language specialists, studying one or two languages. The range of provision in modern languages was narrow. The degree programmes all followed broadly similar patterns, being geared primarily to mastering the literary variety of the language in question and to reading the authors of its country's literary canon. Language-learning methods were very largely restricted to pen and paper. Modern languages were for the 'happy few' and were seen primarily as a discipline in their own right.

With the development of the Common Market and the resurgence of Germany and France in the early 1960s it became clear that the UK was lagging far behind its competitors in the provision of higher education. The Robbins Report (1963) signalled the first wave of 'new universities' (such as Stirling, Essex, UEA, Lancaster), soon to be followed by the 'technological universities' (the former colleges of advanced technology, like Bradford, Aston, Heriot-Watt). Shortly afterwards the polytechnics entered the higher education scene, and in the 1990s transformed the system completely when the abolition of the 'binary line' gave them full university status.

Each wave of university expansion brought a new perspective on the nature of modern languages in higher education. The pre-Robbins universities for many years resisted curriculum changes and continued to offer courses constructed around the traditional literary canon of the 'nations' concerned, normally with a strong historical bias. The new universities retained a pronounced literary flavour, but tempered it as a rule with a synchronic bent, limiting the time-depth in the cultures studied largely to the nineteenth and twentieth centuries. The major break with the past came with the technological universities and the polytechnics. Here particular emphasis came to be placed on the development of language proficiency and the transmission of knowledge with strong instrumental value. Language was to be taught in the context of 'area studies', often with a strong business orientation. Elsewhere, places like Bradford and Heriot-Watt concentrated heavily on professional language skills (Lutzeier, 1998).

Diversification is of course excellent, but its value is diminished if it comes about principally through hierarchisation. The Funding Councils which replaced the old University Grants Committee are more strongly interventionist than their predecessor, but they have only the blunt instruments of the Research Assessment Exercise (RAE) and the Teaching Quality Assessment (TQA) to work with and clearly find the balance between competition and co-ordination in the system extremely difficult to manage. The close-knit structure of roughly equal universities which pertained in the 1950s and early 1960s has, sadly, given way to a fragmented and hierarchised system. The club-like environment of the old regime, with its system of inter-university co-operation, has been broken down into a Hobbesian world of competition and rivalry tinged not infrequently with resentment. Not all parts of the modern languages river have flowed along at the same rate – rapidity of change has, broadly speaking, been in inverse proportion to the social cachet possessed by the institutions involved. The university system has now become quite rigidly, if unofficially, stratified – if not up and down a single continuous scale, at least between several bands of universities of roughly parallel status. All universities may bear the same label, but their status, funding levels and (dare one say it?) academic standards are by no means equal.

Students

The social range and the ability span of students entering modern languages courses are obviously much wider now than they were a generation ago. The old adage that 'more means worse' is absurdly irrelevant: a modern society needs to mobilise the capacities of all its members and make suitable provision for all levels of aptitude. However, one important part of the student profile has remained virtually unchanged: the student body in modern languages is as much dominated by females now as it was a generation ago. Here is not the place to discuss the issue of language and sex (see Coates, 1993) or to attempt to explain the gender imbalance in the subject at university level (are we dealing with nature or nurture?). However, it is perhaps appropriate to point out the dangers inherent in this situation: given the way society is currently organised, major decisions still tend to be taken predominantly by men. Pending a radical change in the distribution of social roles between males and females, the fact that the male British population is heavily monolingual can only impede our collective decision-making capacity. While doing all we can to promote access to top jobs among bilingual females, at the same time our universities should be actively seeking ways of making the learning of languages more accessible to males.

Course structures

Let us now turn to the great changes which have come about in the structure of modern languages courses over the past 30 years, as a result of the drive for wider access. An up-to-date digest of current statistics relating to modern languages in higher education is to be found in Towell (1998).

Pressure for expansion of language provision has come primarily not from specialist linguists, but from non-specialists seeking to upgrade their language skills for instrumental purposes. Towell (1998: 46) indicates that the number of undergraduates studying languages as non-specialists far exceeds the number studying them as specialists. Institutions have responded to this pressure in different ways. Some (for example Cambridge, Hull, Oxford, Newcastle) have set up language centres with their own staff quite separate from the traditional modern languages departments. Others (for example the School of Management in Abertay) have drafted their language teachers into the non-language departments requiring tuition. The majority have induced their modern languages departments to expand the provision of language courses for non-specialists.

The courses on offer to non-specialists comprise, on the one hand, voluntary add-ons which are often paid for by the student (these can comprise personal tuition in the form of evening and lunch-time classes, but they also include a wide range of self-access courses) and on the other, language courses which 'count' in various proportions towards the student's overall degree (most of these are 'off the peg' courses available to all; a few are 'tailor-made' to suit particular degrees). The growth of major–minor degrees with languages providing the minor third has been particularly spectacular. Such degrees are usually an object of pride for their universities, but they seem to be a peculiarly British phenomenon. In Europe, students studying subjects outside the humanities are normally expected to sort out their problems independently. Here in Britain we feel the need to motivate such students by building a language component into the degree. The hidden cost may well be a reduction in the level of training received in the major subject by comparison with that given to our European partners/competitors.

Course provision has become more flexible and almost entirely demand-led. The old 'table d'hôte' system of degree structures has been progressively replaced by a modularised 'à la carte' one which offers greater power to the student/consumer. Indeed, the state of provision for modern languages in British universities in the late 1990s resembles an educational hypermarket. The modern languages 'product' comes in a wide range of varieties, and customers can combine the study of languages with that of most other university products, in whatever mix they prefer, provided they 'shop around'.

This has not been a value-free development: it chimes in closely with the 'free market' ideology which became dominant in the 1980s. For the time being it is not politically correct to question the 'freedom and empowerment' produced by the new ideology, but we can nevertheless point to some of the less desirable consequences which competition and consumer power in the university system are now beginning to have for modern languages. The system encourages students to vote with their feet, shunning unpopular courses. The less accessible subject areas are being increasingly jettisoned.

In this market-oriented context it is easy to see how parity of degree standards between universities is becoming increasingly difficult to maintain. The time has now probably come for a standardisation of levels of language proficiency across the university system, at sub-degree level as well as at degree level. Such a standardisation of levels already exists in the teaching of English as a foreign language (TEFL). Perhaps moves in this direction should now be made in the other modern languages.

Content of Degree Programmes

If the institutional framework in which modern languages are taught has become highly diverse, so too has the content of degree courses that involve languages. The range of languages taught remains pretty much as it was, but technological change has produced major innovations in teaching methods, and ideas about what the modern languages discipline entails have evolved considerably. Let us consider these issues in turn.

Which languages?

The label 'modern languages' is in some ways rather anachronistic, for the term embraces by no means all the important languages in use in the modern world. The label is in fact reminiscent of the seventeenth-century 'querelle des anciens et des modernes'. The academic study of 'modern' languages emerged a century or so ago as part of the move to give the 'modern' standard languages of Europe academic respectability alongside the more prestigious 'classical' or 'ancient' ones. Ex-colonial varieties of Spanish, Portuguese and French have gained honorary membership of the club, and Japanese has made some headway towards admittance, but in the main 'modern languages' remain firmly Eurocentric – Oriental, Middle Eastern and African languages are still felt to belong elsewhere.

Even today, of those students studying a modern language as their principal degree subject more are taking French than all the other European languages combined (Towell, 1998). There is clearly no scientific way of determining which particular foreign languages should be taught in preference to others. However, allowing the choice of language to be dictated primarily by tradition and by the availability of teachers and teaching materials is perhaps not the best long-term solution. The languages we collectively choose to teach/learn should relate to some extent at least to the density of our interactions with speakers of the languages in question. Globalisation of the world's economy and projections of the relative importance of particular languages in the middle of the next century (for example Chinese) call for some re-evaluation of the range of languages we teach. The number of Spanish-speakers across two continents is already increasing demand for tuition in that language. The reunification of Germany and the centrality of that country in the new Europe give German a particular claim to an increased share of the modern languages cake. It is looking increasingly obvious that the traditional dominance of French in the British modern languages system cannot be maintained.

Language teaching methods

Moves made by universities over the past decade to disseminate language skills more widely across their communities can only be applauded. If sufficient language skills are not developed at secondary level, it is vital that the deficiency be made up in higher education. Moreover, this development has coincided with undreamt-of improvements in language-teaching technology and methodology across the university system.

Use of the target language as the medium of instruction has expanded. The development of ERASMUS/SOCRATES links with Europe has not only permitted greater immersion of British students in communities speaking the languages they are learning, but it has also brought a large influx of French-, German- and Spanish-speakers into our universities. The Internet is providing an ever-increasing supply of authentic foreign-language written material, while video and satellite are doing the same for aural material. Processing this material through language laboratories and computers represents progress on an unprecedented scale.

The development of new technology over the past decade has indeed transformed the way languages can be taught. For the teacher and the motivated student, this represents a major advance. However, an unfortunate by-product of this development is the belief (particularly among university administrators) that language teaching can be automated and the teacher dispensed with. Laypersons (i.e. non-linguists) all too often entertain highly simplified notions of what a language is and how it works. They commonly believe, often with strong conviction, that language teaching is a fairly simple process which can be automated. Such naive views of language led to the expensive failures represented by behaviourist language laboratory programmes in the 1960s and 1970s. Some of the CALL courses currently being developed seem inspired by similarly reductionist views. There are, unfortunately, no 'quick fixes' in language learning. For the average undergraduate, particularly those studying language as an ancillary to a main degree, the personal guidance provided by a competent teacher remains indispensable, all the more so when languages are not part of the student's normal business.

There is little evidence that university decision-makers are developing a more realistic appreciation of the knowledge and skill required in the language-teaching process. The past decade has seen a widespread move on the part of universities to employ part-time teachers of language on an hourly-paid basis. This development has been intensified by pressures from the RAEs to concentrate the work of research-active staff on the research front rather than on 'mechanical' teaching activities. While most of the part-time replacements are no doubt excellent, questions can legitimately be asked concerning the qualifications of some of them. Occasionally the mere fact of being a native speaker of the language in question is taken as sufficient qualification to teach it. Whereas in TEFL there exist internationally recognised grades and qualifications, the accreditation of higher education teachers in the modern languages is much more patchy.

This brings us to what is perhaps the central issue in language teaching: its theoretical basis. The expansion of foreign language teaching in universities in recent years has taken place with a near-total absence of funding for applied linguistic research into how this should best be done. Over recent decades foreign language teaching in Britain, at all levels, has been at the mercy of violent oscillations in fashions of language pedagogy. The 'grammar/translation' method gave way to the 'direct' method which gave way to the 'communicative' method which is about to give way to the 'computer' method. Teachers and administrators alike seem constantly on the look-out for a new panacea which will eliminate the 'language problem'. The very belief that such a panacea could exist is indicative of a misunderstanding of the complexity and mysteriousness of natural languages. Its prevalence implies a level of theoretical understanding of the nature of language which is less than adequate – even among teachers of modern languages themselves. Linguistics, even applied linguistics, is still widely viewed as a discipline quite removed from modern languages. In Britain we are particularly fortunate in possessing a large pool of expertise in the teaching of English as a foreign language. We are particularly unfortunate in that there is little cross-over from these ideas into the teaching of other modern languages.

A cliché circulating among modern languages teachers maintains that although today's students' control of the grammar of the foreign language is shakier than before ('today's students are not very accurate'), nevertheless they are much more able to express themselves orally ('they are much more fluent'). This glib formulation is not only self-contradictory, but contains two fairly fundamental misconceptions about language: first, that spoken language is less rule-governed than written (that is, accuracy is not required when using a language orally), and second, that mastery of any language is remotely conceivable without acquisition of that language's grammar. It is hard to see how improvements in language pedagogy can come about while teachers' own knowledge of their subject is so deficient.

Universities pride themselves on conducting high-level teaching in the context of research. But where is the research currently being carried out into the languages we are teaching and which are the expression of the cultures we study? No more than one in 15 of the academic staff of language departments has the investigation of language as their central concern. Very often these 'linguisticians' are working in isolation from solid intellectual support elsewhere in their department. No more than half a dozen of the 150 or so professors of French would call themselves linguists. No more than one in 30 research publications in French purports to analyse the language as language, and no more than one in 15 postgraduate students is working on theses directly related to language.

The discipline

The increased allocation of resources to the teaching of modern languages over the past decade is to be applauded, but it has not automatically strengthened the position of the subject across the university system. More language learning is happening, but the emphasis on instrumentality has normally been at the expense of modern languages as a discipline. Symptomatic of this development is the massive decline, mentioned earlier, in the proportion of students taking honours degrees in a single modern language. While it is true that a sizeable number of students continue to combine two modern languages in their degree, in recent years the possibilities for combining a degree qualification in a modern language with subjects outside modern languages have expanded considerably. From the individual student's point of view this can be extremely beneficial, certainly vocationally, and probably educationally too. However, such a development is not without its dangers for the discipline. Joint honours students engage, naturally enough, in cherry-picking: they receive their intellectual formation in the 'other subject' and draw from the modern language little more than that which is instrumental (i.e. practical tuition in the language), leaving untouched the whole question of familiarity with the foreign culture.

Does this matter? From the individual student's point of view it could be argued that the absence of a coherent discipline on the language side of their degree matters little, provided serious training of the mind takes place in the 'content' subject. The problem encountered here is twofold: it concerns on the one hand what we mean by 'competence in the foreign language', and on the other how we are to achieve a proper understanding of our target cultures. Let us take these questions in order.

Linguistic competence

We have seen how non-linguists tend to entertain a highly simplified and superficial notion of what linguistic competence entails. If we are aiming no higher than at well-developed communication skills, a profound understanding of the target culture is probably unnecessary. But if with our honours-level linguists we are aiming at something closer to true bilingualism, much more is required. It is undoubtedly the case that attempting to convert our undergraduates into full bilinguals is as unnecessary as it is futile. The linguistic needs of the learner of a second language will be more restricted than those of a native speaker. It is our responsibility, none the less, to move such learners as far along this road as circumstances permit. Lyons (1968: 434) makes the point that 'true bilingualism implies the assimilation of two cultures'. A high level of language competence requires a high level of cultural knowledge, too. A long-standing debate exists concerning what we are to understand by 'culture'; it is not our intention to discuss this here, but regardless of how we choose to define the term, in this perspective, study of the foreign culture is not an optional, dispensable part of the language-learning process. If we remove it, the learning of the language will reach a significantly lower level. Perhaps we are reaching a point where we need to revise considerably what we mean by honours-level language proficiency.

Cultural understanding

The diminution in the proportion of specialist modern linguists has consequences not just for individual learners. The social importance of modern languages in Britain extends a good way beyond its capacity to produce competent practical linguists. Modern languages are the country's window on the world. In a community surrounded by sea and thoroughly caught up in an Anglo-American world-view, it is essential for the universities to feed into society a sizeable pool of graduates who have a profound understanding of foreign, non-Anglo-Saxon cultures. This implies specialist knowledge and understanding of the central pillars of a foreign country's way of thinking and how it got to where it currently is. Unfortunately, a serious understanding of such rich and diverse societies as those of Europe (given that, rightly or wrongly, modern languages are oriented primarily towards our European neighbours) cannot be acquired in a quick course of lectures in cultural studies in between the language laboratory and a management seminar. It requires detailed, systematic study.

Since the 1960s modern linguists in universities have become progressively less adept at presenting our subject to students and to the outside world as a coherent, credible and challenging discipline meriting specialist study. English and history can attract students without the carrot of instrumentality, but modern languages apparently no longer can. If a degree in modern languages is to remain intellectually comparable with degrees in, say physics or economics, it must embody a high level of skill in analysis and synthesis, developed within a coherent intellectual framework.

A generation ago there was a consensus about what made up the basic coherence of the discipline: the supreme expression of any culture was to be found in the works of the community's great literary authors. Subsequently this consensus has been broken, with only some institutions such as Oxford and Cambridge remaining true to the old ideal. The technological universities have espoused a new ideal in the analytical framework offered by the social sciences and area studies. In perhaps a majority of institutions, however, various half-way houses have been constructed to appeal to as wide a range of applicants as possible. These consist of variable mixtures of literary studies, cultural studies and area studies. In such programmes, from which progression is frequently absent, it is not always easy to see what level of intellectual coherence the discipline still retains. It is often claimed that through modularisation students create their own 'coherence', but the nagging doubt remains that unrestricted 'pick-'n'-mix' implies a loss of faith among the teachers, a severe weakening of the discipline.

The fragmentation of the discipline in undergraduate courses reflects what has been happening on the research level. It is noteworthy that in the RAE, departments can choose between the panels pertaining to individual languages and the interdisciplinary panel of European studies. Fissiparous tendencies are the strongest in French, the biggest of the modern languages and the one with the highest critical mass. Ten years ago there was just one mainstream British journal dedicated to publishing academic research across the field of French studies: the *Journal of French Studies*. Since then, no less than three new titles have appeared, each carving out a separate and, it should be said, important sector of the discipline: the *Journal of French Language Studies*, *Modern and Contemporary France*, and *French Cultural Studies*. This is to be applauded as a sign of intellectual vitality, reflecting the need of researchers to connect up work in French with theoretical developments elsewhere. At the same time it poses very considerable challenges to the maintenance of French studies as an autonomous discipline.

The convergence of the peoples of Europe in the past half-century has brought with it a weakening of the sense of the national cultures which gained fullest (and most destructive) expression in the nineteenth century and in the first half of the twentieth. The old consensus in modern languages based on the cultural histories of the 'nations' of Europe is no longer in tune with our 'synchronic' preoccupations. Traditional agreement about the notion of 'culture' has given way to the dichotomy between the literary and aesthetic on the one side and the social and anthropological on the other. The modern languages discipline has become quite heterogeneous, with each university department mixing the various ingredients in its own particular way. With no sense of a common core the discipline ceases to have a coherence of its own; its various components become no more than sub-branches of literary studies, cultural studies, politics and economics, accompanied to a greater or lesser extent by the teaching of our respective languages.

Many would argue that this diversity is not only inevitable but entirely laudable, provided that each department imposes on its programmes of study a powerful intellectual rationale of its own devising. The difficulty lies precisely in constructing such a 'powerful intellectual rationale' as will unite the study of the language with study of the 'culture' (however this is defined). Is it possible for modern languages to provide a distinctive approach to literary, cultural and area studies which would in some measure protect the status of the subject as an autonomous discipline?

A New Prescription for Modern Languages?

There is, I believe, a prescription which would more effectively maintain the status of modern languages and which would assert their fundamental unity amid all this diversity. This prescription would proclaim the simple but oft-forgotten truth that at the centre of all our activities in modern languages is *language*. What sets modern languages apart from all other disciplines is our concern for language. What society expects our graduates to be above anything else is linguists. The wonder is that we, as linguists, have come to overlook this fact. It can be explained historically.

Linguistics and modern languages

The beginnings of modern languages as a recognised university subject are to be found about a century ago. At that time linguistic study found itself right at the centre of the discipline, in the form of traditional grammar and historical philology. Scholars were striving to establish a new discipline of modern languages distinct from that of the ancient classical languages, and the new-found historical philology of the time enabled them to do so. Late nineteenth-century linguistics, driven predominantly by the German *Junggrammatiker*, fed upon and reinforced current ideas about language and nationhood in the great nation-states of Europe. They endowed the study of modern languages with scientific credibility, while simultaneously warding off accusations of new-fangledness emanating from the classicists, by concentrating on their deep historical roots.

So powerful was the impetus of nineteenth-century linguistics in the growth of the discipline of modern languages that traditional grammar and historical philology remained at the heart of modern languages studies until the 1960s. Indeed British modern linguists such as Pope, Orr and Ullmann made significant contributions to the general linguistics of their day. Right up to the 1960s, and in many universities beyond this time, modern languages studies remained primarily historicist in orientation, tracing the emergence of the great national identities of Europe via their languages and the literary monuments sculpted from them. However, the important point to note is that language study, traditional as it was, remained central (see Campos, 1989).

In the meantime, of course, thinking about language was moving on. Early in the twentieth century Saussure had opened up new perspectives when he demonstrated that, as well as being studied historically, or 'diachronically', as he called it, language could also be analysed as a structure operating at a single moment in time – 'synchronically'. From here there grew up in Europe, and more importantly in America, a whole school of structural linguistics which gradually undermined the theoretical base of both traditional grammar and historical philology. Accordingly during the 1960s and 1970s both were gradually eliminated from the core of modern languages courses.

But what came in to take their place? Unfortunately for our discipline, the demise of historical philology and traditional grammar has, for a generation now, left a sizeable gap at the centre of modern languages which has not been continuously replenished with a regular injection of up-to-date linguistic ideas. The disparity in the knowledge-base between modern languages and linguistics has now reached serious proportions. Who is responsible?

The blame lies partly with linguists themselves. Structural linguists in the 1960s, in their desire to affirm their scientific credentials, were often sectarian and exclusive. Those working in Chomsky's 'generative' tradition devoted their attention explicitly to the construction of theoretical models located far from the preoccupations of scholars interested in natural languages. The researches of this group have increased our understanding of the phenomenon of 'language' immeasurably, but not without cost. The success of this deductive, quasi-mathematical linguistics in the 1960s and 1970s had the effect of crowding out different approaches to language analysis which were more empirical and grounded in the observation of naturally occurring linguistic data. Linguistics became and still remains in many people's minds synonymous with impenetrable formulae and the ubiquitous tree-diagrams of generative syntax. Sadly, and perhaps not surprisingly, few in modern languages departments could see the link between this abstract theorising and the real languages they were dealing with day by day. Theoretical linguistics took itself out of modern languages departments altogether and entered specially created Departments of Linguistics.

But theoretical linguists must shoulder only part of the responsibility for the divorce between modern languages and linguistics. The staff of modern languages departments did not see the departure of linguistics as posing any sort of threat to the intellectual underpinning of their discipline. Encouraged by the iconoclastic spirit prevalent after 1968, which was implacably hostile to the mandarins' traditional grammar and philology, specialists in literature and area studies exploited the opportunity, not to renew the study of language, but to expand their own fields. The expansion of literary studies and area studies after this time was not in itself a mistake. The mistake was to weaken the links between modern languages studies and linguistics.

This has not only weakened the coherence of the subject at university level, but over the past 30 years has had knock-on effects on the way languages are taught to the much wider public in the nation's secondary schools. For a generation now the universities have been producing modern languages graduates who have received little systematic training in the analysis and description of their chosen language and in the principles which govern its operation. Few people would be happy to see physics taught in schools by teachers possessing no theoretical understanding of physics, yet most people seem content that languages are taught in schools by people with little or no theoretical understanding of language. Practical mastery of the target language is of course a necessary prerequisite of the effective language teacher. However, it is not in itself a sufficient prerequisite: an effective teacher also needs to understand how the language functions and, should the need arise, be able to describe it accurately. This issue, in my view, underlies much of the current debate about the place of 'grammar' in school syllabuses and the decline in standards of 'accuracy'.

What linguistics brings to modern languages

The new prescription which I am proposing is then to bring back nearer to the centre of modern languages the study of language, invigorated by the findings of general linguistics. It is my contention that such a move would invigorate not just the instrumental side of our activities, but the disciplinary side too. A necessary first step in this process is to allay the fears and overcome the prejudices of non-linguists in the profession concerning the scope of linguistics. This involves convincing them that there is much more to linguistics than the stereotyped views of the subject which many still entertain (these usually refer to the mathematical theorising which characterises the generative tradition). Despite the views of some of Chomsky's less gifted disciples, linguistics is not to be restricted to a particular mode of syntactic analysis. Linguistics cannot be reduced to a set of arcane technical terms and abstract symbolism.

Linguistics is a broad discipline embracing the whole of human communication and extending into every activity carried on in modern languages departments. The seminal nature of research in linguistics should not surprise us: language is central to all our experience as human beings, whether as individuals or as groups. This is currently recognised in many areas of scholarship – with the conspicuous exception of modern languages. If proof is needed, one has only to look at the readiness with which specialists in literary criticism and politics have recourse to terminology and analytical frames created by linguists, for example the word 'discourse' which nowadays finds itself in every paragraph of academic writing in these fields. (It is even recognised by sixth-formers, if the popularity of the new

A-levels in English language are anything to go by.) Moreover, linguistics has not stood still since the 1960s. Of all the disciplines in arts and social science, linguistics has been one of the most dynamic.

So I shall conclude with an attempt to show the breadth of what currently goes on under the heading 'linguistics', relating the various branches of the subject in cursory fashion to what could be going on in modern languages departments. My personal way of visualising the field of linguistics as a whole is to divide it basically into two principal approaches, with a third providing the interface between them. The two main areas investigate language on the one side as a *system* and on the other as *behaviour*. When we look at language as a system, we look at it as a set of sound-patterns (phonetics and phonology), as a set of word-patterns (morphology and syntax) and as a set of meaning-patterns (semantics). When we look at language as behaviour, we investigate the functioning of the brain in the acquisition, production and processing of speech (psycholinguistics), and the functioning of language in society (sociolinguistics). Providing the interface between language as internal system and language as behaviour in the real world we find that relatively new branch of linguistics, pragmatics. What do these aspects of linguistics have to contribute to the principal activities of modern languages departments?

Language as system

The branches of linguistics concerned with the internal system of language (phonetics, morphology and syntax, semantics) clearly have major implications for most of what we do in modern languages. I will mention first of all the analysis of literary texts: we would all agree that what makes a literary writer good is that he or she makes highly effective *use* of the linguistic system. However, it is hard for us to evaluate such use if we have only a sketchy understanding of the system itself. It is not easy to see how sensible analysis of an author's style can take place without a coherent terminology and the analytical frame provided by linguistics.

Even more obviously than in the study of literature, a linguistic understanding of the system of our language will have a direct bearing upon our teaching of that language. 'There can be no systematic improvement in language teaching without reference to the knowledge about language which linguistics gives us' (Pit-Corder, 1973: 15). It is not sufficient, if one is to be an effective teacher of a foreign language, simply to have a sound, practical knowledge of it. This is not to say that a good descriptive knowledge of the language acquired through linguistics will make a good teacher out of a bad one – there is indeed plenty of controversy about the value of explicit instruction in language teaching. However, we can be sure that it can only improve what we do. As I have suggested above, it would be inconceivable to ask someone to teach a physics course at A-level who had not devoted a large part of their degree to developing a theoretical understanding of the subject and acquiring appropriate terminology. Yet no one considers it at all odd that most of our modern linguists teaching A-level French or German have had no training at all during their degree course in even the most elementary descriptive linguistics of their target language.

Whenever we set about teaching an aspect of a language we activate an implicit model of that language contained in our heads. This may be an *ad hoc*, impressionistic one, or it may be a relatively sophisticated one informed by serious study. However, there is more to linguistics than the description of the internal linguistic system. Language can also be seen as behaviour.

Language as behaviour

Here we have to report that enormous progress has been made since the 1960s in both psycholinguistics and sociolinguistics. Developments in *psycholinguistics* have big implications for us on several levels. First we need to be aware that a large amount of research is being conducted on language acquisition – whether first or second language – and this cannot be ignored by language teachers with any level of professionalism. If we find it difficult to persuade research councils about the seriousness of our proposals for research in language-teaching methodology, it could be because of the fragility of the theoretical frameworks behind our funding applications. Secondly, psycholinguistic work on the relationship between language and cognition has major implications for other modern language activities too: how far can we think without words? How far does the language we speak determine the way we think? This question is central to much literary criticism and the vexed issue of the separability of form and content. It also has implications for cultural studies and area studies, since the greater the role we attribute to language in cognition, the greater must be the role we attribute to language in culture and society.

The implications of recent work in *sociolinguistics* for modern languages are even more obvious. Sociolinguistics is concerned to examine the functioning of language in society. It is developing sophisticated analyses about the role of language in the creation of identity at the level of individuals, groups and nations which are of critical importance to people working in area studies and politics. It has refined tools for the investigation of language variation – both inter- and intra-speaker – which are highly interesting in themselves, but which could lead literary critics to re-evaluate their methods of analysing 'style' in creative writing.

Pragmatics and discourse analysis

And this brings us finally, to the interface between language as system and language as behaviour – *pragmatics*. Pragmatics is the most recent branch of linguistics to emerge, and for this reason there is, as yet, no firm consensus about its scope and terms of reference. One of the functions of the linguist is to make explicit a speaker's internalised knowledge of the linguistic system (their grammatical competence). Another is to uncover the rules which govern the speaker's ability to apply their language to real-life situations (their communicative competence). This at least is one view of the scope of pragmatics. Pragmatics thus undertakes an analysis of the relationship between language and its real-world context. It concerns itself with speech situations, speech events and speech acts, issues central to the study of *rhetoric*, currently a great concern of literary critics. An important sub-branch of the subject is *conversation analysis* – it is clear that language functions quite differently in interactive conversation from how it does in writing, where only one person is immediately involved. Is our teaching of oral communication not likely to be improved by assimilating the findings of research into how conversations work? A further sub-branch of pragmatics is *discourse analysis* or text linguistics. This topic concerns itself with the study of extended texts and embraces much of what was contained in traditional rhetoric. Social scientists and literary critics have been quick to see the significance of these new methodologies for revitalising their own disciplines. After all, literary criticism is in the last analysis a linguistic activity: whereas the natural sciences are concerned with observing and analysing naturally occurring phenomena (as opposed to artefacts), literary criticism is concerned with human representations of our experience expressed in language.

Conclusion

In this chapter I have drawn attention to the acute tension existing in modern languages at university level between language as instrument and language as discipline. It may well be that in future the two functions will have to be split, with languages being taught in language centres with little or no cultural context, and cultures being taught in other departments with little reference to the relevant languages. For the reasons put forward earlier I would consider this to be a serious loss to our higher education system, particularly since it is possible to relieve the tension between instrument and discipline and to reinject coherence and distinctiveness into modern languages simply by reaffirming the centrality of language.

The affirmation of the centrality of language in modern languages calls for more than just highly developed communicative competence: it implies reintroducing an informed understanding of how languages work and how they impinge upon every aspect of our lives. Bringing back to the centre of modern languages the methodology and discoveries of general linguistics would not involve converting modern languages degrees into degrees in linguistics, merely the acceptance of the principle that the basics of general linguistics are the stock-in-trade of any modern languages graduate. Such linguistic knowledge would not provide the totality of our graduates' knowledge – far from it: literary studies, area studies and so on would remain of critical importance. It would, however, provide the common core of knowledge which all of them would share.

I suggested that recent developments in linguistics have taken place on a very broad front and that they all have major implications for our work in modern languages. Raising the level of theoretical awareness about language could revitalise the subject in all its aspects – in language teaching, in literary work and in cultural and area studies. It could above all help to strengthen the coherence of our discipline. Without a discipline our struggle for resources and for students will be much impaired. We will be increasingly viewed solely as an instrument, and a not particularly efficient instrument at that.

References

Campos, C. (1989) L'enseignement du français dans les universités britanniques. *Journal of the British Institute in Paris* 8, 69–108.

Coates, J. (1993) *Women, Men and Language* (2nd edn). Harlow: Longman.

Lutzeier, P.R. (1998) *German Studies. Old and New Challenges*. Bern: Peter Lang.

Lyons, J. (1968) *Introduction to Theoretical Linguistics*. Cambridge: CUP.

Pit-Corder, S. (1973) *Introducing Applied Linguistics*. Harmondsworth: Penguin.

Towell, R. (1998) Languages in Higher Education. In: A. Moys (ed.) *Where Are We Going With Languages?* (pp. 44–53). London: Nuffield Foundation.

Chapter 7

Logging on to Learning: ICT, Modern Languages and Real Communicative Classrooms?

PHILIP HOOD

CALL Redefined? Why *is* ICT Important for Learning?

It is often asserted that obsolescence is in-built to all matters concerning information and communication technology (ICT). We know that last year's computer already looks dated, that periodically there are surges forward into new media which at first sight seem to make everything previous to them invalid. Yet change is not always as total as we might think. A review of the advantages and disadvantages of computer-assisted language learning (Ahmad *et al.*, 1985) contains what might be at first sight a surprising number of still relevant as well as the more expected outdated points. This is significant, as it shows that many of the arguments for and against the use of ICT in modern languages teaching and learning will remain important however far we move along the cutting edge. It will be helpful to rehearse these arguments at the beginning of this chapter and to remind ourselves that all that dazzles technologically is not automatically of gold standard learning quality. Rather, as ever with equipment, it is what you do with it that matters.

In their introduction Ahmad *et al.* (1985) divide the advantages of the computer into three: its inherent qualities, its benefits for the teacher, and its benefits for the learner. Under the first heading they discuss such factors as the wide range of activity types a computer can handle, the key quality of interactivity, the computer's power to assess and choose appropriate pathways for individuals. Under the second, benefits for the teacher, they point out that computers can take over many aspects of presentation and practice, thus leaving teachers more freedom to be creative and imaginative. Under the third, benefits for learners, they cite greater access, including the potential for distance learning, and speed of assessment. Such advantages are mainly for individuals working alone, but they also remark on the potential for group-based learning as an important factor. Finally, they demonstrate that the computer can be a great motivator.

Clearly now 15 years on these same advantages are still valid, although in concrete manifestation some have probably moved a lot further forward than the authors envisaged. The disadvantages Ahmad _et al._ explore centre mainly on the state of development of computer-assisted language learning (CALL) packages then available, and the non-transferability of programs between different platforms. They mention that the computer is not really capable of open-ended dialogue with the student, and that the type of learning is restricted therefore to material based around rules practice (although simulation and role-play can be initiated by computer input). At that time authoring programs were just emerging and Ahmad _et al._ note their potential. It is interesting, then, that the most common piece of software in modern foreign languages (MFL) departments during the 1990s has probably been Camsoft's _Fun with Texts_.

Since 1985 we have seen great advances in many aspects which Ahmad _et al._ saw as potentially disadvantageous, for example the development of compatible systems and the power to involve audio-, video- and graphic capability in CALL software, but interestingly the capability of the computer to engage in open-ended dialogue is still seriously wanting. This theme re-emerges wherever we look, and cannot be ignored, although perhaps the emphasis is now on the computer and all its peripherals enabling open-ended dialogue between _people_ (rather than with itself) – people who would otherwise not find it easy to get in contact.

Another example of writing from the mid-1980s (Brumfit _et al._, 1985) includes a chapter by Martin Phillips entitled 'Educational Technology in the Next Decade: An ELT Perspective', which prophetically charts out likely developments over the short, medium and long terms. Phillips anticipates both general trends, such as the growth in parallel processing capacities and the convergence of audio- video- and computer-based technologies, and more specific developments, such as speech synthesis and testing and profiling. He too expected more from a computer's interactive potential than we have seen so far: 'the increased power of software ...will facilitate the development of sophisticated interactive simulations. These will offer learning experiences which present lifelike contexts changing in real time according to the learner's input' (1985: 115). We have only very limited versions of such a capability available to us at present. Perhaps therefore we should also quote his general summary of the problem with ICT in the 1980s: 'Too often promising technologies are used in methodologically impoverished ways because our thinking is rooted in the use of earlier outmoded techniques' (1985: 102). But of course vision, execution and affordability are three rare bedfellows!

Although the term 'computer-assisted language learning' and some of its practical applications can still summon up the idea of a pedagogy centred on the 'practice mode', particularly as part of the more behaviourist-influenced audio-lingual drill method of learning (Laurillard & Marullo, 1993), many researchers in the 1990s have looked at it from much broader perspectives. On a theoretical research level there have been many attempts to seek a principled methodology for the design and evaluation of CALL programs. Examples of these are Legenhausen and Wolff, (1992), Holland *et al.* (1995), Salaberry (1996) and Chapelle (1997; 1998). On a practical level there are review articles in journals and on the world wide web (www) which point interested teachers and/or learners in the direction of available packages with a perhaps less theoretically based rationale. An example of this would be Leloup and Ponterio (1998), who review and provide links to packages delivering multimedia-based learning on the web (so combining two very currently fashionable aspects of ICT: materials, typically to be found on a CD-ROM platform, and the Internet).

Carol Chapelle (1997: 21), after listing the many subject-area perspectives from which research on CALL is written, sums up the need for research as follows: 'What is needed then is a perspective on CALL which provides appropriate empirical research methods for investigating the critical questions about how CALL can be used to improve instructed SLA [second language acquisition].' This is an important statement, as it points to the need to prove that CALL packages actually work with language learners, and are not just theoretically justifiable. The evaluation of such packages needs to be very firmly founded in valid measures. Chapelle describes the following two questions as critical (1997: 22): 'What kind of language does the learner engage in during a CALL activity ? How good is the language experience in CALL for L2 [second language] learning ?' She notes that the first question is significant because the instructor needs to decide how much time a particular CALL activity should be allocated, and that the second demands that the instructor has a well-defined view on what kinds of manifestation of language in lessons actually do assist learning.

In a subsequent article (1998) Chapelle analyses very clearly the potential of multimedia applications for language learning. She first presents a synthesised model of second language acquisition, which in turn indicates seven features which are important in the language-learning process and therefore relevant for multimedia CALL packages. This is followed by an indication of how CALL packages could meet these criteria. Briefly, her seven features are that learners need to:

- have the linguistic characteristics of target-language input made salient;
- receive help in comprehending semantic and syntactic aspects of linguistic input;
- be given opportunities to produce target-language output;
- notice errors in their linguistic output;
- correct their linguistic output;
- engage in target-language interaction whose structure can be modified for negotiation of meaning; and
- engage in second language tasks designed to maximise opportunities for good interaction.

Teachers of MFL will immediately see that this is engaging in practical commonsense criteria for language learning, and that subsequent application of such criteria is likely to be valuable in formulating good-quality ICT packages. Chapelle suggests that computers can meet these criteria in simple ways, for example by highlighting certain parts of texts in different colours on screen to enable learners to focus on them deliberately. She adds more complex demands, too, such as that the software package should be able to recognise any version of a well-formed response made by a learner, rather than just a single version of that response which just happens to have been programmed. Again we find ourselves looking for interaction capabilities which will come close to those of a human rather than an electronic speech partner.

If packages do meet Chapelle's criteria (and these are by no means unrealistic) then the facility for more intense, more stimulating and enjoyable practice with individualised feedback is clearly advantageous – not to replace a teacher, but to support and extend the opportunities teachers can give. In being able to offer the multimedia experience in a comparatively seamless way CALL is reflecting the expectations of late twentieth-century lifestyle, and therefore has great relevance for our young learners. Chapelle concludes by showing how a computer-based package can also monitor whether learners are making full use of the features offered, thus demonstrating a further benefit of the medium, which will offer teachers more information and in a well-structured format.

As we move into the new millennium, and as increased sums of money are allocated to educational institutions for hardware, software and training, it is vital that computer use in modern languages learning is rigorously evaluated, and that the results of such evaluation are disseminated to teachers and to companies producing the hard- and software. Of course there should be space for experiment and innovation both in products and in methodology, but there also need to be clear guidelines for teachers who do not have the time or the ICT knowledge to plough an individual furrow. In this the role of agencies such as BECTa (British Educational Communications and Technology Agency) are vital.

Where Are We Now?

ICT in modern languages departments approaching the millennium

ICT provision in modern languages in the schools of the UK varies dramatically from an extreme of virtual non-use (or should we say non virtual-use ?) to a pattern of use which is coherent, frequent and fruitful. Within the very broad range of hardware and software provision there are similar extremes. So we could say we have departments who have very little and use very little, departments who have little and exploit it to the absolute maximum, departments who have a lot but use it very inefficiently and departments who have wonderful facilities, used wonderfully. And all stations in between. But it seems worth describing the positives, and taking two fictional departments, one which makes the most of limited provision and one which is well equipped but has shown that the money was well invested. (For a range of genuine case-studies, which are intended to be updated regularly, see the National Grid for Learning's Virtual Teachers' Centre.)

Limited provision

Let us imagine a department with three stand-alone machines, two Acorns surviving from the previous era, and one a multimedia PC bought recently after a bid from the head of department. The teachers do have access to the IT suite (of non-multimedia PCs), but realistically could book each class in at the very most once a term, if all MFL groups were equally targeted. The school library has one multimedia PC and the department has asked for electronic dictionaries for French and Spanish to be available there. The Acorns can still run comfortably the original *Fun with Texts* programs (Camsoft) in French and Spanish which have been available for some time. Over a few years teachers have created a large number of texts, based in all the major topics and covering levels of ability from near beginners to GCSE. These are seen as a resource specifically targeted at the school's own students and reflecting their needs and their strengths. They are made available in the departmental area at lunch-time and are used very regularly by all classes specifically as an extension or consolidation tool towards the middle or end of the topic cycle. The Acorn machines also run an original *My World* (SEMERC, now Granada Learning) in both languages; this is principally used for learners with special needs, who require extra vocabulary consolidation through matching labels to pictures, sequencing dialogues or creating their own simple text. The multimedia PC is used to support the CD-ROM *En Route* (Heinemann) which supplements the school's main French coursebook, and, as an experiment, an encyclopaedic CD-ROM in each of French and Spanish. Also installed on it is the school's own generic word-processing and database software. The most eager ICT MFL teacher has installed a trial copy of a multimedia authoring program and is experimenting to see whether it would justifiable for the department to buy it.

The department decided that coherence, some form of progression and an eye to what was needed by the students at specific times in their experience of secondary education were the most important considerations in their ICT planning. Therefore they opted for the multimedia PC to be prioritised for Year 7 students when they are on timetable for modern languages with the *En Route* program giving consolidation and extension. But of course only two students can realistically use the machine at any one time, so to build on the enthusiasm which it has engendered there is now an opportunity to use it also during a Year 7 Creative Languages Club, which occurs one lunch-time a week and is staffed in rotation by all members of the department. The ICT co-ordinator has encouraged the department to use the database facility, so (after an initial experiment on the stand-alone machine) Year 8 have entered some personal information into the database in either French or Spanish. This year-group now uses the network room for a lesson each half-term, during which they compile statistical data about the cohort, to be written up in subsequent lessons. The information is entered in the foreign language, although for the present time the software is the English-language version.

Year 10 have priority in the network room, principally for word-processing. The teachers enter texts to be factually or linguistically corrected, or as a stimulus for productive writing by the students either individually or in pairs. The students redraft or create correct versions of tasks marked by teachers, often in pairs, so that they can evaluate another person's writing as well as their own. There may be scope too for GCSE coursework to be written in this way. The ICT staff are also using this opportunity to check that all Year 10 students are completely independent as regards word-processing skills. Again the software being used is the English-language version, but the department is now beginning to ask for a French and a Spanish version to be bought so that a better target-language context can be created for such work. The department's next priority is Year 9, and the intention, as soon as the school goes on-line, is to develop e-mail linking with partner schools, which it is hoped will offer a boost to motivation at a crucial time by creating really personal links for each student with a target-language speaker of their own age.

Generous provision

The well-equipped department, which is running at full strength, is doing all of the above types of work together with some extra refinements such as an emphasis on desk-top publishing (DTP) as well as on word-processing. The ICT department leads some projects which involve small groups choosing a curriculum focus – one such group has worked with the *PowerPoint* program (Microsoft) to create a presentation about the exchange town in Germany, while another has created a practice game for younger students which involves them hearing and reading short texts in the target language and answering multiple choice questions on them. The department has clearly defined policies and a coherent plan to involve its students in ICT at all points in their learning from Year 7 onwards. Greater access to a network room, to multimedia and to communications technology will also create extra flexibility and benefits. The department has chosen three CD-ROM titles to be networked and used regularly, although they can obviously alter these programs from time to time if they wish. The networked titles include the problem-solving situational CD-ROM *Ça y est*, which motivates learners in pairs to use the target language in a listening/reading mode and has been seen to elicit speech in the foreign language amongst the most able. There is also a more text-based program, *Perspectives françaises*, from AVP's *PictureBase* series, and they have a small collection of other CD-ROM-based materials which they can offer as either a lunch-time or an after-school study aid (the multimedia suites are staffed by technicians throughout the day and the strongly implemented 'responsible behaviour' policy seems to be working!).

The collection includes some language titles which involve a speech synthesis element, an electronic dictionary in all three languages offered, three *Living Books* titles, two in both French and German and one in Spanish, and encyclopaedic CD-ROMS such as Encarta and science, history and geography titles, based on materials produced by Dorling Kindersley. A further major initiative is the use of e-mail, which the students accept as a natural part of life in English – using Internet-based e-mail addresses, they e-mail each other regularly. The MFL staff are building on this by encouraging a five-minute e-mail message-writing slot each time a class is in the network room for a languages lesson. The messages are sent to a partner school's teacher, as this has proved more efficient. Some classes write in English; these messages are used for teaching in the partner school. Others write in the target language, and students from the target-language school correct them and add some information either in English or in the foreign language before sending them back to the teacher in England. Thus replies can have a language-learning value on two fronts – one lexical/grammatical, the other by providing a brief reading stimulus.

The Internet is the final piece of the ICT jigsaw and is regarded as a resource for both teachers and students, predominantly through the use of search engines to find items of everyday interest in the foreign language. Alta Vista, for example, allows the specification of a language, so it is possible to type in the name of a sports or pop music personality who may be English-speaking, but specify that the returns should be in French or German. The MFL staff have found that such items have motivated students to read longer and more difficult texts, because of their inherent interest value.

Developments in the Immediate Future

So where are we likely to go from here? The features that we might realistically expect to see becoming much more readily available during the next five years include:

- all schools on-line;
- e-mail turned first to synchronous read/write, later to audio contact, and eventually to video-conferencing – the first universally available, the last in use in the very well-equipped departments, probably of language and technology colleges;
- increased Internet use, commonly leading to the creation of an 'intranet' facility;
- networked multimedia packages that allow both learning and 'testing' via personal profiles.

The features which even a short time ago (the beginning of 1997) were considered very unusual, but which as we enter the millennium will begin to be considered standard in most schools, will need to be refined as the new century settles in. Schools tend first to go on-line via a limited connection, but the move to multiple connections to the Internet and therefore to e-mail as well is already seen as important for both staff and students, and this pressure will become ever more intense. Along with this development will come the need for ICT technicians to be considered by senior management teams just as necessary as are laboratory technicians in science departments. Such personnel will need to be able to work with learners to some extent, and to have the ability to advise staff about possible innovations, and their status will need to reflect this.

E-mail will become so common that it will probably be seen much less as a motivator than as a necessary part of communication, both to those nearby and to people further away. Attention will then turn naturally to real-time simultaneous connection by mail, so that genuine conversations can begin to unfold, at first just in writing, but later also with an audio connection and thereafter via video-linking so that the process can become more personalised and motivating. It is easy to underestimate the power ICT has to break down cultural as well as linguistic barriers. At a time when there may be more educational visits abroad taking place but take-up of conventional exchange programmes still seems rather limited, the facility to write to, talk to and even see a 'partner' from a target-language country could become much more available. Emphasis on the computer as facilitator of a richer communication between humans, rather than as partner in communication and learning, would then be much clearer. But this does not mean we should lose sight of the value of equipping the computer to be such a partner if possible. That role, even if it is seen as a pre-communicative practice opportunity for later 'real' communication between people, is still potentially a highly positive one.

Similarly any programme which causes learners to think about their understanding of language, either as individuals or in pairs, will continue to play an important role. Text manipulation will always be useful, precisely because it has this effect. Learners choosing words to fill a gap or complete a sequence, or reading and resequencing a paragraph of jumbled text, must in so doing consider elements of meaning, syntax, grammar and even style. How well they articulate these may be crucial to their developing ability to generalise and transfer knowledge to new contexts; hence paired work will almost always increase awareness, strategy use and eventually the creative ability to manipulate and express meaning. Computers can make this process more efficient in terms of opportunities to repeat and redraft, of feedback, task storage and differentiation. In addition the computer screen can be a convenient focus for discussion. This is noted by Davis *et al.* (1997: 25):

> Group work around a computer may be more genuinely collaborative than other group work, thereby enabling more focused group talk. This in turn may enable learners to go further in developing their pow-

ers of hypothesising and problem solving without needing to resort to the teacher for help.

In this type of material and this mode of working we can perhaps trace a thread which will demonstrate concretely for ten years either side of the millennium the assertion that not everything in current ICT use is destined to become outdated.

The intranet facility will allow teachers to make available quickly and reliably material which has proved to be useful, although such internal systems will need to be regularly updated to ensure currency and vitality. There is a potential role here for post-16 students who are researching coursework to make available to the intranet materials which could also be used lower in the school. Also, and very importantly, the development of CD-ROM sophistication should allow the current good practice of individual profiling to be extended to all language practice materials. Teachers and learners can only benefit from tracking their path through a series of learning and practice tasks, and such a system, if readily available, will help both learners and teachers to create more independent ways both of working and of learning.

Beyond the Next Five Years

The ideal to aim for?

Features which will certainly appear further into the new century, although perhaps only if MFL departments mount pressure to have them introduced, include:

- interactive whiteboards, for example the Promethean _Quora_;
- 'virtual classrooms', i.e. lesson-linking between home and abroad;
- personalised practice between home and abroad;
- real-interest reading/viewing;
- real-interest communication with partners; and
- work handed in electronically.

Earlier in this chapter we noted Carol Chapelle's (1998) principles for evaluating the learning enhancement potential of multimedia materials. We repeat that list again here, but this time reordered and with some possible implications 'bound in'. It comes in two broad chunks:

- _The linguistic characteristics of target-language input need to be made salient; learners should receive help in comprehending semantic and syntactic aspects of linguistic input; and learners need to notice errors in and_ *be able to correct their linguistic output.* This could be interpreted to reaffirm that when learners are meeting new language, especially in the early stages of learning, they do need a 'commentary' of some sort, either from a teacher who presents and explains new material, or from self-access materials which perform the same function. In other words the image of learners simply switched in to computers and learning in isolation is not part of a positive vision. Through organisation of the structural/grammatical aspects of language as well as of the meaning-centred elements, learners will become aware (just as now) of the need to monitor their foreign language output. Computers may well have a role in helping them to do this on an individual and more intensive basis than is possible for a teacher working with a large group.

- *Learners need to: have opportunities to produce target-language output; engage in target-language interaction whose structure can be modified for negotiation of meaning; and engage in L2 tasks designed to maximise opportunities for good interaction.* This reiterates our theme: will computers be able to offer the real-life variation in response that is essential to properly sophisticated output and interaction opportunities? We simply do not know. It has not happened so far, though the importance of computers has been signalled for the past 15 years. But we return again to the notion that as a medium the computer and its associated hard- and software *can* enable real interaction between real people.

So what means might help us to achieve these objectives at a more intensive and motivating level than is available at present? How crucial will ICT be in such a process?

The interactive whiteboard has an immense potential to enrich the teacher's choice of language input. It is a highly significant, if still at present very expensive piece of new technology. Its capabilities are: to act as a conventional whiteboard, but to allow material written on it to be captured subsequently on disk; to act as a screen for projections from video or computer; and to function as a 'terminal' for the connected computer, so that from a touch on the board itself items can be called up from the PC hard disk, from the network and even from beyond the institution, for example from the Internet. The potential contribution of this to 'conventional' language teaching is immediately obvious. We are accustomed to presentation techniques ranging from the use of visuals, to audio, video and text, but we often find ourselves as teachers limited to a single mode which we can easily control. This development would offer us the chance to present a range of types of stimulus on a single screen, and to build perhaps from using simple images (flashcard/overhead projector equivalents) to teach a simple set of vocabulary, through to generating those images at random for repetition and guesswork practice. A teacher could then link the vocabulary set into a short text to be sequenced, or to a series of interviews such as those that BBC video packages such as *Ici Paris* often use (but which should also be made available in time in CD-ROM format). Finally maybe the teacher could turn to an Internet page which linked into the topic concerned.

Through this multimedia approach we would be giving learners a variety of types of comprehensible input to suit their own varying learning style preferences, and to some extent would also perhaps be combining the presentation and practice stages of the learning cycle. Since it is quite difficult to decide arbitrarily at which point exactly any individual moves from meeting new input to manipulating it, such a process, still quite firmly under teacher control, would allow individual learners within a lesson to move more easily at their own pace. By meeting the new language and structures in several ways and thus being more easily able to decide when they were able to respond to questioning (and hence begin to practise), individual learners would build up confidence, both specifically, about that particular language set, and more universally, about the manageability of the learning process as a whole.

The interactive whiteboard has a value beyond the presentation/practice stage mentioned above, as it could also form the screen for projection of video-conferencing images. This is at present not generally available except as a customised system and still requires a separate large video-screen, but clearly the potential for development is there. The virtual classroom is already a reality in several contexts, and projects such as MERLIN, based at the University of Hull (Marsh *et al.*, 1997), have shown the benefits of computer-linked tutoring systems for individual learners scattered over a wide area. There is no reason why, if broad-band communications become more affordable and therefore more available, classrooms should not link via video-conferencing so that partner classes could share a part of a lesson, perhaps using a dual language focus initially to compare the learning of a topic in, say, science or geography in the two countries. The major factor in making this appealing to teachers and learners is the size of display. From such linking at a class level it will be easier to link on a small group or even individual level through e-mail, audio and video-conferencing. Once a relationship is formed, technology may step back a few paces and allow encounters via the telephone or even in person to take over! There is already in 'tandem learning' (Little & Ushioda, 1998) a system for linking (mainly) adults between countries who wish to learn one another's language. This approach, which allows learning to be individualised, certainly as regards the topics covered, could supplement the more formal learning programme with a range of extra language in which the learner has a real interest. Similarly, easy access to the Internet, which will contain a large number of audio- and video-files as well as textual material, will ensure that learners have access to the very type of material they wish to see, hear or read. Reading and listening at all levels could then become much more personalised, with learners logging their material and responding to it in the target language in a manner more akin to the style of work in mother-tongue English lessons.

The language-learning cycle, from being a linear process from presentation through practice to production, would thus become much more a natural, needs-led growth within each broad topic area. Teachers would still have control over the initial stages and could recap and consolidate with learners who lacked confidence. There could still be class tests of 'minimum competence' where these were needed. But there would also be opportunities for learners to explore language through all four skills (listening, speaking, reading and writing), either directly with a computer or by using material gathered from a computer with other students. The comprehensible input, certainly, and probably both the real intake and the concrete output, too, would grow considerably as a result of this broadening of access and exposure to interesting materials in the foreign language. The content, rather than the message format, could become the major focus, allowing acquisition to take place to a far greater extent than is often now the case. Clearly teachers will still need to intervene with most, if not all learners, but perhaps more infrequently with those who develop independent learning skills, guided by personal interest rather than by a standard lesson plan. Possibly the most important developments in modern languages in the years either side of the millennium will come from those responsible for training teachers (both new and established), who will design programmes that will enable all of us to see the potential role of ICT for learning in an even sharper perspective than we already perceive the role of ICT in teaching.

References

Ahmad, K., Corbett, G., Rogers, M. and Sussex, R. (1985) _Computers, Language Learning and Language Teaching_. Cambridge: Cambridge University Press.
Brumfit, C., Phillips, M. and Skehan, P. (1985) _Computers in English Language Teaching_. Oxford: Pergamon Press.
Chapelle, C. (1997) CALL in the year 2000: Still in search of research paradigms? _Language Learning and Technology_ 1 (1), 19–43.
Chapelle, C. (1998) Multimedia CALL: Lessons to be learned from research on in-

structed SLA. _Language Learning and Technology_ 2 (1), 22–34.

Davis, N., Desforges, C., Jessel, J., Somekh, B., Taylor, C. and Vaughan, G. (1997) Enhancing quality in learning through IT. In B. Somekh and N. Davis (eds) _Using Information Technology Effectively in Teaching and Learning: Studies in Pre-service and In-service Teacher Education_. London: Routledge.

Holland, V., Kaplan, D. and Sams, M. (eds) (1995) _Intelligent Language Tutors: Theory Shaping Technology_. Mahwah, NJ: Lawrence Erlbaum Associates.

Laurillard, D. and Marullo, G. (1993) Computer-based approaches to second language learning. In P. Scrimshaw (ed.) _Language, Classrooms and Computers_. London: Routledge.

Legenhausen, L. and Wolff, D. (1992) STORYBOARD and communicative language learning: Results of the Düsseldorf CALL project. In M. Swartz and M. Yazdani (eds) _Intelligent Tutoring Systems for Foreign Language Learning_ (pp. 9–23). Berlin: Springer-Verlag.

Leloup, J. and Ponterio, R. (1998) Using www multimedia in the foreign language classroom: Is this for me? _Language Learning and Technology_ 2 (1), 4–10.

Little, D. and Ushioda, E. (1998) Designing, implementing and evaluating a project in tandem language learning via e-mail. _ReCALL_ 10 (1), 95–101.

Marsh, D. _et al._ (1997) Project MERLIN: A learning environment of the future. _ReCALL_ 9 (1).

Salaberry, M. (1996) The theoretical foundation for the development of pedagogical tasks in computer-mediated communication. _CALICO Journal_ 14 (1), 5–34.

Scrimshaw, P. (ed.) (1993) _Language, Classrooms and Computers_. London: Routledge.

Software/Internet references

Alta Vista: http://www.altavista.com/

Ça y est (1996) Hodder and Stoughton.

En Route (1996) Heinemann.

Fun with Texts 3 (1998) Camsoft.

My World 2 (1994) SEMERC.

National Grid for Learning (NGFL) Virtual Teachers' Centre: http://vtc.ngfl.gov.uk/

Perspectives françaises (1996) AVP _PictureBase_ series.

Chapter 8

Vocational Languages: An Analysis of Current Practice and Suggestions for a Way Forward

JOHN THOROGOOD

Vocational language teaching, or to use the preferred European terminology, 'vocationally oriented language learning' (VOLL), raises some fundamental issues. Some employers claim that language teaching and learning through the mainstream education system have failed to produce the linguists they need for dealing with foreign language-speaking clients and associates, but there is a counter-claim that many of the courses offered, notably in the national vocational qualification (NVQ) programmes delivered post-16, while addressing circumscribed vocational needs, do not give the linguistic grounding for 'real' language learning.

There is also a tendency to suggest that there is a divide between 'vocational' language learning on the one hand and 'generic' or 'academic' language learning on the other. This is echoed in the notion of a training/ education divide which seemed to be emerging over the last two decades, but which, witness the recent merging of the Education and Employment Departments, is perhaps due for reconsideration.

Where We Are Now

Against this broad background, teachers and lecturers in languages have continued to deliver language courses in a range of contexts to a variety of audiences. By some of them the alleged vocational/academic divide has been practically ignored; for others it has been a source of some anxiety and confusion; for others still, something they have taken effortlessly in their stride. At one end of the extreme are some teachers in schools who are grappling with VOLL for the first time; at the other are tutors working for dedicated business language-training providers who have extensive experience of working to highly specific training briefs based on thorough training needs analyses.

Vocational versus academic

It may be more helpful to stress 'convergence' rather than 'divergence' between the vocational and academic language learning pathways. When all is said and done, much of what people say and write to each other in the workplace may differ little in linguistic content from what they say and write in social settings. A recent Midlands-based English as a Second or Other Language (ESOL) project was set up to train non-native English-speakers in communication within a range of highly specialised trades. Trainers had expected that a high percentage, possibly 80%, of 'technical' language would be taught. In practice such language constituted barely 20% of vocabulary and structures covered. In the broader range of work-based communication it would be surprising if as much as 10% of language used were in any real sense specialised. Foreign language training for work purposes regularly includes language intended for social interaction, which at many levels of work-responsibility is a vital element in the trans-acting of business. Many foreign business cultures regard as discourteous the premature discussion of the negotiator's commercial objectives, and many others would see as over-serious and unsympathetic an undiluted launch into 'heavy' technical detail. The National Language Standards (NLS), which we shall refer to later, explicitly include reference to language required for social purposes, notwithstanding their work-related application.

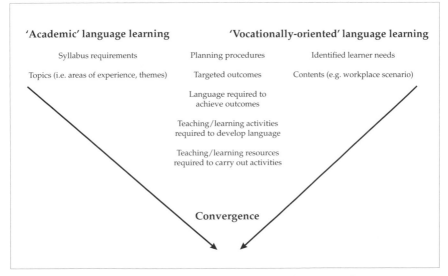

Figure 8.1 Academic and vocationally oriented language learning

Under the heading 'Programme design', below, we shall consider in more detail ways of embarking on vocational courses, but it can be said at once that the principle of convergence applies to this process.

VOLL versus business language training

It would be wrong to infer that vocationally oriented language learning and business language training are mutually exclusive, for their content in individual cases could be very similar, but by VOLL I understand the various courses of study more often associated with full-time education and devised with the aim of laying a linguistic foundation for workplace use; business language training I regard as training done in the context of full-time employment.

There is a tendency for VOLL to be more broadly based, aimed at developing a repertoire of vocational language on which the learner can build in more specific ways once in a particular work situation. VOLL is most commonly represented in such courses as FLAW (the London Chamber of Commerce and Industry Examination Board's 'foreign languages at work' scheme), the GNVQ language units developed by QCA, the RSA's Certificate of Business Language Competence, and so on. Teaching programmes are based either on an appropriate workplace scenario or on a thematic selection of documents and situations that covers most occupational eventualities.

In recent years universities' 'institution-wide language programmes' (IWLPs) have burgeoned. In many of these courses designed for non-specialist language students a VOLL approach has been favoured. Accreditation for such courses is generally internal, though the level of the award may be benchmarked by such external criteria as the NLS. In some cases dual accreditation is now being sought, to give students access to a nationally recognised award for use in employment.

VOLL is most likely to be delivered in the traditional 'drip-feed' pattern associated with educational institutions, for example regularly timetabled over an academic year. Business language training may range from drip-feed to intensive training, depending on company need. The delivery style may also reflect whether the training is broad-based or focused on a specific future role or task.

Such a specific brief may not necessarily cover the requirements of a formal qualification and the learner's achievement may not be formally recognised beyond the needs of the company. Increasingly, though, both as a result of the move towards Investors in People, whereby more employers see themselves as having a duty towards the personal development of employees, and of the possibility of the latter achieving NVQ units through the NLS, employers may take a broader view of language competence in the workforce.

This would certainly be true of enterprises with non-English-speaking parent companies, where internal liaison could be enhanced by the acquisition of foreign language skills among the English-speaking workforce. The UK is high on the list of countries targeted for foreign investment and take-over, not least in the automotive industry where there are instances of employees receiving financial incentives to become qualified in the language of the parent company. As business language training providers become increasingly skilful at conducting language-training needs analysis among their clients and at dispelling certain unrealistic or simplistic perceptions of what can be achieved in a given time, employers stand to gain a fuller understanding of the benefits and implications of having a corporate language policy.

The Department of Trade and Industry has for a number of years conducted a Languages for Export campaign which among other activities has generated some excellent guide booklets on foreign language support and training and has annually staged an awards event at both regional and national levels, recognising excellence and innovation in language training. The Languages National Training Organisation (LNTO) has extended sponsorship of awards to the education sector, with a number of schools, colleges and universities being recipients.

It is tempting to think of language-training need as applying only to exporting activities (selling goods and services abroad), whereas in fact a significant part of the trade of many companies is dependent upon foreign language speakers visiting this country. If we take the instance of the tourism and leisure industries alone (including hotels, catering, entertainment and the arts, the retail trade, sport and recreation), there is a potential market of nine million non-English-speaking visitors to Britain per year. Bearing in mind the predominance of reception and sales-counter contacts in this economic sector, we can readily see the need for a comparatively modest level of foreign language competence for a large number of employees, in addition to the more esoteric negotiating abilities required for management and export sales representatives.

It is not only linguistic competence in the general sense which determines how effectively an employee deals with work-tasks. The range and scope of tasks to be accomplished may so vast and so unpredictable as to require a comprehensive repertoire of language strategies, or so limited and so predictable as to need little more than a phrase-book repertoire with a few job-related manipulations and substitutions. Going back to our thoughts on education versus training, or 'academic' versus 'vocational', it is easy to see how some may take a sceptical view of some vocational language courses on educational grounds. The argument, as put against certain other vocational qualifications, is that there is insufficient requirement of 'underpinning knowledge' for the training process to count as 'real' language learning.

Under the heading 'Scales of attainment' (below) we examine the various approaches to measuring competence in the vocational language field, and consider which levels are most applicable to the various learning needs.

Qualifications

Should an individual or company require formal accreditation for language competence, there is a bewildering diversity of qualifications relating thereto. In his handbook _Vocational Modern Language Qualifications: A Quick Reference Guide_ (1995) Professor Stephen Hagen identified 25 different schemes of varying complexity, run by 13 awarding bodies. Some progress has been made towards simplifying the routes to accreditation, in that a number of key awarding bodies for vocational qualifications, having been approved to accredit NLS units, have tended to promote those units rather than pre-existing schemes. Even where longer-standing schemes continue to flourish, they have been, or may soon be, 'mapped' on to NLS levels to achieve better national standardisation.

The distinction between 'standards' and 'qualifications' is worth making at this point. The language standards setting body for business and industry is the LNTO, formerly the Languages Lead Body. The NLS which are developed by the LNTO are overseen by the Qualifications and Curriculum Authority (QCA) which also scrutinises and approves qualifications. Qualifications are developed by awarding bodies (ABs), who are responsible for packaging, marketing and running them. ABs are the vocational counterpart of what have traditionally been called 'examining boards' (though it is an interesting sign of the times that many ABs have now gone into partnership with examining boards – ULEAC + BTEC = Edexcel!). Qualifications in vocational languages may or may not be NLS-linked. GNVQ language units (from September 2000) will be broadly mapped on to NLS Levels 1, 2 and 3. OCR's (Oxford, Cambridge and the RSA's) Certificate in Business Language Competence or CBLC is 'calibrated' to match levels of the NLS, with one level, 'Basic', set below NLS Level 1. The LCCIEB's FLAW scheme has been independent of NLS at present, but is soon to reflect the NLS levels to bring an element of standardisation into this popular scheme.

Assessment approaches

On the 'academic' language-learning side there is an established examining tradition which stems from an intuitive selection of examination tests for each prescribed level (GCSE, A-level, final honours) developing through precedent into an agreed pattern. The marking of each successive examination is based on discussion of expected outcomes and on agreement exercises using sample candidates' papers. Grading is completed on a combination of the application of performance standards based on precedent and a norm-referenced expectation of the distribution of grades. Linguistic detail plays an important part in finalising mark schemes and numerical values have an equally important role in arriving at grading.

A continuous or periodic assessment approach has also been adopted in certain qualifications, such as modular public qualifications, the latest 'certificates of attainment' for Key Stage 4 and, for a time, the graded objectives schemes adopted by local education authorities and institutions for internal accreditation.

On the 'vocational' side there is both 'examination' in the traditional sense and 'assessment' in the sense of 'continuous assessment'. For instance, the LCCIEB FLIC (Foreign Languages in Industry and Commerce) is a test of oral/aural skills conducted at a pre-arranged time, and the OCR's CBLC scheme is formally examined like the GCSE. On the other hand, units of the NLS (the required units for NVQs and SVQs, but also assessable as free-standing units) are assessed through the evidence of competence generated by the candidate and accumulated in his or her portfolio.

It is worth considering the respective merits of both the examination-based and the continuous modes of assessment. Table 8.1 summarises these. This provides a generic analysis of pros and cons, but in the vocational context we could add on the continuous assessment side that for full-time employees this method has two major benefits, namely that:

- it can be difficult to take time off for externally imposed examinations, whereas evidence for a portfolio can be generated at times to suit learners and their employers; and
- evidence generated in the workplace (tasks performed under real working conditions) can be included in the portfolio without additional time being taken.

Table 8.1 Examination versus continuous assessment

Examination	Notes	Continuous Assessment	Notes
Syllabus structure provided.	Less work – but not negotiable.	Tutor/student negotiate needs and determine content of programme.	More work, but more sensitive to specific needs.
Set, marked and moderated externally (with variants, especially for oral).	Less work – but exam may not reflect personal targets of learner.	Tutor is first assessor (subsequently subject to verification).	More work than examined course, but latter requires regular marking and feedback, and CA may better reflect the aims of a negotiated course. Tutor must exercise judgement against criteria.
Tests performance on only one occasion.	Convenient. Limited sampling of syllabus. Can create high levels of anxiety. Takes no account of individual's state on the day. Able candidates can prepare at last minute and may be less motivated earlier on.	Tests performance on a number of occasions.	More work than exam, but see above. Can sample the course more fully. Less stressful. Gives more representative view of competence. Each assignment counts – more motivation to all abilities to sustain good work throughout course.

Scales of attainment

In the UK the use of commonly recognised scales for assessing foreign language performance is a comparatively recent one, although in the EFL field and elsewhere in Europe the value of such calibration has been recognised for some time. The use of level and grade descriptions in the National Curriculum and the GCSE in the 1990s is probably the first instance of the use of any scale of attainment in modern foreign languages in the UK, although a few localised pioneering attempts at defining attainment were made in the GOML (Graded Objectives in Modern Languages) era.

The teacher/tutor/assessor of work-related languages is becoming increasingly familiar with the NLS. These are based on the NVQ framework, which has broad generic descriptors reflecting levels of skill and responsibility at work. The scale, although expressed in one instance in linguistic terms, relates more to 'outcome' – what the user of the language 'can deal with' by using the foreign language assessed.

Table 8.2 National Language Standards levels

Level 1	Deal with predictable tasks
Level 2	Deal with routine daily activities
Level 3	Deal with varied work tasks
Level 4	Deal with complex work tasks
Level 5	Deal with specialised tasks

These are obviously very broad outcomes and the detail emerges through the various sections. *Unit titles,* for example, include (Listening, Level 2) 'Obtain information about routine and daily activities by speaking'; *element titles* include (Reading, Level 3) 'Read effectively to extract specific details from a variety of sources'; *performance criteria* (defining level) include (Speaking, Level 4) 'Can respond appropriately to questions and comments from the audience arising from the presentation'; and *range statements* (defining areas such as scope and content) include (Writing, Level 5) 'Published texts including those for general readership'. Exemplification of tasks likely to be achievable at each level is provided by 'charts of typical attainment' appended to the standards themselves.

Levels are only broadly comparable with traditional qualifications such as GCE A-level, because the assessment process associated with the NLS is different (see under the heading 'Assessment'). However the following is a helpful guide:

Table 8.3 NLS and 'academic' qualifications compared

National language standards	'Academic' qualifications
Level 5	Postgraduate: degree competence enhanced by work-related experience – professional linguist standard.
Level 4	Good honours degree.
Level 3	Good A-level.
Level 2	GCSE upper band (C–A*).
Level 1	GCSE lower band (G–D).

The NLS are intended to be read by employers seeking a commonly accept-able definition of various levels of competence, by employees seeking to evaluate their own competence or determine personal learning targets and by trainers seeking appropriate training targets. Other aspects are dealt with under the headings 'Assessment' and 'Qualifications'.

A scale which will increasingly impinge on our perception of linguistic attainment is the global assessment scale developed through the *Common European Framework of Reference for Modern Languages* (1996). The latter re-sults from an initiative undertaken over a number of years by the Council of Europe's Council for Cultural Co-operation and is in concrete terms a comprehensive publication addressing all aspects of the learning, teaching and assessment of modern languages. The assessment scale takes account of a range of approaches to defining language competence, including the UK's NLS. It embraces six levels, with the possibility of a further three be-ing added. Some levels, for example 'threshold' and 'waystage', have their origin in earlier Council of Europe publications such as Van Ek's *Un Niveau-seuil* (*The Threshold Level*, 1975). The scale is reproduced here from Draft 2 of the *Framework*.

Table 8.4 European global assessment scale levels

| C2 'Mastery' | Shows great flexibility in reformulating ideas in differing linguistic forms to convey finer shades of meaning precisely, to give emphasis, to differentiate and to eliminate ambiguity. | Maintains consistent grammatical control of complex language, even while attention is otherwise engaged (e.g. in forward planning, in monitoring others' reactions). | Can express him/herself spontaneously at length with a natural colloquial flow, avoiding or backtracking around any difficulty so smoothly that the interlocutor is hardly aware of it. | Can interact with ease and skill, picking up and using non-verbal and intonational cues apparently effortlessly. Can interweave his/her contribution into the joint discourse with fully natural turn-taking, referencing, allusion-making etc. | Can create cohesive discourse making full and appropriate use of a variety of organisational patterns and a wide range of connectors and other cohesive devices. |
| C1 Effective Operational Proficiency | Has a good command of a broad range of language allowing him/her to select a formulation to express him/herself clearly in an appropriate style on a wide range of general, academic, professional or leisure topics without having to restrict what he/she has to say. | Consistently maintains a high degree of grammatical accuracy; errors are rare, difficult to spot and generally corrected when they do occur. | Can express him/herself spontaneously, almost effortlessly. Only a conceptually difficult subject can hinder a natural, smooth flow of language. | Can select a suitable phrase from a readily available range of discourse functions to preface his/her remarks in order to get or to keep the floor and to relate his/her own contributions skilfully to those of other speakers. | Can produce clear, smoothly flowing well-structured speech, showing controlled use of organisational patterns, connectors and cohesive devices. |

Table 8.4 (continued)

B2 'Vantage'	Has a sufficient range of language to be able to give clear descriptions, express viewpoints on most general topics, without much conspicuous searching for words, using some complex sentence forms to do so.	Shows a relatively high degree of grammatical control. Does not make errors which cause misunderstanding, and correct most of his/her mistakes.	Can produce stretches of language with a fairly even tempo; although he/she can be hesitant as he or she searches for patterns, there are few noticeably long pauses.	Can initiate discourse, take his/her turn when appropriate and end conversation when he/she needs to, though he/she may not always do this elegantly. Can help the discussion along on familiar ground, confirming comprehension, inviting others in, etc.	Can use a limited number of cohesive devices to link his/her utterances into clear, coherent discourse, though there may be some 'jumpiness' in a long contribution.
B1 'Threshold'	Has enough language to get by, with sufficient vocabulary to express him/herself with some hesitation and circumlocutions on topics such as family, hobbies and interests, work, travel and current events.	Uses reasonably accurately a repertoire of frequently used 'routines' and patterns associated with more predictable situations.	Can keep going comprehensibly, even though pausing for grammatical and lexical planning and repair is very evident, especially in longer stretches of free production.	Can initiate, maintain and close simple face-to-face conversation on topics that are familiar or of personal interest. Can repeat back part of what someone has said to confirm mutual understanding.	Can link a series of shorter discrete simple elements into a connected, linear sequence of points.
A2 'Waystage'	Uses basic sentence pattern with memorised phrases, groups of a few words and formulae in order to communicate limited information in simple everyday situations.	Uses some simple structures correctly, but still systematically makes basic mistakes.	Can make him/herself understood in very short utterances, even though pauses, false starts and reformulation are very evident.	Can answer questions and respond to simple statements. Can indicate when he/she is following but is rarely able to understand enough to keep a conversation going of his/her own accord.	Can link groups of words with simple connectors like 'and', 'but' and 'because'.
A1 Breakthrough	Has a very basic repertoire of words and simple phrases related to personal details and particular concrete situations.	Shows only limited control of a few simple grammatical structures and sentence patterns in a memorised repertoire.	Can manage very short, isolated, mainly pre-packaged utterances, with much pausing to search for expressions, to articulate less familiar words, and to repair communication.	Can ask and answer questions about personal details. Can interact in a simple way, but communication is totally dependent on repetition, rephrasing and repair.	Can link words or groups of words with very basic linear connectors like 'and' or 'then'.

Although the scale is not exclusively work-related, its upper five levels map tolerably on to the NLS, and awareness of its existence is desirable as it should increasingly be of value in providing a benchmark of language competence in a mobile Europe-wide workforce.

European language portfolio

In conjunction with the *Common European Framework*, the concept of a European language portfolio (ELP) has emerged and pilot trials of experimental material have been undertaken in a number of European member states. An adult, vocational version of the portfolio has been developed with the support of the LNTO and a number of institutions have undertaken trialling work. When an acceptable format has emerged, it is hoped that this document will become a universal vehicle for the personal recording of language competence. The ELP has three parts: a 'passport', in which formal and informal accreditation is recorded by the bearer; a 'language biography' in which all manner of foreign language encounters and experiences, whether or not resulting in accreditation, may be recorded; and a 'dossier' which may include samples of evidence of the bearer's competence in languages recorded in the other sections and actual certificates of qualifications gained, attendance on courses and so on.

It is intended that the bearer should be able to produce the ELP or relevant parts of it in pursuit of employment. The document is also intended to raise the status of language competence and encourage mobility within the European workforce. The European scale is included in the portfolio and bearers are encouraged to refer to it in evaluating their competence in the languages recorded.

Programme design and the vocational context

As already suggested above, this may vary according to whether the teacher/trainer is delivering a broad-based VOLL course or a highly focused company training course.

In the former case, there need not be a great divergence of approach from the design of a general language-teaching course.

Context

This may be generally commercial or may have a sectoral focus, such as leisure and tourism or hospitality and catering, as with Advanced GNVQ language units. In the latter case, consultation with the GNVQ programme leader on suitable links with the main course will take place. Where the teacher of the course is following a published textbook, this will provide its own context, though many teachers find that they need to adapt such material for their own purposes. If it is the intention to devise one's own programme, the following process may be found helpful.

Aims and objectives

These may be defined as a very general context and outcome, e.g. 'Make contact with a French company', with subsidiary objectives, such as 'Receive a French visitor to your UK company' and 'Undertake a visit to your French customer's company'.

Target tasks

Each of the objectives decided upon will be achieved by completing a group of tasks covering a range of skills, such as telephoning, writing to confirm appointments, reading background literature on the customer's or supplier's firm or product, viewing a promotional video, booking accommodation and so on.

Essential language

This can be related to each target task. Essential structures for carrying out the task are listed, together with categories of vocabulary ('terms for key company roles/products') likely to arise in the course of completing it.

Teaching, learning and assessment activities

A sequence of activities to present and practice necessary language forms, followed by communicative tasks to enable them to be practised in context would follow on from the identification of language forms. Assessment material would reflect the latter and would be introduced at the point of readiness for candidates taking portfolio-based qualifications.

Activities could include both teacher-led classroom work and self-access independent learning material.

Resources

Both published and institution- or company-designed material to support the planned activities would be listed against these activities. Such material would be selected for both classroom use and private study. (See 'activities', above). CILT provides information sheets on vocational language teaching and assessment materials. The process detailed above is summarised in Table 8.5 overleaf.

A model of business language training course design might follow a similar process, but would need to be more closely dependent on the original proposal drawn up with the training provider. Whereas the VOLL course would normally lead to a qualification and would therefore follow either a syllabus or the full requirements of the NLS, a specific training contact might only be required to prepare employees for a defined project. The VOLL programme would assume a core of likely objectives, whereas the business proposal could be narrower and more prescriptive, relating, as it would, to the language-needs analysis carried out for the company. With many institutions, universities, colleges and even schools extending their services to the local business community it is worth their bearing in mind

Table 8.5 Planning a programme of study for vocationally oriented language learning

Topic: making contact with a French company

Sub-topic	Task	Element(s) covered (NLS)	Essential structures	Categories of vocabulary	Training/ assessment activity	Resource (published or school-produced)
Visiting company in France.	Making initial telephone contact and proposing visit.	Speaking/ listening (identify from NLS)	(Particularly those which students should understand and manipulate.)	Key words; headings, e.g. words for positions in company.	Identifying activity from coursebook/ assessment pack, e.g. Assignment BUS5	e.g. 'Assessment tasks for Vocational French'.
	Writing to confirm intentions and to request further information.	Writing (identify from NLS).		Polite conventions, e.g. in letters.	Activity 3.5.	e.g. departmental assignment pack.
	Reading reply to your letter.	Reading (identify from NLS).		Structures not yet understood or manipulated.		
	Listening to answerphone information from French tourist bureau	Listening (identify from NLS).				
Arranging to receive visit from French colleague	Dealing with telephoned request for appointment.	Speaking/listening (identify from NLS).				
	Writing a letter giving information about your company.	Writing (identify from NLS)				
	Understanding text of French company's promotional video.	Listening (identify from NLS).				
	Talking about things your French colleague could do while in your town.	Speaking/listening (identify from NLS).				

the importance of being seen to meet company needs, even though the most circumscribed of language-training programmes will necessarily incorporate a significant core of 'generic' language.

Modes of delivery

As mentioned before, there is a tendency for the institution-based course to deliver its programmes through the 'drip-feed' hours-per-week, times weeks-per-year model, though even here, there may be pressure to respond more flexibly (and more intensively) to local business needs. The trainer who deals exclusively with enterprises will need to be prepared to adapt creatively to accommodate a client who may, among other things:

- have an unrealistic expectation of what can be learnt in a given time;
- be unwilling to release personnel during work hours, or at least only be able to afford limited work-time release;
- want the trainer to work in-house on the company premises; and
- need to reach a competence target in much less than an academic year.

Some tuition, especially at higher levels and for specific projects, may need to be on a one-to-one basis, though where the company has a generous language-training policy it may actively encourage group sessions at lower levels for a wider cross-section of its workforce. Many language-training providers offer in addition to pure language tuition 'cultural briefings' in which both the social and business cultures of countries to be visited are explained to the client.

Linguistic competence

Comparisons are drawn above between outcome-based scales of competence which relate to tasks achieved checked against criteria, and academic qualifications which are normally marked according to marking schemes relating to specific points of grammar and lexis and then graded on the basis of numerical marks earned. The criteria which apply to the NLS do not dwell in detail on the minutiae of linguistic accuracy and it is up to assessors to apply their professional judgement to candidates' performance for the level being attempted. Such judgement should take account of the actual or imagined role of each candidate in question and the medium or channel of communication. To what kind of work role might each level be ascribed? The following is a guide to the appropriateness of each NLS level (see Tables 8.2 and 8.3) to a work role.

Level 1 Linguistically similar to a lower GCSE grade (G–D).Users can command a range of simple, set expressions in familiar settings. Grammatical control is limited to a few variations. In work contacts involving highly predictable exchanges, certain reception/retail encounters could be handled, as could survival in a travel or accommodation situation where no unexpected problems were introduced.

Level 2 Linguistically similar to a higher GCSE grade (C–A*).Users can command a basic vocabulary with some alternative expressions to cope with routine situations. They can manipulate the language to generate original sentences using simple common structures and respond to occasional unpredictable interventions. They can socialise simply, describe their work and organisation and survive in the foreign country, coping with minor variations in the information handled. They could undertake a straightforward business visit in which exchanges of factual information, simple opinion and uncomplicated transactions were all that was required.

Level 3 Linguistically similar to a good A-level pass. Users at this level could begin to function quite effectively even where the full work role was performed through the medium of the foreign language. They would have the linguistic control to express and follow most ideas relevant to their work and to negotiate simply, though they would still be in the process of acquiring work-specific terminology and structures. They could integrate with a foreign language-speaking environment if colleagues made allowances.

Level 4 Linguistically similar to a good honours degree. Users would have complete control over the language system and an almost complete command of terminology and structures both generic and relevant to workplace requirements. With this level of competence they would be very quick to absorb new items into their repertoire and would be developing as a matter of course towards the highest linguistic level. They would be able to negotiate and interact sensitively in their work and most social situations. They would be able to carry out most management and supervisory tasks convincingly through the foreign language.

Level 5 Linguistically similar to a good honours degree, with the benefit of experience in using the language to carry out responsible and specialised tasks. Users would have the positive attributes of a Level 4 user, but would have linguistic skills to handle practically all eventualities in and beyond their own work situation. They could, to the extent of their personal skills, perform the highest level functions, such as those involving sensitive negotiation, management and the supervision of others' professional development.

We would have a commonsense notion of what was acceptable accuracy in each of the work contexts mentioned above. In one sense it is determined by the expectations of the language user in the designated role. In another it may be determined (see above) by the type of communication. Even at Level 1, where the candidate may be doing little more than making noun substitutions in a template company-headed letter, the letter format would require that there were no embarrassing mistakes. Yet in an informal spoken communication at a higher level there could be some tolerance of error.

Although the NLS do not address the linguistic detail of a competent performance, it is recommended that for any given assignment the teacher/trainer prepare an outline mark scheme, to forestall issues which may emerge from the performance and to make prior decisions with regard to expected outcome. For example, where a receptive (listening/reading) skill is assessed, it should be clear what factual extraction or gist understanding is required of the candidate. Where a productive (speaking/ writing) skill is assessed, the assessor should be clear in his or her own mind what will be an acceptable level of accuracy for the channel of communication (letter, fax, etc.), relationship (formal/informal) and level attempted. There would also be a minimum requirement for the amount of information requested and/or supplied in this assignment. As a general rule, the assessor should be asking whether the outcome is satisfactory, that is, whether a message is conveyed and understood adequately for the given context. Lower levels of the NLS tend to be such by virtue of the simplicity of requirement; it is assumed that simple tasks will none the less be carried out fairly accurately.

Vocational Language Training: The Future

The foregoing, a quite detailed picture of things as they are, has implications for the future – whether the 'inevitable' future of the pessimist or the 'potential' future of the optimist. What might be the 'worst-case' and 'best-case' scenarios for the UK as a whole and for individual players in the vocational language training game?

Worst-case scenario

Responding to simplistic arguments about English as a world language and capitulating to teacher recruitment difficulties and reports of poor learner motivation, the mainstream education system abandons the dream of 'languages for all' and reverts to pre-1990s – or even pre-1960s – provision for modern foreign languages. This move is bolstered by statements from the business

community to the effect that the school system does not and cannot deliver the
sort of language competence required in the workplace.

But, we may ask ourselves, is this bad for vocational language teaching? Will the absence of mass language learning in the compulsory sector not lead to a burgeoning of demand for pre-employment (i.e. tertiary sector) or employment-based language training? This is possible, though many present business language trainers would acknowledge a debt to the school grounding in language teaching as a basis for making progress in vocational programmes. It would be hard to predict just how far the recipients of business language training might be set back by a lack of prior language-learning experience. Although the skills acquired at school are not always transparently applicable to work situations, this is defensible in that effective language learning depends on the learner working in relevant and identifiable contexts, and for the 14-year-old the office setting does not provide such relevance. To condemn the child-centred topical content of classroom learning in MFL would be as unjust as to condemn the use of nursery rhymes in the development of the native language. The fact is that many supporting skills such as grammatical analysis, comparison between languages and enhanced awareness of one's own language, memorisation of vocabulary and the like are developed in MFL classes. There is also the matter of even broader skills, such as general communication and personal confidence. At the time of writing, research is being carried out in higher education into the transferability of MFL skills for enhanced employability.

We should also take into account the possible effect on attitudes to language learning of a compulsory five years of languages at school. The progress in terms of numbers experiencing language learning over the last 30 years has been remarkable, with a fourfold increase (from pupils in grammar schools only, some 25% of age group, to virtually all pupils in secondary schools). While this may not have led to a higher quality of attainment it has undoubtedly meant that a generation of children will soon be born of parents for whom foreign language learning was 'normal', like English and maths, rather than for the select few.

On balance, it would seem ill-advised to assume that language learning can be left to needs-related training for the employee.

Best-case scenario

The whole-hearted pursuit of language learning for as much of the compulsory
education phase as possible begins to receive more than lip-service from policy-
makers. Languages are included as a Key Skill within the qualifications frame-
work, and funding mechanisms acknowledge that the pursuit by an individual

> *of any course of language training which for that person provides a pathway for progression should be financially supported.*

While European documentation on educational policy abounds in references to the importance of linguistic competence throughout the Union, comparable UK government utterances reveal a conspicuous absence of such commitment. In a best-case scenario the UK would embark on a staged programme to secure immediate and lasting improvements in MFL provision. This would not be without its difficulties, one of which would certainly be recruitment, but a series of realistic steps over a sensible time-scale (such as the 20-year period for achieving a national language capability suggested by the Nuffield Languages Inquiry) could be contemplated if only the political will were there. One such step could be to resist all potentially retrograde legislation on the National Curriculum.

It is almost a decade since the HMI paper 'Core skills 16–19' advocated the inclusion of languages as a core skill. Although such a radical advocacy has clearly fallen upon deaf ears, it is encouraging to note that vocational or vocationally oriented language training has helped to keep the idea alive. Through the incorporation of NLS units in the NVQ (and by extension the GNVQ) framework, there has been continued language-learning activity in the post-16 phase and on into work and adult life. NLS-related accreditation in the academic year 1997–8 has reached in excess of 27,000 unit certificates. The Open College Network in the further education sector has generated a number of defined language progression schemes culminating in recognised qualifications. However, a significant problem in maximising such positive progress has been the obscuring factor of muddled qualifications systems and complex funding mechanisms. Notwithstanding the potential standardising influence of the National Curriculum and the Dearing framework, there has been endless *ad hoc* tinkering with and addition to qualifications in the 1990s, with the result that a simple and co-herent framework is only just beginning to emerge in such developments as Curriculum 2000.

A qualifications vision of the future? There could be:

- A unified system of school-based qualification and progression without the incongruity of National Curriculum levels at Key Stage 3 being discontinued in favour of GCSE grades at Key Stage 4.
- A simplified system of available qualifications at Key Stage 4.
- A planned progression between what is required to achieve school language qualifications and what is later identified as important for the world of work.

Table 8.6 An idealised National Structure of Standards

Education (process recognition phase)		*Training (outcome recognition phase)*	
Personal attainment phase *National Curriculum compatible*	*General qualification phase* *GCSE/A-level compatible*	*Pre-vocational training* *National Language Standards compatible*	*Vocational training* *National Language Standards assessed*
Key Stages 1 & 2 A consistent provision for MFL learning, combining primary-focused activities with the foundations of language awareness (e.g. 'part of speech' awareness) and linked with literacy policy, exploring levels 1–3 of the National Curriculum. Recognition of progress through a personal record, such as the European Language Portfolio (see above).			
Key Stage 3 Learning programmes recognising KS2 progress and offering more adolescent focused activities, especially based on authentic material. Continued language awareness development, (e.g. addressing structure and morphology through relevant and interesting materials and activities). Levels 1–3 of the NC generally assumed from the outset and a conscious effort made to forge well into the GCSE range of attainment. Continued personal record building.			
	Key Stage 4 Providing increasing intellectual challenge, developing competence towards higher levels, both 'pure' and 'applied' where appropriate for the learner.	Offering a prevocational 'applied' emphasis to selected learners. Outcome based, task-related vocational qualification target (GNVQ model).	**Full time employment** Work-specific training offered to employees. Outcome-based, task-related vocational qualification target (NVQ model).
	16-19 full time education/training Advanced courses.	As for KS4, with progression suitable for individual learner.	
	19+ HE and beyond Specialist degree courses. Adult Education continuation courses (e.g. OCN).	As for 16-19, with progression suitable for individual learner (e.g. institution-wide language programme in HE).	As above, with progression suitable for individual learner and context to match work needs.

The third of these is vital. Too much of 'vocational' language training depends in its early stages on phrase-book learning without the learner understanding the principles of what is learnt. Such learning is useful for survival in the absence of deeper understanding, but it is to be hoped that in the future, a majority of work-based trainees will have a better grasp of what it means to learn a language.

A National Structure of Standards which would support a continuum of language learning, with early enjoyment, confidence and awareness of language as a starting point and where necessary expert and highly specialised use at its ultimate stage might look something like Table 8.6. I have made some important distinctions. Language qualifications for vocational purposes ought to be *outcome*-based, since language as a work-tool must achieve a range of tasks in employment. On the other hand and particularly where the foundations are being laid, qualifications and criteria for progression should acknowledge small steps towards true linguistic competence as do the National Curriculum criteria.

Chapter 9

Meeting the Challenge: Developing the 3Cs Curriculum

DO COYLE

> Rather than producing a curriculum that most students can cope with, there is a strong case for building a curriculum that changes the learner, so that they become effective learners and have access to a demanding curriculum.
>
> David Leat, *Thinking through Geography*

The End of an Era

Writing in the 50th anniversary review of the Central Bureau for Educational Visits and Exchanges (CBEVE), *A World of Understanding* (1998), the British prime minister Tony Blair stated: 'The new millennium demands that we develop international understanding, heighten awareness of Europe and the wider world, and strengthen the concept of world citizenship in our schools and colleges.'

If effective communication is to be at the very heart of this international understanding, then raising the level of our national linguistic competence is indeed a priority. There is of course nothing new in this statement: given the state of modern foreign languages (MFL) teaching and learning in the UK at the end of the twentieth century, the most ambitious challenge for our language educators in the next decade is probably that laid out in the 1995 European Commission white paper which had as one of its priority objectives proficiency in *three* European languages for all European citizens.

In order to go some way towards meeting that challenge, I should like to explore some pathways in MFL teaching and learning which until recently have remained unexploited and which may well offer feasible and realisable alternatives to the status quo.

There seems to me to be a profound paradox in the current debate on the lack of success or otherwise of MFL teaching in our schools. With an increased emphasis on the development of key skills and communication, learning to use languages to communicate is a well-rehearsed and uncontentious aim of the languages curriculum. Yet the whole essence of communication is rooted in the messages or the content which need to be communicated. Therein lies the rub! It seems to me that the 'what', the content of communication, has been overtaken by the 'how', the process of communicating. Teachers encourage young learners to use their foreign language skills for communication, but the nature of that communication appears to be determined by neither teacher nor learner, but by the dual processes of communication itself and of meeting syllabus demands.

The main thrust of the 'graded objectives' movement (GOML) of the 1980s was to move language learning into the 'communicative' era, and this was most welcome. However, its legacy was to leave the next generation of language learners in the apparently safe hands of the communicative approach – one which is still prevalent in today's classrooms. As the educational climate has evolved, so the interpretation of this communicative approach has potentially led to a fossilised orthodoxy of accepted practice. It is one thing to parcel up language into functions and notions which encourage transactional communication in terms of getting things done, but quite another when it comes to real communication, which we all know is not like that. The approach may serve a pragmatic, perhaps an essential starting-point for teaching purposes, but does not appear to take learners far enough into the world of real communication to enable them to function independently in the future.

There is also in my view a growing body of evidence to suggest an urgent need for a critical review of the content of communication (what learners are *told* to talk, read or write about), while teachers are still concentrating largely on the means through which this is communicated. As long as the content of communication is narrowly defined in terms of topics, which are in most cases repetitive, at least by comparison with the mother-tongue curriculum in the primary school, and contain little in terms of cognitive challenge and 'new' knowledge, then it will be difficult to break out of the current language-learning mould, the content of which has variously been described as trivial, inconsequential, anodyne (Powell, 1986) and pedestrian (Salters *et al.*, 1995): 'The pendulum has swung from a literary syllabus bearing very little resemblance to everyday life to one which is totally utilitarian and transactional in nature, but still manages to be largely irrelevant to pupils in the secondary sector' (Salters *et al.*, 1995: 6).

A recent shift in emphasis in pedagogical thinking from teaching to learning has brought with it an interest in investigating the potential of the role of social interaction in the classroom: where learners and teachers work together to co-construct a learning environment, where learning is challenging rather than 'fun' and where students create meaning and teachers encourage thinking. One of the core principles underlying a more socio-cognitive perspective on the learning environment brings to the fore an aspect of language which seems to have been forgotten in the modern languages classroom: that as well as learning language to communicate, we also use language to learn. By acknowledging that language must serve the purpose of learning, we are also acknowledging the fundamental principles of an individual's entitlement to learn, contained within the UNESCO report *Learning: The Treasure Within* (1996). The report echoes Tony Blair's wish to strengthen global citizenship, and yet as Coyle (1999a) points out:

> The current modern foreign languages curriculum and ensuing methodologies which developed in response to communicative principles and teacher accountability – examination results, testing and a drive to raise standards – are no longer entirely relevant and motivating to many young people. That is not to say that all the many good aspects of current practice need to be thrown out. On the contrary, they must not only be retained but developed alongside dynamic and evolving perspectives of types of learning and environments which encourage competent, confident communicators.

The two key elements, therefore, in moving current practice forward to the challenges of the millennium, are, I believe, those which will be instrumental in increasing learner motivation and commitment to languages. These fundamental requirements, both of which should in fact respond to an entitlement to learning, are:

- an examination of the boundaries of the modern languages curriculum in order to redefine the *content* of communication; and
- a reappraisal of how communication and learning skills (including metacognitive and thinking skills) can be developed within the confines of the classroom and the curriculum – the *context* of communication.

In my view the period of discontent with modern languages which marks the end of this century both for teachers and learners can be replaced in the next decade by more relevant and appropriate experiences, where adolescents find a voice and teachers are engaged both with and in the process of exploring ways to develop and extend current practice.

I shall base what follows on the premise that the school curriculum both *can and should* provide young people with a variety of opportunities, not just for learning to use languages, but for using languages to learn – and to communicate.

Modern Languages and the Whole School Curriculum: Exploring Boundaries

Reappraising the content of the MFL curriculum

The MFL National Curriculum draft proposals set out in the 'Green Book' (DES, 1990) prepared the ground for extending the confines of the modern foreign languages curriculum. The document was explicit in its recommendations for cross-curricular linking, acknowledging that traditional subject boundaries are in many ways artificial: 'the full potential of the National Curriculum will only be realised if curricular planning involves identifying the overlap of skills and content across the different subjects' (DES, 1990).

The notion of a whole curricular perspective of learning is already familiar. The Bullock Report (1975) laid the ground for the 'language across the curriculum' movement of the 1980s – 'all teachers are teachers of English'; the information and communication technology National Curriculum of the 1990s promoted the delivery of and responsibility for the ICT curriculum within all subject areas. So why not extend this to include a vision of how modern languages, too, may contribute to the whole curriculum? Not through being reduced to the service of other subjects, but through extending their communicative repertoire, exploring their potential for cognitive challenge and increasing their relevance to learners.

This is not of course to suggest that current practice in language lessons fails to provide the essential foundations of linguistic and cultural knowledge, skills and understanding. What it does imply is an increase in the potential for communication, with opportunities for the learner's attention to be genuinely focused on the content of what is being communicated rather than being confined to either its form or its simulated context. In *Communicative Language Teaching* Littlewood warned (1981: 95):

> Foreign language teaching must be concerned with reality: with the reality of communication as it takes place outside the classroom and with the reality of learners as they exist outside and inside the classroom. Because both of these realities are complex and so poorly understood, nobody will produce a definitive teaching methodology.

I agree that it is neither possible nor desirable to have a definitive teaching methodology. I would argue, however, that we do know a lot about the realities of the classroom. We know that many learners become frustrated by the repetitive nature of their linguistic experiences, funnelled as they can be into spurious topic areas, and perceive what is taught as irrelevant to their potential communicative needs. We know that many teachers feel constrained by examination syllabuses and textbook approaches. We know that teacher–learner classroom interaction and spontaneity in the target language are limited and that the occurrence of 'display questions' is high (this is where teachers ask questions to check whether learners can demonstrate linguistic understanding, rather than engaging in genuine dialogue). We know that textbook demands made on 13-year-old adolescents to state their likes and dislikes of school subjects and to describe daily routines are perceived as inconsequential. We also know that we are still some way from achieving conditions which will encourage the kind of learning potential outlined in the Green Book. Indeed, given the latest National Curriculum reforms we seem in some ways to be moving further away from a vision which believes (DES, 1990) that:

> the main reason why the study of modern languages can make a major contribution to cross-curricular activity is that it enables learners to talk and write in a new language about issues of great importance to their whole future, topics in which they have a special interest and activities in which they are currently engaged, both within and outside the school curriculum. This encourages them to think again about what they want to say and about how to say it, and their personal involvement helps them in their learning of the language.

Extending the skills and competence base of the MFL curriculum

Having made a case for re-examining the content of the modern languages curriculum, the Green Book identifies another 'missing link' between the MFL and whole school curriculum as follows (DES, 1990):

> The study of modern foreign languages also has an important contribution to make to cross-curricular skills and competences. These skills include for example social, through communication and co-operation; personal, by developing creativity and imagination; study, through observation, research and planning using a variety of media; and vocational, through communicative competence, independence, problem-solving and decision-making.

The promotion of transferable skills such as problem-solving and learning to learn could be fundamental to effective curriculum organisation. In an extensive and somewhat depressing American study (1988), Nickerson concluded that it was possible to finish 12 or 13 years of public education in the United States without developing competent 'thinking' skills. Similarly, Leat (1998: 157) makes reference to the many students who leave school underachieving: 'Whilst a Grade D, E, F or G at GCSE may represent a great effort by a student and his or her teacher, it is a sad reflection on eleven years of compulsory school .. [and] .. many able students do well at GCSE but without becoming effective learners.'

Tied up with the phenomenon of underachievement is the notion of the appropriacy of the knowledge and skills promoted by the current educational system. The 1991 OECD report *Learning to Think: Thinking to Learn* identified major trends in modern European society that call for a whole new range of cognitive skills. Such trends include the need for a flexible workforce capable of being retrained and having an understanding of technological rather than manual tasks; increasingly intricate communication between human and machine systems; the emergence of enterprise skills; and the complex demands of citizenship in a society where intersubjective truth has become less easy to identify. From this perspective, the teaching and learning of modern foreign languages has an increasingly crucial role to play in the broader education of our young people and thereby within the whole school curriculum. Ironically it is precisely this dimension which is in danger of becoming overlooked in the drive to raise standards in a re-active rather than a proactive way.

Curricular boundaries

I should therefore like to explore further the implications of adopting a broader and more flexible approach to modern languages learning in the next century. Three permutations of curricular boundaries can be defined, as follows:

- *redefining* curricular boundaries through work developed within modern languages courses;
- *crossing* curricular boundaries through co-operation between modern languages and other departments; and
- *breaking* curricular boundaries through teaching other subjects mainly or entirely in the foreign language for a specific period of time (three weeks to three years!).

The three models may have a different focus, but all are underpinned by a common principle – to encourage the development of communication, cognitive and metacognitive learning skills, whilst exploring different ways of using language.

There are many excellent examples of these models which are currently operating in our schools and colleges. Some have attracted outside funding through the European SOCRATES or Lingua programmes, others are small-scale classroom projects which have crucially contributed to changing the direction of everyday practice. There is a comprehensive account of cross-curricular work to date in the CILT publication *30 Years of Language Teaching* (Hawkins, 1996). Such approaches to MFL work are creative and motivating. They range from developing topics such as the environment, racism and local community issues beyond the textbook, organising electronic class-links for exchanging thematic data and joint field studies between geography, history and MFL departments, to MFL coursework or GCSE presentations based on another curricular area of study (for example a comparative study of localities in Spain and England), studying history through the medium of French in Year 10, taking GSCE business studies in Spanish, or as in the case of one comprehensive school, experiencing almost the entire Year 7 foundation course through the medium of French.

One could even argue that the MFL National Curriculum itself is open to flexible interpretation and to adaptation of the content to be covered. The areas of experience to be covered are wide and non-prescriptive, including 'the world around us' and 'the international world', and the *Programmes of Study Part I* focus on communicating, language skills, language-learning skills, and cultural awareness. It would thus appear that in terms of statutory requirements the MFL National Curriculum is not a stumbling block to developing alternative models and in fact could even be said to support a cross-curricular way of organising student learning.

Redefining curriculum boundaries

The idea of incorporating a cross-curricular dimension into the MFL syllabus is of course not new and is familiar to language teachers. However, drawing a poster to illustrate the slogan 'Sauvez l'environnement' or designing a leaflet entitled 'C'est bon pour la santé' simply stays at the surface level of the issues and is unlikely to generate a genuine desire to communicate. It also ignores potential for the transfer or extension of knowledge and skills developed in geography studies (environmental issues) and food technology classes (healthy eating). In other words, cross-curricular work suggested by modern languages coursebooks tends to remain at a pre-determined linguistic level to accommodate the linear design of the language syllabus. There also seems to be an in-built principle that the learners' level of linguistic competence determines the level of cognitive operations. Learners clearly need to have an entry-point into the language of a theme or topic, but analysing the content for potential conceptual and linguistic demands (rather than analysing the language for potential content requirements) creates a richer learning environment. In this learning context the teacher moves from initially directing the language taught to a situation where he or she is less in control, and the students play a greater role in determining the language needed to carry out specific tasks. Quite simply, as the students find they have an active role to play in directing their own learning, they also find a voice.

In the CILT Pathfinder No. 27, *New Contexts for Modern Language Learning: Cross-curricular Approaches,* Brown and Brown (1998) suggest a series of steps that an individual teacher can take towards adopting a more fully integrated cross-curricular approach to the teaching and learning of modern languages. A first step is to examine the potential for shared *resources* – the French revolution, say, or the world war of 1940–5, and the history department; a second step might be to identify a joint *topic* – the francophone world and the geography department; a third step is to focus on *learning skills* across the curriculum, such as ICT and an electronic class link; the next stage might be to share common *teaching and learning strategies* such as role-play techniques in history or English and MFL; and the final stage could focus on different areas of the curriculum which share a concern to raise awareness of *social and cultural issues,* such as personal and social education (PSE) and drug abuse.

Pathfinder No. 27 and its support materials (CILT *Resource File 1(1998)*) give concrete examples of how cross-curricular activities not usually associated with the MFL classroom can be organised to have broader learning outcomes as well as language-learning outcomes. An illustration could be the use of photographic evidence as a basis for enquiry. This is a common activity in both geography and history lessons – however, if in the languages classroom the learning outcomes are to do with enabling students to learn about different communities and alternative experiences, encouraging them to gain a sense of perspective and identify similarities and differences, as well as letting them practise formulating questions in the target language in response to a visual stimulus, asking for new information, vocabulary and structures in response to the photo, then the process has really started – small steps, but manageable and effective measures.

Although adopting a more cross-curricular approach makes many demands on teachers, such as finding alternative resources, careful preparation and monitoring, and time taken from tightly planned schemes of work, none the less it has the potential to offer a valuable pay-off. If this work can be seen as 'adding to' rather than 'detracting from', if it encourages planners to analyse language from a different perspective, if it allows thinking skills such as problem-solving, reasoning, hypothesising, predicting and analysing to be developed at the same time as linguistic skills, then this can only serve to enrich the languages classroom and make communication, for at least some of the time, authentic and engaging.

Crossing curricular boundaries

A whole-school approach to learning initially lends itself to an analysis of the curricula of all subjects, so as to identify areas of commonality and share ideas for collaborative teaching across departments. The geography National Curriculum contains a list of countries to be studied from selected areas including Europe and Africa and is hence a potential source of countries where the target language is spoken. Geographical thematic studies also cover weather and climate, ecosystems and environmental issues – all of which might be reinforced or developed through and in language lessons. The point here however is not to replicate what might go on in other subject areas, but to ensure that modern languages learning too has a part to play in extending the range of knowledge, skills and understanding traditionally associated with other subject areas.

The geography curriculum places great emphasis on the value of the skill of question-asking, referred to by Postman (1979) as 'our most important intellectual tool'. More generally, according to Battersby, learning in the context of geography is about enabling learners to develop a broad range of thinking skills: 'The role we have as teachers is to provide opportunities which encourage pupils to think about the same thing in different ways and different things in the same way' (1997: 5). In particular, Battersby suggests that when teachers ask questions they should be asking themselves what kind of thinking a question is generating and how it will help learners engage with the subject matter. The types of question generated in geography classrooms are based on developing the following skills: articulating knowledge, comprehension, application, analysis, synthesis and evaluation.

For example, in geography classes the most appropriate vehicle for creating a 'sense of place' is enquiry, where typical questions might be: What is this place? Where is it and what is it like? How did it get like this? How is it linked to other places? How is it changing? What do local people feel? What would it be like to live in? From a linguistic point of view such questions could easily form part of the language classroom repertoire, yet the absence of an authentic purpose might well result in a potentially powerful learning experience being reduced to decontextualised language practice. In other words, in linguistic terms *meaningful language* is language which conveys information that allows an activity to be completed. I would argue, however, that any classroom activity needs to have more than just completion in mind – it needs to have *purpose*. Burden (1998: 87) explains this as follows:

> A purposeful activity is more than an activity involving meaningful language. It not only uses language that conveys meaning, but also contains some value to the learner. This may be an educational value,

such as learning about the world or about a subject through the target language, or the activity might have value to the learner through enjoyment or interest or need ...learners are frequently asked to engage in activities in the target language that are cognitively superficial and unchallenging, merely because the learner does not have a proficient grasp of the language, or in tasks that are boring, childish, too simplistic, unrelated to their interests and often just insulting to their intelligence.

It might be that cross-curricular activities could well serve to bridge linguistic demands with educational purpose. For example, during a geography investigation into a 'sense of place', students had to create an instrument to measure individual perceptions of place. This involved them in developing a descriptive tool. Students began by brainstorming a range of adjectives which might be used to describe a place. Antonyms were then added to construct a sliding scale – such as noisy–calm, beautiful–ugly, dense–sparse. Such a language-focused activity could easily be carried out in a foreign language and the enquiry based on a shared sense of purpose – as well as a sense of place.

Developing this idea of the role of questioning and its interrelationship within a cross-curricular context, Collingwood was describing questioning as early as 1946 as 'the spark in the engine which drives forward historical enquiry'. Key questions underpinning a typical historical investigation might aim to develop the following skills: chronology, continuity, change, cause, consequence, interpretation, situation, sources, communication. Such questions might be summarised as follows: When did it happen? How long did it last? What changed? Why? What was the result? What are the differences between accounts of the same event? What was it like? What evidence is there? How convincing is this as a piece of history?

If questions are indeed 'at the heart of historical learning', as Collingwood suggested, then there is clearly potential for developing the skill of question-asking through the use of historical sources in a different language. Studying source documents from the period of the Enlightenment for example, or the Norman invasion, provides both teachers and learners with opportunities for developing their thinking, for transferring skills and extending their linguistic as well as their historical knowledge.

Another example of curricular linking combines sciences and modern languages in the 'Science across the world' project run by the Association of Science Education. This involves students working on and discussing environmental science issues of universal concern with students elsewhere in the world. The themes focus on global problems such as drinking water, food, energy, global warming and health, but with wide regional variations. The director of Nuffield Curriculum Projects, Andrew Hunt, asserts that 'Science must make connections and face up to issues that really matter' (so too must modern languages!). Students work on the same global theme in different countries, then exchange and compare their data with each other. Since the units are available in a wide range of languages it is feasible to exchange the data in another language, to receive data in a different language or to work through the whole unit in a language other than the mother tongue. In other words the theme could be worked on in Spanish, for example, or partly in English by the science teacher and partly in Spanish by the linguist. With an in-built collaborative framework and communications network the possibilities are endless.

The Tacade Directions project involves students in drug and alcohol education through the medium of a foreign language (French, German, Spanish). Students take part in problem-solving activities, trust-building scenarios, active listening, clarifying concepts, role-plays, simulations and so on. The link between the personal, social and moral education curriculum and MFL is not only clear but also well planned. The language demands become progressively more complex as students gain confidence and practise using the language. Materials such as these serve to illustrate a crucial point – that however creative the cross-curricular link might be, however motivating it may be work to alongside other colleagues to explore means of using language for a real purpose as well as for learning and thinking, nevertheless without carefully defined aims and objectives and long-term integrated planning, ideas such as these are destined to remain peripheral to the school curriculum.

Breaking curricular boundaries: Teaching through the medium

The third and most challenging model for widening the scope of the MFL curriculum is to use the medium of a modern language for the delivery of other elements of the National Curriculum. Ten years ago this approach was clearly the domain of the international or European schools, with only a handful of pioneering enthusiasts in other schools. Though it could be argued that Britain already has a successful tradition of bilingual education in its Welsh- and Gaelic-medium schools, the teaching of subjects through a European language which is not a heritage language has remained largely outside British mainstream education. However, times change – and in this instance, rapidly. The 'bilingual' movement is now well established in other European countries, particularly Germany, France, Austria, the Nordic countries and the Netherlands. There the focus is usually on teaching subjects through the medium of English. Now it is our turn.

Perhaps one of the more controversial of recent government initiatives, one which was covertly instrumental in encouraging language-medium teaching, was the setting up of a small cluster of schools with specialist 'language college' status and backed by commercial and government sponsorship. By the end of the century there will be over 60 such schools, with many more planned. The guide for language colleges (DFEE, 1995) stated:

> 37. Some schools may wish to focus on offering a broad range of modern foreign languages ..and incorporate ...the teaching of particular subjects through the medium of a foreign language, at least for specific pupil groups, or through opportunities for pupils to practise and experience modern foreign languages outside formal lessons.

> 38. Some may wish to go further in adopting a bilingual approach, specialising in the use of a particular modern foreign language throughout the school and across the curriculum.

Whilst the DFEE guidelines only cautiously promoted language-medium teaching, it soon became clear that if such schools were to attract more students, then offering some kind of bilingual experience would clearly be a selling-point. Moreover, there is still no one model for bilingual education in operation, since schools are all developing programmes according to their individual circumstances. As Beardsmore (1993) notes, 'There is no blueprint for bilingual education. No model, however successful, is for export.' A programme may range from a ten-lesson module to a term, from a core syllabus lasting two years to a proportion of lessons – say two out of three per week – for an extended period of time. It may consist of a Year 7 foundation course or GCSE history taught in French. Science, geography, history, drama, ICT, PSE, sport, business studies are all represented.

Clearly, such radical departures from traditional practice require careful consideration, planning and organisation. There is a certain irony in the fact that the bilingual movement in the UK is led by language teachers, whereas elsewhere it is the subject teachers who are turning to bilingual education as a means of enhancing their programmes.

The teaching and learning of other subjects through the medium of a foreign language is not, however, a panacea. It certainly raises very challenging issues – not least that of who should or could deliver the curriculum. And yet, what we do know from the few case-studies which exist in the UK is that learners become comparatively and relatively competent linguists, and that their achievement in the discipline over a period of time does not appear to fall behind. According to research carried out in two

English comprehensive schools, targeting Year 9 learners (Coyle, 1999), the indications are that bilingual classes may have potentially positive outcomes, among them that:

- there is an increase in linguistic competence, since using the target language to learn also builds on language learning in MFL lessons;
- some students are capable of taking their GCSE language examinations one year early;
- learners show evidence of operating at a linguistic level which goes far beyond the transactional;
- after only three years of language learning, many students have the confidence to communicate effectively, initiate conversation and participate in work experience or field studies abroad;
- learners are involved in subject tasks which engage them in hypothesising, analysing, discussing and exchanging views;
- there is an acceptance of the 'normality' of working in an alternative language;
- students develop study skills involving concentration, learning strategies, increased motivation and collaborative learning;
- bilingual experiences encourage individuals to take risks and engage in spontaneous discourse;
- expectations of both students and teachers are raised; and
- the bilingual experience results in an enhanced individual learner profile (future career, cultural awareness, key skills).

However, breaking down curriculum barriers is about much more than enhancing linguistic skills through increased exposure to the language. In one comprehensive school where Year 8 learners followed a science module through the medium of French, students were able to read and understand science texts in French at two National Curriculum levels higher than those in their language classes. As more schools become involved, networks flourish, practice is shared, confidence increases and (crucially) support systems are put into place. Not only is the range of subjects taught extending, but so is the age and ability range of the learners. Medium-teaching is no longer an elite passport for a small group of able linguists, but a pragmatic opportunity to create motivating and challenging learning environments within the confines of the school. According to Christ (1993), 'More children, or even all children, could be offered the experience of using the foreign language as the working language by offering modules in the foreign language in as many subjects as possible.'

The MFL curriculum

However good the case for redefining, crossing and breaking curricular boundaries the modern languages curriculum itself remains the essential base – for learning to practise and use language in a variety of different ways, whether drills and exercises or high-level cognitive processing ; for understanding an alternative linguistic system and comparing it with others; for identifying the building-blocks which help learners to communicate effectively; and for exploring and developing cultural awareness. The cognitive skills involved in processing language input and output are themselves extremely complex: working out structural rules, understanding norms of use and appropriateness, sequencing utterances as well as developing communicative competence, and so on. In addition, building up a vocabulary, memorising new chunks of language and learning to listen, speak, read, write and think using another linguistic code, with its own rule system, are themselves demanding and challenging.

Furthermore, unless some linguistic and communicative tasks are rooted in a meaningful and purposeful context their potential for developing cognitive and metacognitive skills will be lost. Mindful of such inherent difficulties, Prabhu (1987) experimented with meaning-focused tasks in his language classroom. These tasks were based not only on the commonly used 'information gap' method, but also on reasoning and opinion gap activities. He discovered that:

> Reasoning brings about a more sustained preoccupation with meaning than information transfer does on its own, since it involves deriving one piece of information from another (working things out in the mind), not just encoding or decoding information .. the interaction resulting from this is a public, dialogic expression of the working out which learners have found difficult to do on their own which, as a result, they are likely to be able to do more independently in a subsequent task. (Prabhu, 1987: 48)

Prabhu's work suggests that for the modern languages classroom to be effective as a learning base, tasks which promote learning must involve real communication, must be meaningful, challenging and have purpose in the eyes of the learners.

The Context of Communication

Much has already been said about the pivotal role which communication plays in the modern languages classroom: pivotal in that it is at the same time both the aim as well as the means of learning. However, it would appear that genuine communication in the target language, hallmarked by spontaneity or 'banter' and a real desire to 'talk' rather than just 'speak,' is far from commonplace. Unless we find ways of increasing the immediacy of the communicative context, learners will continue to find little relevance in their modern languages lessons. Increasing immediacy entails developing methods that encourage learners to communicate in the 'here and now' of the classroom, whilst extending their communicative repertoire for operating in the wider world at some time in the future. Without an emphasis on the immediate context, modern languages learning could, at its worst, be summarised as a no more than a rehearsal for a play which may or may not take place.

It is perhaps salutary to revisit the recommendations of the report *Languages for Communication – The Next Stage: Recommendations for Action*, published by the then DES and CILT in 1987 (Salter, 1987). This underlines the importance of classroom strategies to maximise the use of both teacher's and learners' use of the target language. It also draws attention to the need for greater emphasis on genuine language use rather than mere practice, and on the means for taking learning objectives beyond the transactional, which clearly highlights the developing of communication skills and ultimately presages a move from speaking activities (one of the four National Curriculum discrete skills) to *talking*. For me, what distinguishes talking from speaking in the languages classroom is founded on the distinction between *reaction* and *interaction*. During speaking activities learners are often told what to say – the 'dead bodies talking heads' syndrome described by Legutke and Thomas (1991). When they are engaged in talking, on the other hand, they are continually interacting, not only with what is being said but also with their interlocutor.

For many years now, Krashen's (1981) language-learning and acquisition theories, based on the notion of 'comprehensible input' – making what we do and say comprehensible to our learners – have gained popularity amongst teachers, reflected in the common practice of breaking language down into manageable chunks. Far less emphasis has been placed on what the learner might do with that input in order to transform it into participatory output. If learner output involves genuine participation, then the way ahead must lie in finding ways of extending opportunities for interaction within the classroom. Are we in danger, due to the paucity of social interaction in the classroom, of educating learners, in Donato's harsh words (1996), 'towards communicative incompetence rather than competence'?

Allwright (1984: 169) advises us that 'Interaction is the process whereby everything that happens in the classroom gets to happen the way it does. Let us make the most of it.' 'Making the most of it', however, may require a more fundamental shift in our thinking than first appears. Interaction is not about reviewing the 'speaking' activities which go on in classrooms, but about examining the social conditions, the interrelationships between the teacher and learners, the roles and the 'voices'. It is about reviewing the number of teacher–learner exchanges which follow the pattern of teacher question, learner response (usually limited to one or two words or a short phrase), followed by teacher evaluation: 'Where is the post office?' 'Next to the bank.' 'Well done!' In traditional French classes this might appear as (T = Teacher; P = Pupil):

T: Tu aimes le fromage?
P1:   Oui, j'aime le fromage.
T: Très bien! C'est bon pour la santé?
P2:   Ça dépend.
T: Et toi tu aimes les fruits?
P3:   Oui, c'est bon pour la santé
T: Excellent!

Interaction is about finding ways of encouraging learners to *initiate* talk and to find a voice. It is about relevance, immediacy – and, as we move into less controlled situations, about taking risks.

The extract that follows is taken from a Year 9 French lesson transcript of a group of learners in a comprehensive school. It serves to illustrate the potential of an environment where learners are encouraged to 'talk'. Whilst the theme is one common to a typical Year 9 syllabus – healthy eating – the language explorations revolve round individuals making contributions, with learners occasionally initiating the conversation as well as responding to lead questions or comments from the teacher. There is evidence of learners 'playing' with language, talking to themselves and to their peers as well as practising key phrases such as 'c'est bon pour la santé'. There is also evidence of the learners directing the flow and nature of the talk and building on what others say. There is humour, there is spontaneity and above all there is interaction. The teacher's script also demonstrates that whilst he takes an active role in leading the discussion, he neither dominates the exchanges nor limits questions to the closed recall or display types. An extract such as this lies in sharp contrast to more familiar classroom exchanges. Transcripts such as these could serve as a guide for developing classroom practice.

T: Oui, J?
J: …l'ail [*lots of noise*]

T: L'ail, il y a un opinion sur l'ail, oui? [*lots of reactions*]

F: C'est bon pour la santé mais c'est pas bon pour les amis.

D: pas bon pour …[*to friend; voice tails off; everyone laughs*]

H: C'est pas mauvais pour la santé.

T: Sauf pour les amis qui aiment l'ail …si vous mangez tous les deux l'ail vous ne sentez pas.

L: C'est très très très bon pour le cœur et c'est bon pour …

F: [*to self in reaction, exasperated with same student talking*] Tais-toi!

J: Quand c'est cru c'est dégoûtant mais quand c'est cuire c'est délicieux.

A: [*to Ab*] Oui mais c'est dégoûtant

Ab: [*replies*] Non

H: [*singing to herself*] Il fait beau …

F: C'est pas …

T: …cru et quel est l'autre, le contraire de cru?

F: Monsieur! [*hand up*]

A: …avec la salade, la salade mixte

L: cruire

T: 'Cuit', pas 'cruire' – cru et cuit. [*To R*] Qu'est-ce que tu penses de l'ail?

R: Hmmmn,c'est vraiment délicieux

D: C'est dégoutant.

T: 'C'est dégoûtant', voilà les deux extrêmes – dégoûtant et délicieux – tu es d'accord avec J, que c'est bon pour la cuisine et pour le cœur. F, allez.

F: Erm j'aime bien le le pain de de l'ail [*lots of reactions*]

D: [*in agreement with 'pain à l'ail'*] Oui.

T: Ay oui mais vous savez, on dit 'le pain à l'ail', c'est pas français, ça. Les Français ne connaissent pas. On donne ça aux Français quand ils viennent en Angleterre et ils disent 'Ah bon mais qu'est-ce que c'est? Ça n'existe pas en France!' [*everyone laughs*]

A: C'est bon pour la la la

F: gorge

T: pour la gorge

A: Oui parce que quand je suis allée à la er er er oh, Polande …

T: en Pologne

A: Pologne et oh er j'ai un mal mal au gorge, et il a dit 'Tu manges ça' …et c'est ...[*inaudible; coughs*]

T: Tu avais ..?

A: J'avais, oui [*laughs*]

F: mal au gorge

T: mal à la gorge

A: mal à la gorge

T: Et tu as mangé ça, alors toute ta famille a fait comme ça [*makes a pushing gesture*] et après, et après ça allait mieux? Oui? Très bien!

L: Eh il y a quelque chose avec le pain à l'ail ...le pain à l'ail?

T: Est-ce que c'est vraiment bon pour la santé, ça? [*lots of opinions and noise*]

D: L'ail est ...Mais ...[*tails off*]

T: Ça fait grossir, pain à l'ail? OK c'est bon le cœur. Pourquoi ça fait grossir?

A: Le beurre

D: Oui, parce que le pain ...[*again lots of noise*]

A: [*in a whisper to neighbour*] Qu'est-ce qui pain à l'ail? Qu'est-ce qui pain à l'ail?

J: Parce qu'il y a beaucoup de beurre

Ta: C'est comme une soupe de beurre

F: Monsieur!

T: Oui?

F: K, elle adore le fromage de l'ail

T: Et comment s'appelle ce fromage, K?

F: Roulet?

K: Du Boursin, le Roulet et

T: Quelqu'un sait qu'il y a une publicité pour le Boursin à la télévision [*lots of reaction*]

A: Le pain, le vin du Boursin

Ab: [*shouts out but mispronounces*] Oui le pain, du vin et le Boisin

F: Oui ...du vin du pain et

L: Du vin [*lots of noise*]

F: Du vin du pain du Boursin [*lots of noise, everyone shouting out*]

Ta: [*to friend*] Ah oui, le pain le vin des Bourson

T: Du vin, du pain et le Boursin ...

This transcript is but one example of interactive discourse; a step forward would be for more departments to record lessons and analyse the teacher–learner and learner–learner exchanges in terms of their content and their context. And so it is against this backdrop that the 3Cs curriculum is evolving.

The 3Cs Curriculum

COLT: Linking content and the context of communication

The COLT matrix (Content and Context-oriented Language Teaching; see Figure 9.1) was developed in the mid 1990s as a professional development tool for use by modern languages teachers (Coyle & Leith, 1996). It provides a coherent framework for integrating key aspects of content and methodology. MFL teachers interested in developing their teaching along the horizontal axis (_context_) are those who are working on strategies for promoting interaction during lessons, getting their learners to talk spontaneously to the teacher and to each other – just as they might during other lessons, except in the target language. In other words, the focus is to progressively shift the emphasis from an artificial environment for communication as the locus for talk ('imagine you are in Germany and need to buy some petrol') to the classroom (discussion about a student having been suspended for smoking drugs, or, more usefully, whatever the learners themselves feel is important).

Other teachers prefer to concentrate on the _content_ of their lessons – along the vertical axis – moving from imposed surface-level MFL topics (pocket-money, description of homes) to a deeper level of engagement. The crucial point here is twofold – to work with content which is not only relevant and motivating, but also cognitively challenging, so that learners engage with rather than merely participate in lessons. This has already been discussed under the heading 'Reappraising the content of the MFL curriculum' earlier in this chapter.

The matrix thus enables teachers to audit their current practice and plot future developments. It also acts as a stimulus for professional debate. It is based on an integrative approach which

- wherever possible relates the language that is learnt to the content which is used to learn it;
- considers language as a medium for learning as well as a linguistic system;
- combines learning to use language with using language to learn; and

* acknowledges the role of interaction at all levels, but especially within the classroom.

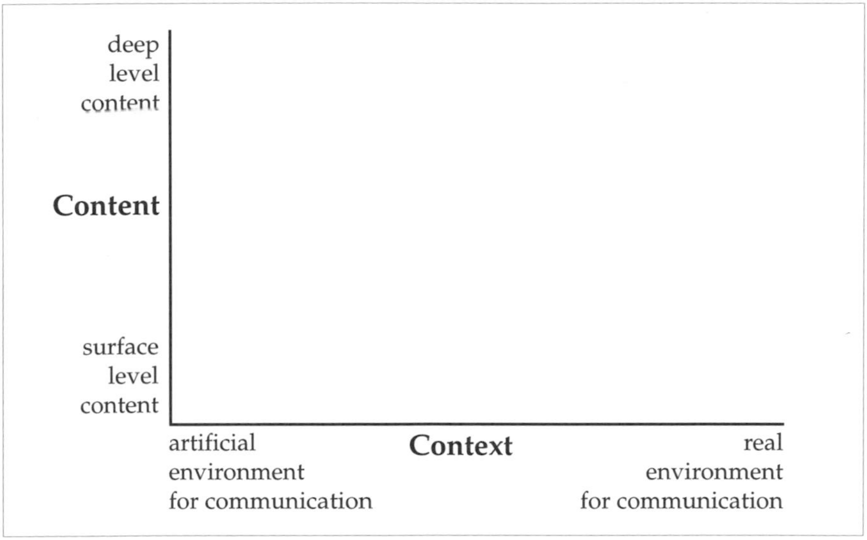

```
deep
level
content

Content

surface
level
content
         artificial              Context              real
         environment                                 environment
         for communication                           for communication
```

Figure 9.1 The COLT matrix (Coyle & Leith, 1996)

The case for cognition and metacognition

A recurrent theme throughout this chapter has been to link cognition and engagement with learning. I have asserted that when learners – whatever their ability – are working in environments they find cognitively challenging, they are more likely to engage with the task. This may seem in opposition to the notion that learning needs to be broken down into smaller units which can be easily digested, but in the languages classroom there is a danger of language units becoming so small and decontextualised that, although undoubtedly accessible to many learners, they are in fact meaningless. Increasing emphasis is being placed on the learners' diet, as Smith and Paterson (1998: 1) have noted:

> Research has shown that cognitively undemanding work, such as copying or repetition, especially when there is little or no context to support it, does not enhance language learning ..by actively involving pupils in intellectually demanding work, the teacher is creating a genuine need for learners to acquire the appropriate language.

One way of carrying out a self-audit of classroom practice is for teachers to consider the cognitive and linguistic demands of the tasks they set for their learners. By creating a matrix (see Figure 9.2) plotting cognitive demanding–undemanding tasks on the vertical axis, against linguistically demanding–undemanding tasks on the horizontal axis, teachers can gain an overview of the linguistic and cognitive levels at which they expect their learners to operate. Such an analysis facilitates planning for progression and individual learning by placing different classroom activities in each quadrant.

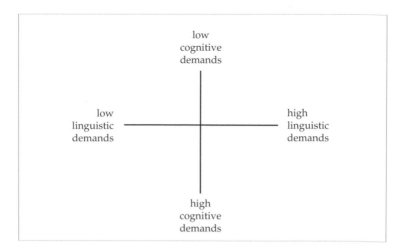

Figure 9.2 Challenging learners: a framework for plotting cognitive and linguistic demands (adapted from Cummins & Swain, 1986)

However, a paradoxical vacuum exists. Whilst issues to do with raising learners' metacognitive awareness (learning to learn) have become part of the language teachers' professional repertoire, along with developing strategies for independent learning, individual target setting and self-evaluation, this has not been mirrored by similar moves to put cognitive awareness on the teaching and learning agenda. The notion of organising the modern languages curriculum according to the kind of thinking skill required to process the knowledge and understanding associated with language learning is indeed an alien concept. The history curriculum for example, draws on a range of thinking skills of both a logical (inductive, deductive and analogical) and associative nature. The geography curriculum aims to develop a broad range of thinking skills such as connecting, arguing, analysing, sequencing, predicting, contradicting, inducing and so on. So what of the modern languages curriculum?

Breaking New Ground

Stoll and Fink (1996: 11) tell us: 'As we move into the twenty-first century, we need to rethink our conceptions of how to respond to our rapidly changing concepts.' Having created a vision of how modern languages might develop in the early stages of the new millennium, our next step is to rethink, reconsider and re-envision what changes must take place in order to allow this to happen.

Reconceptualising the MFL curriculum

Given the case for changing the focus of the content of modern languages learning, retaining essential linguistic elements of grammar and communication but extending and revising the current topic repertoire, a logical starting point might be to relate the subject matter or content of the languages classroom to relevant thinking processes. Those thinking processes could then be analysed for their linguistic demands.

There are many different models for defining structures of knowledge and related thinking processes. Mohan (1986) for example proposed three categories: *classification* (such as defining, applying new concepts); *principles* (explaining, predicting, interpreting, hypothesising); and *evaluation* (ranking, judging, expressing values). A modern languages scheme of work based on categories such as these would demonstrate progression in developing thinking skills alongside linguistic progression, rooted in challenging content. As Van Lier (1996: 69) says, 'Such awareness-raising work, which turns the classroom from a field of activity into a subject of enquiry, can promote deep and lasting changes in educational practices.'

Integrating an MFL thinking skills programme

Another pathway might be to explore successful 'thinking skills programmes' such as CASE (Cognitive Acceleration through Science Education; Adey & Shayer, 1993) and adapt these to the modern languages curriculum. Experimental work in this field is built on the notion that a particular set of teaching strategies can accelerate learners' intellectual development and their ability to think, and in the longer term improve their academic achievement. It was found in the CASE study that it was the very process of constructing personal meaning which enabled learners to develop their general thinking skills and intellectual abilities.

However, a problem-solving basis from which to tackle both linguistic and non-linguistic issues will require a fundamental rethink of curricular boundaries. Teachers will need to be supported and encouraged to investigate their own classroom practice in a principled way. Learners will need support in thinking 'hard', communicating more interactively and learning more effectively. Schools managers will need to be ready to chart the agenda for change. According to Joyce (1997: 142):

> Effective teachers and effective schools take seriously the link between classroom practice and the student learning outcomes, particularly in terms of what the child learns, the pace of learning and the high expectation existing in the classroom. Teaching strategies reflect not just the teachers' classroom management skills, but also the ability of the teacher to help students acquire new knowledge through for example, learning how to extract information, memorise information, to build hypotheses and concepts, to use metaphors, to think creatively and to work effectively with others.

Reappraising the context for communication

In order to develop the context for communication within the classroom beyond tightly controlled role-plays and GCSE scenarios, greater emphasis will need to be placed on finding out more about the social and linguistic conditions which encourage learners to take control and find their own voice. Opportunities for developing talking as well as speaking skills will feature more prominently in the classroom by providing learners with a genuine reason for using their language to communicate and to learn. Since it is unlikely that funding will be made available for extensive INSET, then it must be that the future for MFL lies in firmly embedding the 3Cs curriculum into whole-school development plans, especially those focused on school improvement. I should like to finish with some of my favourite words of advice, addressed to the classroom experts, practitioners and researchers by Leat (1998: 163):

> Hang on to the things that make you good, anyway. These could be good relationships, high expectations, rewards systems, setting targets, good display work, using topical events or drama techniques. These can all happily weld on to the changes implicated here in a 'productive synergy'.

References

Adey, P.S. and Shayer, M. (1993) *Really Raising Standards: Cognitive Intervention and Academic Achievement.* London: Routledge.

Allwright, R.L. (1984) The importance of interaction in classroom learning. *Applied Linguistics* 5, 156–171.

Battersby, J. (1997) *Teaching Geography at Key Stage 3.* Cambridge: Chris Kington Publishing.

Beardsmore, H.B. (1993) Bilingual learning: Institutional frameworks – whole school practice. In *Report on Workshop 12A. Bilingual Education in Secondary Schools: Learning and Teaching Non-Language Subjects through a Foreign Language. Language Learning for European Citizenship*. Strasbourg: Council of Europe Publications.

Brown, K. and Brown, M. (1998) *New Contexts for Modern Language Learning: Cross-curricular Approaches*. Pathfinder No. 27. London: CILT.

Burden, R. (1998) How best can we help children to become effective thinkers and learners? The case for and against thinking skills programmes. In R. Burden and M. Williams (eds) *Thinking Through the Curriculum*. London: Routledge.

CBEVE (1998) *A World of Understanding: Review of Fifty Years of CBEVE*. Available from CBEVE, 0171 389 4886.

Christ, I. (1993) Opening address. In *Report on Workshop 12A. Bilingual Education in Secondary Schools: Learning and Teaching Non-Language Subjects through a Foreign Language. Language Learning for European Citizenship*. Strasbourg: Council of Europe Publications.

Collingwood, R.G. (1946) *The Idea of History*. Oxford: Oxford University Press.

Coyle, D. (1994) Science in French in the National Curriculum: A pilot study. In R. Budd, P. Chaux, C. O'Neil, D. Arsndorf and U. Gaber (eds) *Subject Learning and Teaching in a Foreign Language*. Triangle 13. Paris: Didier Erudition.

Coyle, D and Leith, J (1966) Content-oriented language learning. *Comenius News* 7. London: CILT.

Coyle, D. (1999a) The next stage. Is there a future for the present? The legacy of the 'communicative approach'. *Francophonie* 19, 13-16.

Coyle, D. (1999b) Adolescent voices speak out – if only they would, if only they could. A study of interaction in classrooms where foreign languages are used. Unpublished thesis. University of Nottingham.

Cummins, J. and Swain, M. (1986) *Bilingualism in Education: Theory, Research and Policy*. London: Longman

Department of Education and Science (DES) (1975) *A Language for Life: The Bullock Report*. London: HMSO.

Department of Education and Science (1990) *Modern Foreign Languages Working Group Initial Advice* ('The Green Book'). London: HMSO.

DfEE (Department for Education and Employment) (1995) *Language Colleges: Guidance for Schools* (Specialist Schools Unit). London: HMSO.

Donato, R. (1996) The contributions of Vygotsky to understanding learning in foreign language classrooms. Paper delivered at the AILA conference, Jyvaskyla, Finland.

European Commission (1995) Teaching and learning: Towards the learning society. Objective IV, White Paper. Strasbourg: Council of Europe.

Hall, D. (1995) *Assessing the Needs of Bilingual Pupils: Living in Two Languages*. London: David Fulton Publishers.

Hawkins, E. (1996) (ed.) *30 Years of Language Teaching*. London: CILT.

Johnstone, R. (1989) *Communicative Interaction: A Guide for Teachers*. London: CILT.

Joyce, B. (1997) quoted in D. Hopkins and B. MacGilchrist (1998) Development planning for pupil achievement. *School Leadership and Management* 18 (3).

Krashen, S.D. (1981) *Second Language Acquisition and Second Language Learning*. New York: Pergamon Press.

Leat, D. (1998) *Thinking through Geography*. Cambridge: Chris Kington Publishing.

Legutke, M. and Thomas, H.F. (1991) *Process and Experience in the Language Class-room*. London: Addison, Wesley, Longman.

Littlewood, W. (1981) *Communicative Language Teaching – An Introduction*. Cambridge: Cambridge University Press.

Mohan, B. (1986) *Language and Content*. Reading, MA: Addison-Wesley.

Nichol, J. (1995) *Teaching History at Key Stage 3*. Cambridge: Chris Kington Publishing.

Nickerson, R.S. (1988) On improving thinking through instruction. *Review of Research in Education* 15, 3–57.

OECD (1991) Learning to think: Thinking to learn. Report cited in R. Burden and M. Williams (eds) (1998) *Thinking Through the Curriculum*. London: Routledge.

Postman, N. (1979) *Teaching as a Conserving Activity*. Laurel Press, Dell.

Powell, R. (1986) *Boys, Girls and Languages in Schools*. London: CILT.

Prabhu, N.S. (1987) *Second Language Pedagogy*. Oxford: Oxford University Press.

Salter, M. (ed.) (1987) *Languages for Communication – The Next Stage: Recommendations for Action*. London: DES and CILT.

Salters, J., Neil, P. and Jarman, R. (1995) Why did French bakers spit in the dough? *Language Learning Journal* 11, 26-29

Smith, J. and Paterson, F. (1998) *Positively Bilingual: Classroom Strategies to Promote the Achievement of Bilingual Learners*. Nottingham: Nottingham Education Authority.

Stoll, L. and Fink, D. (1996) *Changing our Schools*. Open University Press.

UNESCO (1996) Learning: The treasure within. Report cited in R. Burden and M. Williams (eds) (1998) *Thinking Through the Curriculum*. London: Routledge.

Van Lier, L. (1996) *Interaction in the Language Curriculum: Awareness, Autonomy and Authenticity*. New York: Longman.

Williams, M. (1998) Teaching thinking through a foreign language. In R. Burden and M. Williams (eds) *Thinking through the Curriculum*. London: Routledge.

Conclusion: Creative Thinking About a New Modern Languages Pedagogy

KIM BROWN

It remains for us in this concluding chapter to reflect on what has been written and to consider the implications for our own research and practice. There is general agreement amongst the contributors to this book that we need to reassess language teaching methodology. But the argument goes deeper than this: there is a sense in which the study of modern languages seems to be losing its identity and the call in this book is for a fundamental reappraisal of the rationale for our practice.

I should like to pursue these two themes, writing from the perspective of a teacher educator engaged in research on the professional development of teachers of modern languages. The biggest challenge for me in this book is how we move from research which appears to be offering exciting new possibilities for language teaching, such as we have here, to an informed change of practice in the classroom. How do we 're-engage the profession', as Mike Grenfell puts it, in an exploration of effective practice so that we really begin to make a difference in our subject area?

And yet a lot of the ideas in this book are not new. There have been calls for the introduction of languages at primary level, for independent learning strategies or for cross-curricular approaches to teaching languages for many years now. Perhaps these ideas have simply become more compelling in the current context of change and reappraisal in modern languages. The millennial date of this publication, in itself, is not as significant as recent inspection evidence or proposed changes to the curriculum or the growing decline in interest in our subject area. There have been lost opportunities and it is time to turn these into creative possibilities.

So what will the role of the modern languages teacher be in the next decade, or even in the next century? This chapter will explore this question, responding to and building on the ideas of the writers in this book. We need to look first at some of the evidence for the need for change and then at what a new pedagogy might look like. It will be argued that the projects described in this book are a first step and that what we need now is to engage practising teachers in an exploration and evaluation of such strategies and approaches in their own classrooms. We all need to find out what works best in the languages classroom and why.

There is currently a lack of consistency in language teaching methodology within departments which I shall explore with reference to my own research findings (see also Dobson, 1998; Whitehead & Taylor, 1999). This may well be a reason for the loss of identity of our subject as well as a reflection of that loss. Above all, we need to work towards a new and shared understanding of the full potential of language teaching and learning. We need to develop a strong rationale for our practice which is based on a broad range of research evidence and which reasserts the importance of modern languages pedagogy in the education of the young person as a whole, an issue more fully explored by Brown and Brown (1996; 1998).

The Breakdown of Pedagogy

There is one preoccupation which is shared by all the writers in this book and that is the nature of communication in the languages classroom. Above all, there is the concern that too much talking *in* the language being learned has led to a loss of opportunities to talk *about* other aspects of language learning, for example, language structure or cultural issues. Anthony Lodge explores this imbalance at the higher education level in terms of *instrumentality* and *disciplinarity*, where instrumentality describes the narrow focus on communication and disciplinarity the call for a broader understanding of what it is to study language. This argument is taken up by both Chris Brumfit and Mike Grenfell in their discussion on secondary classrooms. They suggest that a balance is needed in the use of second language and mother tongue: that pupils need to work in their mother tongue and form an understanding of it in order to gain a full understanding of language, of a second language and of the language-learning process. David Little also places the emphasis on a broad approach to language learning, with a focus on interaction between pupils. In the classrooms he describes, pupils plan and carry out group-work tasks together, working both in mother tongue and in their second language: the educational purpose is to support the personal and social development of young people in the *process* of learning a second language.

These writers are challenging the narrow focus on transactional, communicative activities and arguing for a broader context for talk in the languages classroom. For them, language learning is effective where talking in the target language is only one of many different kinds of exchange in the classroom. With models like these in mind, we can see the ways in which language-learning experiences have been greatly diminished: opportunities for learning about cultural issues, for extended reading, for talking about the ways in which language works are all being lost through a narrow focus on communication.

If the communicative model were successful in itself this might at least make up for some of these losses; it might be thought a compromise worth making. However, even in classrooms where the focus is mainly on target-language activities and where we might expect higher levels of competence in speaking amongst pupils, this is not proving to be the case. In the first place, there is the question of the authenticity of much of what is said. This is explored in detail in two chapters in this book. Mike Grenfell describes the nature of interaction in many classrooms as 'a sham, mimicking the features of communication rather than genuinely communicating'. Do Coyle draws a clear distinction between real communication, *talking*, which involves an element of interaction and response to the interlocutor, and the kind of communication that is so often found in secondary language classrooms, *speaking*, where learners are simply told what to say.

Such communication may not be wholly authentic, but the fact that there is some exchange between pupils and their teacher in the target language might nevertheless be held to indicate a measure of success. However, a more fundamental problem is beginning to emerge from the inspection of modern languages teaching in schools. Recent findings of secondary inspections of modern languages teaching seem to suggest that communicative methodology, as it is being interpreted in language classrooms, is just not working. This is the case for both Key Stages 3 and 4. The report for Key Stage 3 found that:

> Use of the target language by pupils is not developed over [Key Stage 3] and the early momentum of beginning a new language is not sustained in Years 8 and 9. This is due partly to insufficient opportunities being provided for pupils to respond to progressively more demanding tasks and partly to under-expectations by teachers of their ability to respond.

Again, the Key Stage 4 report stated that:

> Many of the characteristics of pupils' performance in Key Stage 3 can also be seen in Key Stage 4. For example, few pupils show confidence and independence in the use of the language outside controlled situations or the ability to apply language previously learned to new situations. Apart from vocabulary acquisition, the range of language used by many pupils does not widen sufficiently, and their grasp of

grammar, particularly the ability to manipulate tenses, is not strengthened. (Dobson, 1998)

When we consider the research findings in this book alongside inspection
findings in secondary schools, it is clear that the challenges facing us go beyond an imbalance in communication. As long as pupils continue to co-
operate with teachers in languages lessons, as long as they will have a go at
the role-plays and information gap activities, for example, then at least
some kind of teaching and learning can take place. The greater difficulties
lie in classrooms where pupils are withdrawing their co-operation entirely,
where it is becoming impossible to establish any kind of interaction at all.
You cannot force pupils to say things in French or German or Spanish if
they do not wish to, 'speaking other people's lines' as David Little puts it,
and even if pupils do make an utterance under pressure, we could hardly
call that an effective communicative activity. The concern is not about an
imbalance in communication but about a complete absence of communication. In schools where growing levels of disengagement amongst pupils
are a concern for teachers across the curriculum, there are specific and fundamental implications for modern language teachers: for them, the
breakdown in communication with pupils is essentially a breakdown of
pedagogy.

Clearly there are teachers who are highly successful in their interpretations of a communicative approach; we need to understand the factors that
contribute to their success if we are to begin to rebuild a successful modern
languages pedagogy. This is the focus of the next section. But before we
look at methods that work, there is one more factor in this discussion of
communication in languages classrooms that we need to consider and that
is the contribution that languages have to make in the education of the
young learner as a whole (see DES, 1990, particularly Chapters 8 and 14; for
a full exploration of whole-curriculum issues, Siraj-Blatchford, 1995;
Radnor, 1994). If pupils find themselves in lessons where the teacher does
most of the talking, where they are not allowed to speak or discouraged
from speaking their own language and cannot or will not speak the target
language, or where they do not speak at all, then we have to ask ourselves
what contribution our subject area is making to the personal and social education of the young people in our classes.

This is particularly important in the current context of change in the education system (a comprehensive overview of current thinking about
education policy will be found in Bentley, 1998). There is a growing recognition by the government that pupils need to develop a broad range of
cognitive and affective skills in order to be successful at school and as

young adults in the future. This has led to a renewed focus on literacy and numeracy skills and to initiatives such as the work-related curriculum, Education for Citizenship and the teaching of democracy in schools (QCA, 1998), and the 'preparation for adult life' (PAL) programme. At the same time there are strong recommendations being made for schools to take a much more active role in anti-racist education, following the publication of the Stephen Lawrence inquiry report (HMSO, 1999). The new agendas for the curriculum are placing the emphasis on the active participation of young people in the shaping of the world in which they live. Central to this democratic process is the role of *talk*. If we are to ensure the place of modern languages in the curricula of the future, we must work towards a new pedagogy which reflects a commitment to the teaching of languages, in particular, and to the education of young people in the broadest sense. This is what David Little means when he talks about the need to 'rebuild pedagogy from first principles'. The single, narrow focus on communicative methodology in many ways reflects a loss of identity for our subject area: the challenge now is to reassert the identity of languages at the centre of the curriculum, and to reaffirm the opportunities for talk in the languages classroom. We shall now go on to think about what a new pedagogy for modern languages might look like in the future.

Rebuilding Pedagogy from First Principles

It is clear that we need to consider the role of the teacher of languages in the broadest terms. This is particularly relevant for those of us working in initial teacher education. Before we go on to consider the issues here, let us look at the role of the teacher as it emerges from the studies in this book. First, there seems to be common agreement that the role of the language teacher is a central one. The pupils in Gary Chambers' study place the teacher as the most significant factor in determining their positive views of language learning, a finding confirmed by other studies in subjects across the curriculum – see, for example, Kinder *et al.* (1996), on the role of the teacher in pupil disaffection. Second, we find a varied picture emerging of what that role might be. In the classrooms that David Little describes, for instance, the role of the teacher is to foster autonomy in pupils. She monitors group work and encourages pupils to develop for themselves projects and activities which meet the demands of the curriculum. In Little's words, pupils 'engage dynamically with the curriculum' and share authority in the classroom with their teacher; whereas in other classrooms, such as those in Do Coyle's study, the teacher is at the centre of interactions, initiating and stimulating class discussion in the target language. Even in situations where the role of the teacher might appear to be under threat, as perhaps in the case of computer-assisted language learning (CALL), Philip Hood makes a strong case for the contribution teachers have to make, monitoring and talking to pupils about their work: 'the image of learners simply switched into computers and learning in isolation is not part of a positive vision'.

We have, in this book, several interpretations of the role of the language teacher. What are the implications of this broad range for those of us working with student teachers? We could argue that it offers our students a rich diversity of models of good practice to draw on as they begin to reflect on the development of their own teaching role. It might be construed as confusing or even as reflecting a lack of consistency in methodology. But there is one aspect that is common to all of these approaches and that is the strong rationale underlying them. This is what we have to help student teachers to understand and develop for their own emerging practice. We have to help them move from their observations of other teachers, perhaps teaching in quite different ways, towards a strong sense of their own individuality in the classroom, with a strong rationale of their own. As we shall see, this is important both for their own professional development and for the future of modern languages.

It is this sense of the individuality of teachers which distinguishes pedagogy from methodology and which we need to explore further here. *Methodology* describes a general approach, a way of doing things: for example, how teachers might use resources to support teaching and learning. *Pedagogy* specifically refers to the role of the teacher in bringing a subject alive: the way in which a teacher might explain fundamental concepts in their subject area, or make links for pupils or help them to spot patterns. Methodology tends to stay on the page, while pedagogy implies a sense of energy; it tells us how the teacher interacts with the methodology to engage pupils in their learning.

While it is possible for teachers to teach without a strong sense of their pedagogical role, it is difficult to see how the experience they offer pupils will give their subject area a strong sense of identity. Mike Grenfell provides a fascinating case-study illustrating this point in his book *Training Teachers in Practice* (1998). He describes a teacher who has developed a methodology, based on classroom organisation strategies such as a carousel, which specifically reduces the need for any input in lessons from her. Wherever she can, she resists entering into any pedagogical interaction with her pupils. It is the difference that an individual teacher can make in helping pupils to learn or understand their subject more effectively through explanation and example, through *talk*, that distinguishes pedagogy from methodology. We can offer student teachers current models of good practice in methodology. But if we want to ensure the future of our subject, we need to help them develop a strong pedagogical role in the languages classroom.

There is a very practical reason why this might be important. My research findings suggest that lack of consistency in methodology within a department is a major cause of disaffection in pupils. This, in turn, is leading to disaffection in language teachers and to a downward spiral for the whole profession. What is beginning to emerge from the findings is that the capacity of newly qualified language teachers to survive this downward spiral depends upon the extent to which they have developed a strong sense of their own professional identity in the classroom.

Although many factors are involved in this, one has particular resonance for the discussion here and that is the importance of positive role models for these new language teachers. If they are going to develop their full potential, they have to have a clear understanding of the possibilities of language teaching. The reflections of one newly qualified teacher illustrate this point well:

> I still remember my first placement with A and B who were, who are brilliant teachers and I can only say it is so important to have these people to look at when you start .. and I think now I am still drawing from that, I still think well I'm not that sort of teacher, but I have seen examples where effective, brilliant teaching is possible and this is what I want, where I want to go.

It is this understanding that will give these new teachers the confidence to accept or reject models of teaching they encounter and to develop their own rationale for their teaching. Another student teacher, at the end of her training year, describes this progression for us:

> I feel your role has changed for me throughout the year, which is good – at first I was very idealistic and thought 'Wow!' at everything, then you became somebody who, not criticised, but would say if I was on the right or wrong track, now I see you as somebody who gives suggestions and now with this year behind me I can decide whether I agree with them or not. I feel this progression is good, because although now I still feel supported, I feel ready to go out and do it by myself.

But the need to help teachers develop a strong sense of individuality in the classroom is not just about personal survival. There is another reason why it is important and this is the contribution that each teacher can make to the identity of the profession as a whole. By encouraging student teachers to gain the fullest understanding of the possibilities of language teaching we are helping to ensure that creative thinking about methodology will keep moving the discipline forward: we are helping to ensure the survival of the subject in the curriculum of the future. This is particularly important at the time of writing with the renewed emphasis on grammar and teaching about language at both primary and secondary levels. The extent to which modern languages teachers will see this as a valuable opportunity to develop new approaches to teaching language across the curriculum, along the lines suggested by Chris Brumfit or David Little, for example, will depend very much upon their engagement with methodological questions and upon their understanding of their role in the curriculum as a whole.

What is emerging from this study is that student teachers of the future will need to know about research in broad educational areas as well as those specific to language learning, and they will need to understand the implications of all of this for their practice as a teacher. They will need to have experience of different teaching and learning styles and active learning strategies; they will need to know about the research on multiple intelligences and emotional intelligence; they will need to understand the contribution that their subject can make to teaching about controversial issues such as human rights and equality issues; they will need to understand the importance of process as well as content in the planning of their lessons. Above all, they will need to be able to understand the relevance of all this for their own practice as effective teachers of young people, as well as effective teachers of language. In the next section, we look at one example of ways in which this broad approach might be developed in the languages classroom.

Talking about Photographs

An example of the creative possibilities available to modern languages pedagogy

In this final section we shall consider an example of a research project based on the use of photographs in the languages classroom. There are several reasons for choosing to end with this. First, the project presents a model of collaborative research involving mentors, student teachers and tutors in an exploration of new approaches to language teaching: if we are to begin to make a difference to the learning experiences of pupils in our classrooms, then it seems that we must involve practising teachers in the kinds of research described in this book. Second, the project aimed to explore ways of encouraging pupils to interact with each other in the target language in group-work tasks – thus picking up the earlier discussion in this chapter on the nature of communication in the language classroom. And third, the photograph activities described are informed by an understanding of active learning strategies and development education principles which reinforce the role that language learning has to play in education of the child as a whole. (On the potential of photographs to enhance pupils' learning about the world, see Pike & Selby, 1988.)

As part of their training, student teachers on the PGCE course at the University of East Anglia are asked to conduct classroom investigations into group work while they are on placement in school. The aim is to help them to develop a sense of curiosity about their pupils' language learning and to raise their awareness of the possibilities that group work offers for extending pupils' confidence and competence in the target language. At the same time they gain experience of conducting classroom investigations and a basis for further exploration of effective methodology once they have qualified. Mentors were aware of these investigations but had not really felt part of them. The suggestion from them that we might all work together in this way has given our training partnership a strong sense of identity and a shared research focus (for a full discussion of the project, see Brown, 1999).

The aim of this project was to explore the way in which using photographs as a visual stimulus for group work might change the nature of communication in the languages classroom. In itself, the use of photographs exemplifies a new languages pedagogy, where the learning aims are both specific to language learning and charged with a much broader educational purpose. Activities such as questions around a photograph, message match or jigsaw photograph activities are all part of a canon of active learning strategies, well known to practitioners in other curriculum areas, which are informed by an understanding of different teaching and learning styles and have the explicit educational purpose of helping to prepare pupils for their role as participating citizens in future society. At the same time they have a clear communicative purpose: to engage pupils in collaborative group tasks or pair work; to encourage discussion, negotiation, agreement, disagreement and other communication skills. We wanted to find out to what extent it was possible to achieve this kind of communication in the modern languages classroom.

Visual stimulus is often offered to pupils in language lessons, in the form of colourful overhead tranparency drawings and cut-outs, particularly to support presentation stages of lessons. But it is much less common for pupils to be asked to practise the language they are learning by talking about a photograph (a point also made by Rosamond Mitchell in conference discussion about the methodology used in the research project she herself conducted into progression in MFL). Textbooks have become much more visually appealing, with many colour photographs and photo-stories. But when you look closely, these photographs are not the central focus of the language-learning tasks and activities in the books. There is no understanding evident in current language coursebooks of the potential that photographs have to stimulate interaction between pupils or of the educational purpose of their use to enhance pupils' learning about the world. By taking activities such as the jigsaw photograph into the languages classroom we are beginning to push thinking forward about language teaching. Photographs hold the potential for rich learning experiences, and yet this is an area of methodology barely explored in modern languages: how they are used represents both lost opportunities and creative ways forward in the communicative classroom.

Students and mentors took brief extracts from transcripts of group activities centred around photographs to study in detail. We learned that it *is* possible to encourage pupils to interact in the target language, and that it is important to prepare them for this in advance by teaching them phrases and strategies to support their interactions. For example, where pupils have been given phrases such as *d'accord, pas d'accord, moi, je pense que c'est ... et toi, qu'est-ce que tu en penses? à mon avis, c'est . „.oui, c' est possible .., ça, c'est certain, non, je ne suis pas sûr, moi,* they are then able to practise these in the group tasks we set them. We also noted how pupils began to take roles in group tasks and to take turns:

A: Was ist das, was denkst du, Jane?

B: Ich denke ein Kleider.

A: Was denkst du, Peter?

C: Ich denke das ist ein Dreiecke.

A: Was denkst du, Laura?

D: Ich denke das ist ein Flag.

A: Was denkst du, John?

E: Ich denke das ist eine Flagge.

There were also occasions where they began to correct each other in the target language:

F: Wie heisst sie?

G: Nein, *er*, nicht 'sie'!

And again:

H: Wo ist der Mann?

I: Ein Tennisspieler.

H: Nicht 'wer'; *wo* ist er?

Most important of all, we learned from the evaluations that the pupils wrote of these activities that they valued them and saw a clear communicative purpose in them:

Q: *What did you learn today?*

PP: What it's like in France with everyone speaking French at you.
I learned many new words thanks to the dictionary and also how to make others understand me.
It makes a change to be able to practise the French we have learned for real.
Not being allowed to speak in English has made me realise how little of sentence structure I actually understand in French

Q: *Would you like to do more activities like this?*

PP: Yes, I feel it would help my French a lot because I would depend on it.
Yes, because it gave me a chance to have a proper (not set-up) conversation in French.

When this last pupil talks of a 'proper (not set-up) conversation', this is not strictly the case: the comment refers to the jigsaw photograph, which is a totally pedagogic activity. The point about this activity though, is that it offers a structured context for interaction in the target language while at the same time being prompted by much broader learning aims.

This collaborative project has meant that mentors have become involved in the same investigations as their students, in their own classrooms with their pupils. As a result we have begun to develop across the partnership a shared frame of reference, a common language with which to talk about language teaching and learning. In time we hope that this will work towards ensuring greater consistency in experience for student teachers on placement in partnership schools, as well as offering enhanced learning opportunities for pupils.

The use of photographs is just one area of activity that holds potential for modern languages teachers and that might become part of a new pedagogy. Mentors and tutors and students might take any number of other such areas to investigate together. The most important aspect is the process of shared exploration and discussion and the engagement of the pupils in these investigations. Above all, we need to devote fresh energy to research into effective pedagogy, if the study of modern languages is to reassert its identity as a discipline in the curriculum in the next millennium.

References

Bentley, T. (1998) _Learning Beyond the Classroom: Education for a Changing World_. London: Routledge.

Brown, K. and Brown, M. (1996) _New Contexts for Modern Language Learning: Cross-curricular Approaches_. London: CILT.

Brown, K. and Brown, M. (1998) _Changing Places: Cross-curricular Approaches to Teaching Languages_. London: CILT.

Brown, K. (1999) This feels much more like a partnership. _Links_ 19. London: CILT.

Department of Education and Science (DES) (1990) _MFL for Ages 11–16: Proposals of the Secretary of State for Education and Science and the Secretary of State for Wales_. London: HMSO.

Dobson, A. (1998) _MFL Inspected: Reflections on Inspection Findings 1996–7_. London: CILT.

Grenfell, M. (1998) _Training Teachers in Practice_. Clevedon: Multilingual Matters.

HMSO (1999) _The Stephen Lawrence Inquiry_. Report of an inquiry by Sir William Macpherson of Cluny. London: HMSO.

Kinder, K., Wakefield, A. and Wilkin A. (1996) _Talking Back: Pupil Views on Disaffection_. Berkshire, NFER.

Pike, G. and Selby, D. (1988) _Global Teacher, Global Learner_. London: Hodder and Stoughton.

Qualifications and Curriculum Authority (QCA) (1998) _Education for Citizenship and the Teaching of Democracy in Schools_. London: QCA.

Radnor, H. (1994) _Across the Curriculum_. London: Cassell.

Siraj-Blatchford, J. and I. (1995) _Educating the Whole Child: Cross-curricular Skills, Themes and Dimensions_. Buckingham: Open University Press.

Whitehead, J. and Taylor, A. (1999) _Teachers of Modern Foreign Languages: Foreign Native Speakers on Initial Teacher Training Courses in England_. Bristol: University of West of England.